The Magical Dilemma of Victor Neuburg

CAMERON'S BOOKS
And Magazines

J.O.F

4.75

336 S.W. 3rd Ave.
Portland, OR 97204
503/228-2391

We Buy Books

5-96

Victor against a background of ferns (by courtesy of Victor's son)

The Magical Dilemma of Victor Neuburg

A Biography

Jean Overton Fuller

Mandrake
PO Box 250
Oxford OX1 1AP
(UK)

By the same author

Biographies and Studies
Madeleine: A Biography of Noor Inayat Khan, GC
Shelley, a Biography
Swinburne, A Biography
Noor-un-Nisa Inayat Khan (Madeleine)
Sir Francis Bacon, A Biography
The Comte de Saint-Germain, Last Scion of the House of
Rákóczy
Blavatsky and Her Teachers

Poetry
Carthage and the Midnight Sun
The Sun's Cart
Silver Planet
Darun and Pitar
Gilby
Tintagel
Prophecy from Helen

Poetry in Translation
Shiva's Dance (From the French of Hélène Bouvard)
That the Gods May Remember (from the French of Hélène
Bouvard)
The Prophet (from the Russian of Alexander Pushkin)

Forthcoming
Sickert and the Ripper Crimes (Autumn 1990)

ISBN 1 869928 12 1 Pbk
ISBN 1 869928 13 X Hbk
First published in 1965 by W H Allen

This Edition, revised, 1990
Printed by Dot Press, Oxford

Poetry in English - Neuburg Victor B - Biography 821'.912
© 1990 Jean Overton Fuller

Contents

Acknowledgements to the original edition

Victor's son, Mr Victor E Neuburg, by his willingness that the book should be written, lifted from my mind the fear that it might cause embarrassment to him and his family. He read it chapter by chapter as I was doing it, in the first rough, and again in proof, and lent me two albums of family snapshots from which I was able to have enlargements made of the pictures of his father and mother, their home, and relatives, which I reproduce. To avoid confusion with his father I have called him in the text by his nickname of 'Toby'. With his name I should like to associate that of his wife, Anne, whose moral support I felt as valuable.

Mr E Hayter Preston(1), Victor's longest standing friend, gave me the benefit of personal recollections of him extending over twenty-five years; he read the whole manuscript, in several of its drafts.

Mr Gerald Yorke, by lending to me, and allowing me to have in my flat for weeks at a time to study and copy, the original typescript of Crowley's (then) unpublished autobiography and the original typescripts of the unpublished magical records entitled *The Vision and the Voice* and *The Paris Working* and a number of other miscellaneous items from his incomparable library of un-published Crowley papers, made it possible for me to put together the almost day-to-day account of periods of Victor's life with Crowley which I present. Mr Yorke, also, read the whole manuscript in draft and vetted it from the point of view of his special knowledge.

Mr David Archer; the late Ethel Archer (Mrs Eugene Wieland); Mrs (Eva) Baker; Mr Francis Berry; Mr Oswell Blakeston; Mr A R Bothwell; Mr H F Burgess; Cmdr and Mrs Eric James King Bull; Mr Charles R Cammell; Mr Raymond Casey; Mr Rupert Croft-Cooke; Mr Herbert Corby; Mr H Cutner; the late Mr Leslie Daiken; Mr Cyril H Davis; Mrs (Ruby) Demusiak; Mrs (Vera) Dennis Earle (née Pragnell) and Mr Dennis Earle; Mrs Edward Noel Fitzgerald; Mr Constantine Fitzgibbon; Major-General J F C Fuller, CB, CBE, DSO; Mr Mark Goulden; Mr Brian Harker; Mrs Pamela Hughes (née Baker); Pamela Hansford Johnson (Lady Snow); Sir Gerald Kelly, KCVO, PPRA; the late KL; Mr Charles Lahr; Mr Hugo Manning; Mr Arthur Calder-Marshall; Mr G D Martineau; Dr Ralph Maud; Mr Somerset Maugham; CH; Mr Ewart Milne; Margaret Morris; Mr Arthur Leslie Morton; Lettice Newman; Mrs (Rose) Odle; the Rev Arthur Peacock; Mrs (DW) Pollard; Mr and Mrs Walter Raeburn, QC; Mr Eric Richmond; Mr Maurice Sarver; Mrs Joyce Saunders (née Haddon); Father Brocard Sewell, O Carm; Mr Frederick and Mr Oswald Carlton Smith; Mr John Symonds; Mrs (Vera) Wainwright; Mr Percy West; Dame Rebecca West, DBE; Mr Louis Umfraville Wilkinson; Miss Margaret Stanley Wrench.

Revised edition

In preparing this revised edition I should like to acknowledge the help of my friend Timothy d'Arch Smith, himself an author on Golden Dawn sub-jects. As always, he has read my proofs.

(1) Mr Preston died in Brighton in September, 1964

Book One

Vicky As I Knew Him

All mystics come from the same country, and recognise one another

De Saint-Martin

For Victor

**lines written in contemplation
of the frontispiece photograph**

A smile upon his face, head in fern,
Respected in an image grey and white
Stays he from whose blue hawk eyes shone the light
Which pierced my memory; who would not learn
The mean ways of the world; but could discern
Within the budding soul the inner sight,
The dream-wrapped spark which wand-touched welled to height
of conscious recognition; lit flames that burn
Yet, on imagination's wick. He,
stumbling, marked, bearing a fierce scorch,
Still, was my true teacher; true torch
On a dark night held high, symbol to me
Of one whose whole life was wholly given
To the mystic way, the poet's, the seer's vision.

Jean Overton Fuller

1

How I Came to Know Him

The morning post brought an envelope containing a narrow strip of paper on which was a Roneoed invitation to a meeting of the Creative Circle, 64 Springfield Road, NW8 at 8 pm, the following Saturday. It was not signed; I did not know what the Creative Circle was; if it was a club or society, the names of its officers did not appear. I might even have thrown it away!

Because the story which I have to tell is a very strange one, it may be well to say something of the teller. I was twenty, for it was the spring of 1935, and I had been born on March 7 1915. I was a posthumous child, my father, Captain J H M Fuller, a regular officer of the Indian Army, having been killed in action before I was born. I was brought up by my mother, whose life was divided between music and painting, and my grandfather, Colonel Frederick Smith, CB, CMG, DSO, RAMC who, being himself widowed, made his home with us while I was a child and really took the place of a father. His much younger cousin, Arthur Overton, an artist who scorned the philistine, was also much with us until I was fourteen.

I had been to the Royal Academy of Dramatic Art, but before finishing my course had obtained my first part on the professional stage. I was just seventeen when engaged to play juvenile leads with a new repertory company opening in Dundee, and within a few weeks illness of the leading lady enabled me to play leads earlier than would have been normal. I was just nineteen when engaged officially as leading lady, first at Porthcawl and then, for the autumn and winter, at Clacton-on-Sea.

While I enjoyed acting, I did not altogether care for the theatrical world and had come to feel that, whereas the author of a play created something, I did not want to spend my life interpreting the works of other people. My real inclination, from childhood, was towards Hermetic and Oriental wisdom but was not reflected in my outer life.

The Magical Dilemma of Victor Neuburg

I had no channel through which I could express myself but I thought I might be able to do so if I became a writer.

This, then, was me on the spring morning in 1935 when I received the slip of paper. I showed it to my mother. She said, 'NW8, that's the St John's Wood area. There are studios up there. They may be artists or unconventional people. I suppose it would do no harm to go and see. If you don't like the look of the house, you don't go in. If you find it's an invitation to pose in the nude, you'll come straight home!'

The last remark had point. Only a few days before while walking down Dean Street I had been overtaken by a running boy who said mysteriously he had been told to ask me to come upstairs. Curiosity overcoming prudence, I followed him up to a narrow, dark flight. What I found at the top was perfectly respectable. It was a commercial photographer's studio with a girl clerk at a desk and a man who explained that he wanted me to sit on a throne and smile, if possible in the way I had been smiling at the sky, when, happening to look out of the window, he had seen me from above. It was to advertise a product.

Before I left, he had induced me to pull a woolly jumper over my head and model for that, too. Unaccustomed to this sort of thing, and hardly realizing it was professional, I would have gone without more ado, but the girl at the desk stopped me and gave me a cheque, which she said was my fee. I thought this was remarkably easy money.

But because no harm had come of it, I had the feeling this spring morning that the world was a place where all sorts of curious and interesting adventures could befall one. I accepted the invitation to the unknown.

I put on a very special dress. My mother had made most my stage clothes and when she asked me what I wanted for a new spring outfit, I said 'A dress the colour of horse-chestnut leaves unfurling, in April, in the Jardins du Luxembourg'.

Surprised by this unexpectedly precise specification, her first reply was, 'I doubt whether that exact shade can be obtained in a fabric.' But she came with me into many shops, where she asked the assistants to show us something 'in apple green'. Many stuffs in light green were produced, but none the colour of the horse-chestnut leaves, just unfurling, which I had so clearly in mind. I almost gave

How I came To Know Him

up hope; and then at last, I saw it! Mother made from it a dress, a jacket to match, and the merest shell of a hat, which sat on my head like a calyx. To go with this, I bought grass green, high-heeled shoes and gloves; and it was this ensemble which I wore when I took the 31 bus to St John's Wood, and walked along Springfield Road until I came to 64.

It was a big house, detached and standing back from the road in a garden. It looked most respectable, and I pressed the bell. The door was opened by a man who, without waiting for me to speak, said, 'I'll take you through,' and began walking. I followed him. He went down a flight of stairs, and I remembered those other stairs in Dean Street which I had gone up on the heels of another guide, and wondered where I was being led this time. I realized I was descending into a private flat, in the basement of the house, but the man walked straight through the sitting-room and out through French windows at the back. Following him, I found myself in a great wilderness of a garden, overgrown with long grass, wild plants and creepers. But this was not yet our destination. The man began climbing an iron staircase on the outside of the house, and having come so far I followed. We reached an iron platform in front of a glass door of a conservatory. 'It's in there', he said. He opened the door for me, retreated, and left me to enter by myself.

In the conservatory were a number of young men sitting on wooden chairs drawn round a china fountain. There was a moment's silence while they all looked at me. Then they moved up politely and pulled up a vacant chair so that I could become one of the ring. I supposed this was the Creative Circle and wondered what it created.

Although they looked at me as though wondering why I had come among them, they did not at once address me directly, but continued with their own conversation; this was about poetry, and the name Vicky was mentioned several times. Then one of them, bolder than the rest, asked me who I was. I told him my name and my interlocutor, who had canary fair hair, asked how I had come to be here. I said I was invited and showed him the slip. He said, 'Oh that must be Geoffrey Lloyd's doing. He isn't here tonight but he said something about sending circulars to contributors.'

'Contributors to what?' I asked

'The *Sunday Referee*.'

The Magical Dilemma of Victor Neuburg

'But I'm not a contributor to the *Sunday Referee*.'

'You must be,' he said, 'or you couldn't be here.' Perceiving I was still puzzled, he explained, 'the *Poet's Corner*. You must have sent something in at some time.'

Suddenly things came together in my mind. The feature to which he referred was a weekly poetry competition, conducted by Victor B Neuburg, who judged the entries and commented critically upon those to which he awarded prizes; these he printed, together with the names of runners-up. I had sent in a poem almost a year ago. Some timidity had caused me to use one of my father's middle names, Middleton, and I regretted having used a pseudonym when I saw it in a group of names which included Margaret Stanley Wrench and Herbert Corby, entrants distinguished by Mr Neuburg as having sent in 'good poems'. But I must have enclosed my real name and my bank address, Lloyd's, Pall Mall, from where the circular had been forwarded to me.

More people began to arrive, including one or two women; all had been brought by slips of paper like that one I had received. There were no longer sufficient chairs and presently the canary fair young man said, 'I wonder if Vicky knows all these people have come to see him. Somebody had better tell him, or he may not come out.' He left the conservatory by a door leading into the interior of the house and presently reappeared with two remarkable looking people. The first to enter was evidently the lady of the house, a tall figure in grey; commanding, lean, striking in profile as in carriage, grey haired.

Though less tall than she, it was Victor Neuburg who made an instant impression of the deepest order.

He was all head, the body being but a slight affair as to its skeletal structure, and was further shrunk by emaciation. Rich brown locks grew from above a broad forehead surmounting finely chiselled, aristocratic Jewish features. But it was his eyes that were everything. They were in shadow from his brows and additionally screened by deeply hooded lids, but opened to disclose an astonishing quality of forget-me-not or celestial blue. I had never in my life before had so strong a feeling of already knowing another being; of there being no need, in the deepest sense, to create a relationship, because it was already there. Inexplicably, I thought of an ibis, with slender legs and delicate curved bill, picking its way with selective tread about the borders of a water. This feeling of the atmosphere of Lake Mareotis gave way to that of an earlier, inland Egypt and he was standing before me in a corridor built with massive, square blocks of stone.

But when he let go my hand, and his eyes were no longer looking into mine because he was shaking hands with other unexpected guests, I felt the Egyptian vibrations in his atmosphere give way to those of a nearer past; his courtliness seemed to me now to belong to the Victorian or Edwardian era.

Yet still, through this, came another layer of associations. Sand. Drifts of it blown by the wind over rock, dry and stinging. The floor of the rock was opening into a cavernous valley. It seemed to be the valley of Hell; and I felt that he had been into it and came out alive.

Yet there was fun in his smile. He and the lady whom I heard called Runia sat down with us and we all drew our chairs together, those who had none squatting on their heels or on the rim of the fountain. I noticed that Victor Neuburg - Vicky - had no socks; his worn flannels ruckled to show ankles and shins of painful thinness. He wore also an ancient tweed sports jacket, frayed at the cuffs and gone at the elbows.

One of the young men explained the idea that we should meet here every Saturday. Vicky and Runia looked at each other; they said there was no reason why not. Whether or not they were at home, we could always use the conservatory and Cyril Moor would let us in, as he had done this evening. Runia became fired by the idea that this was to become the headquarters of an important cultural group, and suggested we should invite well-known people to come and lecture to us. 'And' she declared, 'we must have that hideous fountain removed!'

There was a cry of anguish from Vicky. 'Oh no, I love it because it's so hideous!' Within the rim of the trough was a central pedestal, climbed by coloured china frogs, lizards and water weeds. Vicky declared, 'It's the epitome of the spirit of the people who built these houses, a monument to an age that has almost gone. I realize that by the canons of modern taste it's monstrously ornate. but I like it. Let it remain!'

The lady, laughing as though he were being outrageous, cried, 'We don't all share your perverted sentimentality!' It has got to go, she said. If we were to have well-known people here to address us, we should need to arrange the chairs in rows, which we couldn't do 'with that thing in the middle.'

Vicky transferred his defence of it from the spiritual to a practical plane. 'I don't know that the terms of our lease give us the right to remove fixtures. It's part of the structure of the house.' I gathered they had only just moved in.

Runia wanted us to have a name as a group, and Vicky suggested, Zoists'.

'What does it mean?' we asked.

'*Zoos*, in Greek, means *living*. It could mean people putting more life into things. I only thought of it because it begins with a Z and so few things do.'

There was a thoughtful silence.

'You don't have to have it,' he said.

We agreed to Zoists.

Runia wanted us to have badges, 'so that one Zoist can recognize another, if you meet outside, or if we have provincial centres.'

There was a murmur of dissent. Some of us felt this thing was getting inflated. And we didn't want badges. We weren't boy scouts; just a few people who wanted to come here and sit and talk to each other on Saturday evenings.

'All right, no badges,' she said. 'But it is agreed we have a name?'

It was agreed but there was no enthusiasm for the name, our feeling being for the informal. Before we left Runia made us cups of tea.

When eventually we broke up, and I stood again in the road outside, I felt I could tell my mother I had been among distinguished people. But the truth was I felt something else as well. I felt I had been in ancient Egypt and for this feeling I could find no explanation.

Not all of those who had been present on the first evening returned the following Saturday, but as I attended every week I began to know the regulars. Arriving soon after 8 (dinner at the hotel where my mother and I lived, was at 7, so it was a rush), I always found a certain number of people there already, though there was usually some time

B

to wait until Vicky and Runia came from the inner room. It was
in this waiting time that I had to find my feet, as it were among
the other young ones. Nobody was ever introduced at Vicky's.
One just found out for oneself. I did not find the young men easy
although they made efforts to draw me into the circle, for they
assumed an acquaintance with modern poetry and political authors greater than I possessed; I could not always follow their
allusions, and I had the feeling they all participated in a form of
culture slightly strange to me. I was therefore grateful when a
good looking young man, quiet mannered and of a more ordinarily civilized demeanour, settled himself beside me and asked,
simply, 'How did you come to Vicky's?'

I told him about the circular letter I had received. He knew Geoffrey
Lloyd had sent some out and asked, 'What do you do when you're
not writing poems for Vicky? What's your background, so to speak?'

I told him I had been on the stage since I was seventeen.

He said 'Fancy our having an actress among us!'

'What's your name?' I asked him.

'William Thomas', was what I first thought he said, but then he
added, 'It's a special Welsh name.'

There could be nothing very special about William, and I puckered
my brows.

'You'll never have heard it before,' he said. 'Nobody in England ever
has. It should really be pronounced Wullam, in Welsh.' Or was he
saying 'Dullan'?

'It's a special Welsh name,' he repeated. 'I shall have to spell it for
you. D-Y-L-A-N. In Wales, it's pronounced Dullan. But I'd been corresponding with Vicky for some time before I came to London, and
when I arrived I found he had been calling me Dillan, in his mind. I
thought if Vicky didn't know how to pronounce it nobody in England
would, so I decided to take it as the standard English pronunciation of
my name. Otherwise I'd spend all my time telling people it was Dull
and not Dill, and I think perhaps Dillan sounds more elegant than
Dullan. Only Idris objects and thinks it's frightfully fancy! Because
he's Welsh, too, and he knows! but now I'm getting even Idris trained
to call me Dillan, though it's under protest!'

'What part of Wales do you come from?' I said.

'Oh, I only come from a small town. Swansea.'

Whereas I had previously felt myself to be the most naive member of a group otherwise composed of sophisticated, bohemian intellectuals, I now felt I had, vis-à-vis Dylan Thomas, at any rate, an advantage in being a Londoner. 'I should have thought Swansea was a large town,' I said. 'I was near there all last summer. If you had been to the theatre at Porthcawl you would have seen me on the stage!'

'No, I'm afraid I didn't' he said. 'What a pity!'

Giving the conversation a turn he did not expect, I said, 'Have you ever been down a mine?'

'No.'

'I have!' I explained triumphantly. 'Near Crumlin. I once played a January date in the Rhondda. Or more exactly the Ebbw Vale.' I told him how I had persuaded the men at a pit to take me down the shaft, and how, having arrived at the bottom, I was given a lamp to hold and escorted along a passage which had been hewed through the coal to a point where it became so low that one would have had to proceed on hands and knees. I was shown a fault seam, which I felt with my fingers.

'You have seen something in Wales which I haven't!' said Dylan. He explained that his home was some distance from the mining regions. He described the part of Swansea where he lived, with a detail I cannot now recall, except that it sounded salubrious and agreeable. His father was Senior English Master at the Grammar School. 'Living where I do one doesn't really see anything of all that,' he said, with reference to my allusion to the coal mining (and depressed) areas. 'Idris comes from the Rhondda,'(1) he said. 'I haven't been into those areas.' As though he had been slightly shamed by my adventure, he added, 'Perhaps I ought to have done.'

'It's because you live there that you wouldn't think of it,' I said. 'When one is touring one feels one must see everything in case one never comes again. When I was sixteen, my mother and I made a tour of Italy, Pisa, Rome, Naples, Capri, and back through Perugia, Florence and Milan. We felt we had to go into everything, even the smallest church we passed on any street. We realized we had never "done" London half as thoroughly because we took it for granted.'

I have no 'outrageous' sayings of Dylan Thomas to record. His conversation with me was perfectly drawing-room and unexceptional. I remember him as a polite young man. Friendly, but not at all presuming.

He told me the origins of the circle of which I now formed part. 'First one and then another of us found our way to Vicky's through entering into correspondence with him or something like that, and so a circle grew up around Vicky. We're all very fond of Vicky.' He explained that, 'always reading each other's names in print we began to wonder what the ones whom we hadn't seen were like.' So they had had the idea 'of sending out circulars to everybody who was a contributor. He thought it had brought in some interesting people. 'Well, it has brought you!' Perhaps one could name some kind of a regular thing of it. 'The only thing I don't like is the name Zoists!' he said.

I laughed and said, 'It does sound a bit like protozoa, zoophytes and zoids!'

Dylan pulled a funny face.

'We're always called "Vicky's children",' said Dylan. 'It's a bit sentimental, but I don't think we shall ever be called anything else.'

It had been at the back of my mind while he was speaking that his name, as he had spelled it out, was one which I had read in the *Sunday Referee* in a context more important than that of the weekly prizes. I had not taken the paper regularly before I joined the circle, or I would have known the whole build-up. I said, 'Aren't you the winner of a big prize? I believe you're one of the distinguished people here!'

'It was through Vicky and the *Sunday Referee* that a book of my poems has been published,' he said. He explained that a prize was offered twice yearly, part of which consisted in the publication of the winner's poems in book form. 'The first was awarded to Pamela Hansford Johnson. She isn't here tonight. I was given the second of them.' He said that Vicky had helped him pick out what he thought were the best of the poems he had written.

'What's it called?'

'Just *18 Poems*. It was published just before Christmas, and I think it's doing quite well.' He added, 'I'm very grateful to Vicky. It's a big thing for me. One's first book is the most difficult to get published. Everyone says so. Now that I have one book published, it should be easier to get the next accepted, perhaps by an ordinary firm.'

My sentiment for Vicky was already so strong that I was slightly shocked.

Dylan Thomas saw it. 'Vicky doesn't expect us to stay with him!' he said. 'This is a nursery school from which we are expected to go out into the world. When we can get published elsewhere nobody is more pleased than Vicky!'

Just then the moment for which we had been waiting arrived. The door from the inner part of the house opened and our hosts came out to join us.

Vicky came straight up to Dylan and me. I did not know which of us the distinction was meant for but it gave me joy. He stood by my chair, looking down on us beamingly, and said to Dylan, 'You're entertaining this little lady?'

Dylan said, 'I've been telling her something of the history of the *Poet's Corner*.'

Other regulars included the canary fair one; he was Geoffrey Pollet, a New Zealander, and he had tramped England selling his own poems, from house to house, and written a book about it, *Song for Sixpence*, which was being published by Longmans. Herbert Corby was a cheeky little Cockney sparrow with bright eyes and a neat appearance. Walter Ford aimed at sophistication, wore a drooping moustache, described himself as a Materialist and worked at the Belgian embassy. Idris Davies, whom Dylan had first pointed out to me, was a stocky little man with dark hair and a strong Welsh accent. He was a miner's son. These four constituted a gang which adopted me. As they escorted me from Vicky's, Idris would declaim upon the night air Yeats's 'I will arise and go now, and go to Innisfree', which I shall never now be able to dissociate from his Welsh lilt. Usually they took me to a pub in Great Marlborough Street, and once to the famous Café Royal where we seated ourselves in a row on the red plush and ordered lagers, and Ford said, 'We ought to have brought Vicky, to make it seem real!'

How I came To Know Him

Geoffrey Lloyd proved to be a Left Wing young man just down from Oxford. Prominent also was a young Irishman called Leslie Daiken who was always friendly to me. Brian Crozier and George Rae came together. One evening I talked with Julian Symons through whom I met George Woodcock, who would become leader of the TUC.

Sometimes there was Maurice Sarver, Manager of the Unicorn Press. In connection with my novel I had been tempted by an advertisement from a firm that wanted young authors - but also a premium from them. I told Vicky. He looked grave. He took me over to Sarver, told him what I had told him, and said, ' I would like you to tell this little lady what you think about that proposition.' Sarver said I must have nothing to do with it. 'If your book is any good you will find a publisher who will produce it at his own expense and pay you a royalty'. As he was a publisher I was tempted to ask him to read it, but my mother had always told me it wasn't nice to exploit the professional capacity of people one knew socially.

Then there was Cyril Moore, who had the basement flat, and let us in. He was Advertising Manager of the *Sunday Referee* but interested in Yoga.

But the one who made the strongest impression on me, after Vicky, was Arthur Leslie Morton. He was exceptionally tall and gaunt, with interesting hollows in his cheeks and light coloured hair, a flop of which seemed always before his eye. He wore an open necked shirt and had something to do with the *Daily Worker*. He had no small talk whatever. Indeed, he said almost nothing, which increased his mystery. When asked his opinion on a philosophical or sociological question, he would begin with a hesitation and then say, 'Well, yes and no.'

One afternoon Runia suggested somebody should climb the pear tree and bring down some of the fruit. I volunteered and so did Morton. Runia exclaimed, as though he were too distinguished a person to be sent on such a mission, 'Oh, I didn't mean you, Arthur. I meant one of the children!' Nevertheless, he accompanied me through the garden. When we reached the pear tree, to my surprise, he crouched down on his hands and knees at the foot of it. In this posture, he remained, apparently waiting for something to happen. I did not understand

and stood, simply looking. 'If you mount on my back, when I stand up you will be able to reach into the branches ' he said, twisting his head a little. Though members of the same circle we had not been introduced, and these were the first words he had addressed to me. I did as bid. 'If you hand the pears down to me as you pick them, it will be the best division of labour,' he said.

I had the impression his friendship with Vicky went back to a period anterior to the *Poet's Corner* in which, though it appeared he was a poet, he did not compete. Sometimes he was accompanied by a beautiful, and even more silent, girl, whom I later learned was his wife, Vivien.

The link between all of us was the *Sunday Referee*. Taking it for Vicky's column, we would read others. In particular the centre page sociological article, signed Vanoc II, often formed a subject of discussion. Vicky would hint with affectionate slyness that he knew the identity of Vanoc and there was a general belief that he was the Literary Editor, Hayter Preston(2)

We had been meeting perhaps four or five weeks when we decided that Saturday June 29 should be sacrificed to practical matters. When I arrived I found Herbert Corby, Idris Davies, Geoffrey Pollet and Walter Ford already there. Dylan Thomas and Geoffrey Lloyd came in escorting between them a petite, slight girl, with dark hair and intelligent eyes. From the cheer with which she was greeted I knew she must be someone of consequence. She was carrying a bottle of beer, and Dylan and Geoffrey Lloyd were each carrying bottles. 'How thoughtful of you!' I exclaimed.

'Where's Vicky?' they asked. We told them Vicky and Runia appeared to be out. This caused consternation, as they had expected Vicky and Runia would provide glasses. Pollet suggested we could go into their rooms and get glasses from the sideboard. The girl, whom I heard addressed as Pamela, said she did not think Runia would like us to go into their rooms in their absence.

'We don't need glasses,' I said, 'We can drink from the bottles!'

There was a silence. Everybody was thinking hard. Idris replied. 'There aren't as many bottles as there are of us. There wouldn't be one for each person to drink from.'

Feeling dashing, I said, 'We could give them a wipe before passing round. I don't suppose any of us is suffering form anything contagious!'

Five bottles was an awkward number to share between eight people. Someone said, 'Dylan, you can have a whole one, as you're the fondest of beer!' Ford said he did not feel like having any. That left four bottles between six people, which was still awkward, as we had nothing into which to measure out the contents equally. Dylan said, 'I can simplify your problem still further. I will drink two whole bottles. That will leave you with three between six. Half each.'

So he had two bottles. Pamela shared with Geoffrey Lloyd. Idris said he would share with me and gave me the first drink.

We stacked the empties and pulled up our chairs round the fountain. Pads and pencils were produced; the first question was whether we were going to charge a subscription. At this point Pamela took charge. 'I have a suggestion to make' she said. 'I am in favour of a subscription because it would enable us to provide refreshments. Tea or coffee and biscuits, which could be handed round on plates.' Vicky and Runia would perhaps allow us to use their china, or if we made the subscription high enough we could buy our own. I seconded this proposal and thought we should get our own, for if we used Runia's we should always be terrified of breaking it. This motion having been carried we settled the subscription at 5s per half year, and elected Pollett Treasurer. It had come to be accepted that we were the Committee.

Dylan used the occasion to say he didn't like the name Zoists.

Pamela supported him. 'It suggests we are a menagerie. We don't want to give people an excuse to laugh at us.'

Geoffrey Lloyd recalled he had suggested the Creative Circle; but the others thought this sounded pretentious.

I said 'The Conservatory Club! We always meet in the conservatory!'

'People might confuse it with Conservative', said Walter Ford.

Various other suggestions were put forward and turned down.

Dylan himself had none to make. And we remained Zoists.

The next question was whether we had any aims; if we were going to send out further circular letters these should be stated. We decided we hadn't any. We were not gathered together for the purpose of reading our own poetry to each other. It was embarrassing for the person read to if he didn't think it was good, because he had either to say something insincere or something which would cause disappointment. We made a rule against members reading their own poetry to other members. We just wanted to meet each other and talk.

This brought us to the question of whether we should, as Runia had urged, invite well-known people to come and talk to us. None of us really wanted it. Idris said well-known people weren't always interesting, might not want to be bothered to come and speak to us, or worse, might expect to be paid. Surely we had enough ideas in our own heads to keep each other interested. We could take it in turns to present our ideas on something to the others. Vicky should be our chairman, and he should be asked to give us a talk on *Alice's Adventures in Wonderland* to start the ball rolling, after which the next week's talk should be by one of us. 'Dylan?' inquired Geoffrey Pollett, who had been made responsible for organizing talks.

Dylan said he would in the course of the week be returning to Wales and this would be his last evening with us for some time. We said it was a pity we had wasted his last evening with us in so dull a way; if we had known we would have done something to celebrate; but Dylan said he was glad to have been here while the decisions were taken.

Pollett turned to Pamela. She pleaded she had nothing to say.

'But if *you* haven't, which of us has?' said Pollett. 'You're our shining light.' It was at this moment that I became certain (as the case was in fact) that Pamela was Pamela Hansford Johnson.

After some urging, in a tiny voice she agreed to try.

Pollett turned to me. 'Do you think you could give us a talk?'

'If it doesn't have to be about poetry,' I said.

'Something about the theatre?' he suggested. But I was trying to get away from the theatre and said, 'Something more philosophical, if that isn't too abstract.' It was agreed talks need not be about poetry; they should, generally, have some relation to it, but we would not be hidebound.

We were advancing in our deliberations when Vicky and Runia came in. Runia saw the stacked beer bottles, stiffened, and said 'What are those?'

Pamela rose and said, 'We thought you wouldn't mind our bringing some beer to drink here.' I thought she sounded anxious.

Runia looked about and asked what we had drunk from.

I said, thinking it amusing, 'We drank from the bottles.'

'Disgusting!' Runia said. As she moved about, repeating this word, I thought at first she was mimicking the manner of an angry person in order to be amusing. Then with sudden shock I realized it was real, I was dumbfounded. Dylan sat tight-lipped. He didn't apologize. Neither did I. Then Runia accused us of inconsideration towards Vicky. She said, 'The smell of beer is repugnant to him'.

This did cause me distress. I would not for the world have done anything he did not like. Turning to him I said, 'I didn't know.'

'I don't mind it,' he said.

'He's only *saying* that,' said Runia. 'The fumes disgust him!'

'I'm so sorry,' I said to Vicky.

'But I don't mind it,' he repeated, his eyes open wide into mine, blue and innocent. 'Really I don't! It's quite all right.'

Runia continued about the odour of beer, and suddenly Vicky said to her, 'Oh, do stop making such a fuss!'

I wished his voice were not so frail, hers being so strong, but he maintained our defence, saying she was making a storm in a tea-cup and being a spoil-sport. It was developing into a dissension between them; somebody nudged me, and said, 'We'd better go'.

(1) More accurately, the Ebbw

(2) Mr Preston confirmed to me that this was so

2
Early Days at the Zoists

Vicky accepted the invitation to become our chairman, and also to give the first formal talk, though he began, ' I'll talk about "Alice", but I'm taking as my title "Nonsense Poetry", which will give me a little more scope.' He started by reading:

> Twas brillig and the slithy toves
> Did gyre and gimble in the wabe.

This might be called nonsense, yet to almost everybody it meant something. 'Nobody could be so dull as not to know what a slithy tove is! Probably most people form a picture of some sort of octopus, with tentacles.'

He read from the first chapter, and pointed out how everything became rather peculiar for Alice from the moment when, following the white rabbit - a symbol of intuition, but here also of curiosity - she fell down the rabbit hole, from which the only way of escape seemed to be by following the rabbit farther, through the gate through which it had disappeared, but through which she could not pass. The only aids to hand were magic commodities in bottles labelled EAT ME and DRINK ME; but when she had partaken of the one it made her too small to reach up to the golden key, and when she had partaken of the other it made her too big to get through the gate. ' This is absolutely occult!' Vicky declared. 'The man who wrote this had, consciously or unconsciously, knowledge of occult law!'

He put down *Alice*, picked up another book, and said, ' I'll read you a different kind of nonsense which has meaning.'

> They went to sea in a Sieve, they did,
> In a Sieve they went to sea;
> In spite of all their friends could say,
> On a winter's morn, on a stormy day,

Because I had never before heard this poem by Edward Lear, 'The Jumblies', the effect on me was of something out of this world.

Early Days at the Zoists

Shortly after this he gave us a second talk on *The Idea of Poetry*. From the pile of books he had assembled on the table beside his chair, it was evident that this evening he was going to proceed with more scholarly method. After some preliminary remarks about the early Greek poets' attitude to themselves and the observation that Plato, surprisingly, was rather disappointing on poetry, he began by opening Aristotle's *Poetics*. 'There isn't a great deal in it for us,' he said, 'as it doesn't deal with Lyric poetry.' Nevertheless, he read some of it, ran his finger down the rest of the pages, summarizing the main ideas, and then jumped several centuries to locate in Milton's *Tractate: Of Education* the phrase, 'Poetry would be...simple, sensuous and passionate.' He went on to Wordsworth; 'Poetry is the spontaneous overflow of powerful feeling...emotion recollected in tranquillity.' Then he passed to Shelley's *Defence of Poetry*, with which he became identified: 'A man, to be greatly good, must imagine intensely and comprehensively...Poetry is at once the centre and circumference of knowledge...the mind in creation is like a fading coal...when composition begins, inspiration is already on the decline...Poets are the unacknowledged legislators of the world.'

Reading these lines he had become incandescent. After this he thought it would be too much of a descent into dull clay to quote from Matthew Arnold, though he had marked some passages in the *Study of Poetry*. These he summarized. He warmed back to human sympathy with Housman's *Name and Nature of Poetry*, savouring whimsically the odd phrase, 'Poetry is a secretion.'

Before he closed he quoted a line or two of verse which seemed to me exquisitely eloquent; it was not from a book, and though I listened for the name of the author he did not give it. I thought the lines were probably from some well-known work and did not like to expose my ignorance by asking. Nevertheless, as the gathering was breaking up and I could do so without being overheard by the others, I asked Vicky, saying, 'I thought it was so beautiful.'

Blushing in pleased confusion, he said, 'Oh! it's just something of mine which I printed a long time ago.'

At some point on each Saturday evening the door from the garden would open and Cyril Moore would come in with the tea. He made it on his stove in the kitchen of his flat below, where he housed our provisions. I had offered to come down and make it but he said he had everything to hand.

Generally speaking, there were very few girls at the Zoists. After the evening with the beer I did not see Pamela for a long time. Occasionally a new girl would appear but she never stayed. Most often I was the only one. As so considerable a company of young men would normally have attracted a fringe of girls, I wondered if they found Runia intimidating.

The chairs in the conservatory being hard, I bought cretonne and kapok and made a set of pads with tape by which they could be attached. This won me a measure of Runia's approval, she said it showed the 'Group Spirit'. I did not think in 'group ' terms but I was thankful she was pleased as without being welcomed by her it would have been difficult to continue coming to see Vicky. Although I enjoyed the atmosphere of lively intellectual discussion I did not think of myself as a poet and none of the young men interested me sentimentally.

Runia wanted me to get them to do a play. The garden, she said, would make a wonderful setting for a theatrical performance. I was not eager to put this forward. Having known the professional theatre, amateur theatricals had no attraction for me, and it was plain none of the others wanted to do anything but talk. I mentioned the idea to them but they did not respond, and I had to resist Runia's urging I should push it further.

If Vicky referred to an author's work, it was always to say something perceptive, but I think Runia often referred to authors whose names she had heard on the lips of others but whose work she had not read. I was mindful of my mother's counsel, however, that when dealing with a couple one should distribute one's conversation between them equally; and indeed I tried to like Runia because it was plain Vicky wanted us to do so. It seemed to me that respect for him must include respect for the companion of his choice. To some extent this attitude paid dividends. Although always aware that my acceptance by Runia was precarious, I survived.

Once, when only I and one other turned up, Runia told us all she had done for Vicky. It appeared that she had built up his health from a shadow. 'I wanted to have him psycho-analyzed,' she finished. 'Jung was interested in him...'

'I will not be psycho-analyzed!' Vicky declared. 'That's the point where I put my foot down. I shall take my complexes to the grave with me! I've had them so long they've grown comfortable, like old shoes. I can go one better than the lady who read the Medical Directory and decided she'd got everything in it except housemaid's knee. I read Freud and knew I'd got the lot! In any case, I've never lacked personal friends to tell me I've got an Oedipus complex and that I'm a masochist.'

I was surprised by this word and I must have looked it for Vicky said, 'Yes, really. One person was always telling me I was a masochist.'

I must have looked distressed for he hastened to say reassuringly, 'I didn't think I was and I said I wasn't. But it's impossible to argue with Freudians, because if you deny it they say that proves it. They've always got you, whichever way you answer, on their two-pronged fork. They can tell you you're anything they like to think of. I don't really think I'm a masochist.'

I knew Vicky liked me because he would come and sit beside me, singling me out. The young men of the Zoists talked often about new poets and I sat silent while the names of Auden and Spender flashed between them. Vicky, divining that I had not read a great deal of contemporary poetry, tried me on Dickens. Unfortunately this was not a good field for me. Feeling I must be sincere, I said I had never been able to get on with Dickens because he didn't make his heroines like real girls.

Vicky said, 'Perhaps Dickens didn't know how to make them like real girls.'

I was timid with him because of his great learning; but I realized, with surprise, that he was timid with me. This I could not understand as I supposed him to be a man of vast experience. His movements, also, had a jerkiness which I at first thought to proceed from nervousness, though I later realized that it belonged to a constitutional, almost physical nervous inco-ordination. He would address me out of the side of his head, as it were, in a tangential manner, and in the third person, as 'this little lady', or once, 'this little lady in green.' I always felt I wanted to put on the green dress when I went to Vicky's and persisted, despite my mother's amused remark that they would think I had nothing else and that it grew on me!

Sometimes, when he faced me across a whole roomful of people, his wide eyes made their way into mine with a long, unflinching looking. I felt something I had not done with any other person, that there was a spiritual consanguinity. I believed he felt it, too, for sometimes he would address me to the core of what he was saying, and his eyes would become for me the eyes of the Horus Hawk. Of this, I had seen statuettes in the Louvre and in the British Museum. It seemed to me the poised symbol of Will and Knowledge. But I could not understand why I had this persistent illusion of Vicky's identification with it. There was nothing Egyptian in the conservatory. When he drew his chair next to mine again, he became once more the awkward, learned man addressing a young girl, and my own shyness reasserted itself. I never told him I saw him as the Hawk of Horus. I was afraid it would sound silly. He never spoke of Egypt

One evening, as we were sitting in a semi-circle talking, Vicky suddenly sat straight back in his chair and emitted a high-pitched, unmodulated cackle, sustained upon a single note. I received quite a shock as I realized that this was his laugh. His general speech and manners were so quiet and so courteous that I was unprepared for the utterance of a sound which seemed to me uncouth, and indeed unnatural, for most peoples' bursts of laughter have a beginning and an end, a crescendo and a diminuendo, a rise in pitch followed by a fall, but this was a screech upon a single note, which ceased as suddenly as it had begun. I was almost embarrassed for him; I had been taught that one should not laugh immoderately and I could not reconcile this strange sound with the rest of his personality. It went with a sudden rigidity of the whole person and seemed hysterical or compulsive.

Later, I discovered that other people were disconcerted by this laugh. Runia once apologized to all of us for it, saying, 'He isn't laughing at you. You must none of you ever think he's laughing at you. It's just some private joke of his own.'

I never, in fact, made any mistake about this. But as his chain of thought was unlike other peoples', so his laughter sometimes seemed causeless. As I got to know him better, however, and my mind began to follow the tracks of his, I was often able to anticipate the junctures at which the shrieking laughter was going to take place and to be infected by it myself.

Fragments of his speech remain in my mind: for instance, his saying, as the shadows of the summer evening drew about us (for there was no electric light in the conservatory), with reference to the sonnet as a form, 'There's something *about* those fourteen lines - the four, the four-, the six- the eight, the six. I don't know what it is. It won't

Kabbalize.' (This was a word I had not heard before, and which, like others of his utterance I committed to memory). 'Or at least, I can't make it. Yet I'm sure it's a magical form. That's why the effect is so special.'

I discovered that Vicky detested the practice of teaching children to learn poetry by heart. He was sure that it was because they were made to do this at school that their enjoyment in it was killed. He also maintained that there was no relation between ability to quote long stretches of poetry from memory and appreciation of poetry; often there seemed to be an inverse ratio. Neither did he agree with Auden that the test of poetry lay in its memorability; as he pointed out, by far the most memorable kind of verse is a jingle!

Once Vicky and one or two of the young men, including Cyril Moore, were standing in the French windows outside the latter's flat, when I joined them. Vicky was showing his arm, saying, 'We had to give ourselves little cuts every time we said "I". Just a little discipline. But it was surprising how difficult it was not to do it inadvertently.'

I wondered to what course this discipline referred. The young men were regarding him with great curiosity and one of them said something about 'evoking the gods'.

Vicky said, '*In*voke! you can't evoke what is superior to man. You evoke the little creatures.' Saying this, he made a graceful bow towards the earth, making a beckoning movement, as though a company of gnomes would spring up beneath his hand.

Somebody mentioned superstition; Vicky said there was an element of superstitious - super-standing- structure in all religion. By this he meant forms and procedures which had become divorced from the understanding of their origin. He would tell a story which illustrated the process of religious superstition. There was a yogi who had a cat. The cat worried him when he meditated by rubbing up against him. 'It disturbed the currents,' he said, with a look at Cyril Moore. 'To keep it away he tied it up before beginning to meditate. Another yogi came by, saw this, and supposed that a tied cat was an aid to meditation. Some fifty years later there was in this valley a colony of yogis, none of whom ever sat down to meditate without first procuring a cat and tying it by the leg.'

I was thrilled by the intimation that Vicky had knowledge of meditation and yoga. When I was fourteen I had meditated on the Tibetan prayer-wheel which had been given to my father in 1913 by the Prime Minister of Tibet. Round it were carved ivory Buddhas. When alone I would seat myself cross-legged, in imitation of their attitude, hold it in my lap or against my forehead, and say aloud, 'Please, Holy Men of Tibet, give me teaching.'

I never had any visions while doing this, which puzzled me, as ordinarily I had a good deal of 'coloured cinema,' which was the term I gave to the pictures which formed themselves inexplicably before my eyes at all times. They might be of anything: flowers, persons, scenes, objects, or geometrical shapes. They never had any obvious connection with anything of which I was thinking. I suspected there might be a subtle one, but, though normally in motion, they stopped, or rather vanished, the moment I tried to examine them and only recommenced when I was content to let them pass without trying to understand. I had never known anybody with whom I could discuss these things but I believed that Vicky might know about me. It came to me that he was the person I had always been looking for who would perhaps be willing to teach me. But I did not like to presume, so did not push myself upon his notice by asking questions. If it were as I thought time would unfold it.

Meanwhile, I learned from the merest words he dropped. I had not, at that time, read Plato; but from Vicky had learned that the Real could be considered as that of which the visible and tangible world was the shadow; I came to recognize that he used in a special way the words memory and know. When he said know, his whole being seemed to be brought to a focus.

One evening he asked me, 'Are you related to General J F C Fuller?'

'No', I said.

I did not at that time know anything about General Fuller, and so I did not understand why he said, ' It would have meant something to me if you had.' It seemed to me that he had been groping for the key to something, and was disappointed because he had not found it. He said, 'He's somebody I used to know.' This gave me no clue as to its nature. Suddenly, as though he almost discarded my answer, he exclaimed, 'But there is something! There is! There is! I know I'm not wrong! Strange...'

I was too timid to ask what he had in his mind.

On another evening, I looked up, to meet his eyes, and he said, 'I believe that you remember.'

It seemed to me that he was using the word in the special sense that I only half apprehended.

I found that some people came on Sunday afternoons and had tea in the garden. I brought as my contribution a bag of gooseberries. Vicky came and sat beside me on the grass and began picking them out of the bag, which ceased to be passed round when it became evident he was making his meal from them. This was noticed by several of the others with smiles but without comment for, like a wild bird, he was not to be disturbed while feeding, lest he took fright and flew away. Absorbed and unconscious, he continued until he had eaten them all.

Then, feeling the dampness of the ground, he moved to a low pedestal which must once have supported a piece of statuary. The shadows lengthened, and we still sat. Suddenly George Rae startled the atmosphere with a cry: 'Great Gods, does Vicky look like Pan, or a goblin, or what?'

I supposed it was because in the dusk, sitting motionless, Vicky seemed to merge into the growing, breathing, leafage of the garden that Rae had made his exclamation and did not understand when somebody else said, 'Truth will out!'

I thought there was in Vicky's reaction just the faintest shade of annoyance, though he managed to convert it into a tone of amused petulance, as he replied, 'It's unintentional. Can't I even sit in my own garden...I'm so harmless, really!'

But even Runia looked slightly agitated, although her tone was one of banter as she besought him to come down off the pedestal. 'You look too elfish there for anyone to feel comfortable. Sit on the ground among us.'

'The grass is wet,' he said.

I had my coat, the others rugs. A newspaper was spread out for him and eventually he dropped on to it.

It belonged to the same unaccountable, almost unreal world when on another afternoon in the garden he came beside me and said, ' I have a son...'

I knew by this time that Runia was not his wife. Walter Ford had told me. But I did not know if he had ever had a wife. 'You have a son?' I repeated uncertainly.

'Yes,' he said. There was pride in his voice, the pride of someone who has produced something; but there was also a far away quality as he continued, 'I see him sometimes...when I am able to slip down there...'

There seemed to be some impediment to his visits to the child and I supposed he must be without legal title to it. I pictured him slipping into some house by stealth, or merely peering through the windows from the outside.

Morton gave us a talk in the conservatory. His title was *Poets, Town and Country*, and he began by saying, 'I assure you it isn't an excuse to talk about Housman and nothing else!' He read some Hardy and some Edward Thomas. Then he settled down to Housman.

In the discussion which followed, Vicky said Housman was a stoic philosopher and seemed to him like an old Roman. He was of the breed of Marcus Aurelius, Catullus and Lucretius. 'His only English peer in outlook is Emily Bronte'.

Pollett gave us a talk on selling *Songs for Sixpence*; and somebody spoke about *Men of the Trees*. I spoke on something.

Sometimes discussions took on a political slant; there was a Left Wing of which Geoffrey Lloyd was the most pronounced member. Then provoking sallies began to be heard. They came from a vinegar-like little man with a sandy moustache. Exasperated, somebody said, 'Who are you?' He replied, 'I'm a member of the British Union of Fascists!' An electric current went round. It was as if a spy had been discovered in our midst. One noticed suddenly that the moustache was Hitler-shaped. The atmosphere became threatening.

Vicky, very serious and polite, said, 'It seems this gentleman has something he wishes to say to us. The only way I can see to relieve the situation is to offer him an evening on which to give us a talk.'

Geoffrey Lloyd thought the situation would be met adequately if 'this gentleman' were told his presence was not welcome.

Vicky seemed taller than his usual height as he drew himself to his feet and said, 'I've told you before, I will not have this place made into a Communist Party platform! You've got the wrong idea!' He was so stern, I thought I had never seen him before. Controlling the whole room with his authority he said, 'Either it's a free platform for all, or else all political discussion will have to stop. We should then become like one of those clubs or college halls in which it is forbidden to mention politics, religion, or any lady's name. But that would be rather dull. It assumes gentlemen are incapable of discourse on these heads without becoming abusive.' The price of freedom, he said, was self control, and courtesy towards those with whose views one was not in accordance. Tolerance, if not catholic, was nothing. Speaking with tremendous incision, he declared, 'You should read Voltaire! *I hate what the man says, but I'll fight to the death for his right to say it.*'

There was a silence. Looks were surly. But when Vicky said, 'As your Chairman, I can then invite this gentleman to speak to us next Saturday?' there was no dissent.

I remained for a moment after the others had gone. Runia said to Vicky, 'He'll bring along some of Mosley's toughs and there'll be a roughhouse. We shall have to call the police; and by the time they get here somebody will have been hurt.'

She was frightened. Vicky, though subdued and conscious of the danger he had made possible, was not to be shaken from the stand he had taken. He said, 'Isn't reason a weapon? We shall see which side has the better reasons. It should make an interesting occasion for the comparison of values.'

When I arrived the following Saturday, the first thing I noticed was that the usual composition of the group had changed. Familiar faces were missing. With dismay I realized that Geoffrey Lloyd and the other politicals had chosen to mark their disapproval by absenting themselves instead of being here to present their reasons. Instead there were a number of big, burly figures; they did not look like poets, and I could not help remembering Runia's words.

The Fascist was there. Vicky, nervous but self-possessed, took the Chair, and presented, 'Mr - I don't think I've been told your name.'

The guest gave a name and said, 'I claim to be the only British Nazi!' Of the speech that followed, I remember only one phrase, 'Moses was a good Fascist!' But it was all about superior and inferior races. I felt someone had to help Vicky, and there was only me there to do it. Being untrained in political theory all I could do was take the thing on to another plane. Starting from the observation that the greater teachers of mankind, from Gautama Buddha to Jesus Christ, had chosen to lay their emphasis on what men had in common rather than on what separated them, I produced a second and complementary argument.

'Light, when it's refracted, proves to be composed of the many colours which can be seen in the rainbow. If one of the colours is missing there is no longer the white light, which is the only total and complete light. Perhaps the different races of man are like the colours of the spectrum.'

To my relief, support came from a young man whom I had not seen there before; he had the robust, outdoor look of a hiker. Later I learned his name was Hugo Manning.

Finally the big, burly figures came into tongues; and not on the side of the Fascist. So they were not Mosley's men. Vicky asked them who they were. They gave their names and the positions they held; they were high up members of the Communist Party. They said they had heard there was going to be a 'do' here tonight, and had come, 'in case you needed help'. Geoffrey Lloyd must have asked them to come.

The whole thing finished more or less amicably; our own politicals came in, their arrival coinciding with that of the tea.

The Fascist did not reappear; neither did the burly officials of the Communist Party. It had, however, dawned on me by this time that the feeling of the house was Socialist. My family background was entirely Conservative. It was my first encounter with the Left Wing intelligentsia and I was more ears than voice. Only Geoffrey Lloyd attempted to convert me. He walked down the road with me after one meeting saying that at this juncture of history one had either to be a Communist or a Fascist. 'There is no middle road. I'm afraid you'll have to choose.'

I did not believe him. (Geoffrey Lloyd was a Marxist)

To change the subject, he asked, 'What are you reading now?'

'The second part of Goethe's *Faust*,' I said, 'In translation, of course.'

'If you'll come in and have coffee with me and my friend Harry Maule, I'll give you my copy of Marlow's *Dr Faustus*,' he said.

He did. I still have it. Only in retrospect does it strike me as a curious coincidence that I should have been plunged into the story of Faust at the moment in my life just preceding that which was to follow.

3
The Drama

One evening when I had been invited for a late snack, there was a new arrival, a big florid man, with light coloured hair and eyes. Vicky half rose to acknowledge his entry, and saluted him with a 'Hello, Gussy!' Already with us was a young Left Winger whose name I cannot recall. He and Gussy, whose conversation revealed him to be an Orientalist, came quickly to disagreement. The young Socialist taking umbrage at Gussy's assumption that there existed in Tibet some divine theocracy, accused Gussy of 'spiritual Fascism', to which Gussy retorted that Dialectical Materialists, being conscious on one plane only, understood nothing but their bellies!

This dispute struck Vicky's humorous side. He tried to soothe the contestants but he kept laughing as he said, 'You're talking on different planes. Between Karl Marx and Milarepa there is no common ground. You can never meet!'

Turning to me he said, 'It's funny! and they don't see it!' I saw it. And as the contestants were reft by a further terminological misunderstanding, Vicky and I were simultaneously convulsed.

In addition to being angry with each other, they were now cross at being laughed at. Gussy spun on me and said, 'You've got a Father Complex!'

I supposed he said this because he felt I had joined with Vicky to laugh at him. I replied, 'I can't have. My father was killed before I was born. I was brought up by my mother and my grandfather.'

'Then you've got a Grandfather Complex!'

Vicky exploded. 'Freudians will never let you get away with it. They've always get you on their two-pronged fork. Unless you let them have it their own way they'll give you no peace. The only thing is to avoid them, or at least refuse to be drawn into discussion. It's the only defence I've ever found!'

When I rose to go, Gussy said he would give me a lift in his car. I was not pleased but could see no way to avoid it. He seemed determined to bury the hatchet. He tried now to probe my soul, which I didn't like either. He wrote his real name down for me, Gerhard Heim, or Gerard Heym, and invited me to tea at the Devonshire Club. As I was reluctant he said, 'Are you afraid of me?'

'Of course not', I said, cross and uncomfortable.

When I got in I told my mother I had been badgered in to promising to have tea with a man I didn't feel I could entirely trust.

'Why don't you trust him?' my mother asked.

'In the car he said I had a profound mind.'

'That's not an indecent remark,' said my mother, puzzled.

'I hadn't said anything profound.'

'One can form an impression of profundity on very little acquaintance,' my mother said. 'Where has he asked you to have tea with him?'

'At the Devonshire Club. In St James's Street.'

'It's a very respectable place,' said my mother. 'I *really* don't think anything can happen to you *there*.'

I had to admit it didn't sound like the setting for a seduction and began to laugh with her. Probably I was making an ado about nothing. Mother said, 'If he asks you to go anywhere else afterwards you can say your mother is expecting you back for dinner.'

Reluctantly I kept the date. Tea was served to us in a drawing-room peopled only by elderly, stuffy looking persons. He asked me about my background and family, and when I said my father had been in the Indian army he asked whether he had been stationed near the Tibetan Border, whether he had any contact with Tibetans, and in particular whether he had received any gifts from Tibetans.

I told him about the Tibetan prayer-wheel.

It was as though he had found the confirmation he had been looking for. He was convinced that this object had been given for me so that I should have something in this life to connect me with the land of the lamas; I said my parents had only just been married and at the time the gift was made I would not have been on the way, but this did not make him alter his opinion.

The Magical Dilemma of Victor Neuburg

In a measure, I was gratified that he thought this because I had sometimes thought something of the sort myself.

'I don't know who you *are*!' he said, looking at me in awe.

I would have been more flattered by this suggestion of distinction if I had been able to rid myself of the feeling that he was unbalanced. I decided that it would be best to play the whole thing down and assumed an attitude of scepticism. This did not truly represent me but it was my only defence.

When I said I must be getting back for dinner he did not try to detain me, but asked me to come again for tea, at the same time and place, next week.

When we had tea again, he asked me if I had dreamed during the week. I had dreamed I was on the coast near Clacton inspecting the Martello towers, defences which had been constructed when a Napoleonic invasion was feared, and saw the guns were pointing towards Germany.

He reacted with annoyance. 'It's because I have a German name!' he declared. He said he was an American citizen and not an enemy and not contemplating an invasion and there was no need for me to marshal my defences against him.

I was edgy. To settle me he spoke of Vicky. It had the right effect, because, for me, Vicky was sanity itself, as well as deeply interesting. He said Neuburg knew much about these things. He hinted at a story but did not tell it. He asked me if I would stay and have dinner at the club. It was obviously respectable. Mother was away for some days so would not be waiting for me. Heim said, 'We must arrange a dinner with Neuburg some time. Just the three of us.' That turned the scales. I was always loyal to Runia but I would have given anything to see Vicky alone or in different company. I went with Heim into the dining room of the Devonshire Club.

He did not try to detain me afterwards. I did not mention that my mother was away. And I was back at the hotel early.

Soon after my mother came back we moved to another hotel: Pembridge Manor Hotel, Pembridge Crescent. For me it was more convenient for getting to Vicky.

One evening at Vicky's Cyril Moore told us he had met - in Lyons

Corner House of all places - a young Hindu who was a real yogi. He would be in this country for another ten days or so. Would we like him to come and talk to us?

The following Saturday Mr Rai was with us. He looked extremely well bred, and had regular features from which a wine stain on one side of his face hardly detracted. 'I am not a teacher' he said. I have never done any public speaking. What do you want me to tell you about?'

'What you believe. What it means to be a Hindu'.

'Then I suppose I had better start with Manu,' he said; and it was from his lips I first heard the name. 'There was a great teacher called Manu who gave us the laws which are the basis of our philosophy.'

He explained the main branches of yoga; or ways to union with the divine spark. Raja Yoga, by meditation and exercise of the will, only; Bhakti Yoga, by devotion to Krishna, as the Divine Spirit seen in man. 'Would it give offence here if I suggested that the Christian religion seems to be of the type of Bhakti Yoga?' He was assured he did not offend. Jnana Yoga, or the pursuit of knowledge, was the way of students and scholars; Karma Yoga, or right actions, was for people active in the world. These were the four main types, but there were also some special branches. Mantra Yoga was the use of sounds. As we were poets, he supposed this would interest us, since poetry must consist, partly at least, in a mantric effect. Hatha Yoga was the attunement of the physical body, by means of exercises. 'This is the one which I have chosen,' he said, and explained that it was for this reason that foods and hygiene assumed greater importance on this than on some of the other paths. Complete continence for life was required.

This drew more questions from our young men than anything else. 'Don't you find it difficult?'

'The energy is converted into energy of a finer kind, which opens higher centres of consciousness,' he said.

I asked, 'But if this is the way how is the population of the world to be maintained?'

'It is not a problem,' he said. 'Not all people will choose this way.'

Still puzzled I said, 'But if you have chosen it you think it is the best...'

'Not best,' he said. 'I like it because it makes me feel well. One chooses the way which is in accordance with one's temperament.'

Vicky had been sitting quietly throughout. When he thought we were going to break up he said to Rai, 'It's obvious you know something I've wanted to know all my life. I should like to have a private conversation with you, if I may, before you go back to India. I should like to tell you a bit of personal history and ask you if there is any remedy for a case such as mine.'

Rai said that of course he would be pleased.

We all wanted to see him perform his exercises, but he said they were only for doing early in the morning before the first meal of the day.

'Tomorrow morning, then!' we chorused. 'We can stay here all night!'

Rai still had a reason to hesitate. 'I have never performed them while dressed in a suit. It would be constricting.'

Somebody said, 'Surely somebody has shorts or something!' In the end it was decided we should all go to our homes to sleep and reassemble in the conservatory in the morning at six.

When I arrived - breakfastless myself at this hour of Sunday morning - Rai was already in the bathing trunks somebody had found for him. He had a body of extraordinary beauty, the trained muscles moving with the smoothness of a dancer. Not all of the exercises, however, were spectacular. Some were breathing exercises. He explained each series and said that one should never persist beyond the point at which pain was experienced.

This impressed and startled Vicky. He said, 'In the days, which are very long ago now, when I endeavoured to practise yogic exercises I always thought I had to persist however much it hurt!'

'Oh no! Pain tells one something is wrong. It is a signal.'

Vicky protested that all yogic exercises produced some degree of pain from the cross-legged positions, which strained the muscles, to the breathing exercises, which were excruciatingly painful.

Rai was shocked. 'If there is such pain, it is doing you harm.'

Great amazement was caused when he did the exercise which followed. Seating himself cross-legged he said he would loosen his vertebrae; and as though he had in his back some muscles which controlled the operation, he caused his vertebrae momentarily to dis-joint, one after another, so that a wave went up his spine from the root to the neck, with slight, audible snicks.

When he had finished we all went down to Cyril Moore's flat in the basement for breakfast. 'You can eat toast and butter?' Vicky asked Rai, as if in doubt whether even this might violate some Brahmanical proscription against impure foods. As Rai accepted it, Vicky contin-ued his thought. It would be an achievement if we could keep a yogi in St John's Wood on his proper foods. 'There's fruit in the garden which has not been touched by hand, and which Mr Rai can pick for himself. More fruit can be bought in the shops but of course we can't do anything about the magnetic conditions of that.'

Rai protested that all this trouble was unnecessary: 'On the ship I ate the meals served,' he said. But Vicky was not to be deterred so easily from doing his best. 'I've an idea that the food which in a strict Jewish household would be considered Kosher would be acceptable under your rules, too - excepting, of course, that you don't touch any kind of flesh.' He said he did not observe Jewish or any other food rules; he had a mixed and complicated background. 'I eat anything now.' But he knew of Jewish grocers nearby and would try to interest them in the problem of feeding a Brahmin!

Rai was, in fact, Kshattriya. His father who had a business in Lahore, had asked him to come to England to speak with someone on his behalf. He had no one else he could send, or he would not have asked him to break his yoga training. The upsetting effects of the unsuitable foods and of the crowds were superficial and would wear off when he went back. Had he refused to help his father, he would have brought on himself the far more deeply disagreeable karma of an undutiful son.

Turning to us Vicky said 'I do hope you children realize how good he is being to you!' He reminded us how unapproachable the ascetic of the East generally is. 'And he's the real thing, you know!' He pointed out that it was not easy to answer questions rained upon one from all sides, 'and applying to different planes.' He believed it was unusual for a yogi to submit to such a barrage of questions as Mr Rai had just endeavoured to answer. 'Poor young man! He is a stranger in this country. He has hardly arrived when he is surrounded by a horde of people who ask him every indiscreet question, from what Caste he belongs to, to whether he doesn't find continence difficult! I don't know what impression Mr Rai will take back to India of the behaviour of the English in their own country!'

'I am not offended,' said Rai smiling. 'The questions show me the interest is real. I had not expected to find such interest in England.' He said he had been a little overwhelmed when called upon to expound the sacred philosophy of India, feeling it must seem to stand or fall according to the way he explained it. To Vicky he said, 'Really it is extraordinary. I arrive in this country for the first time. In this huge city, with millions of inhabitants, I go into a Lyons Corner House and look at the menu. Mr Moore is sitting at the same table. He sees I am strange and asks if he can help me. He brings me straight to this house.' From the way in which he pronounced this, looking at Vicky, I could tell he regarded it as a very special house indeed.

They both agreed it had not the hallmark of an accident. Vicky said, 'There are invisible threads which pull....'

Rai said, 'And bring one to a house where one will receive help, or where one can give it.'

Something else struck me. At the usual Zoists' meetings I was hesitant in speaking because in the fields of poetry and politics the other young people knew more than I. Now it was reversed. They sat almost silent while I talked with Rai and Vicky; we made a natural trio.

The following week Rai was there again, but it was his last evening. When the party broke up he asked if he could drive anybody home. I got into the front of his car and two young men got into the back. He drove to my address first and as we stopped outside the Pembridge I asked him suddenly if he would let me examine his palms. He consented. 'It will be interesting for me. No one has ever done it.'

The light inside the car was not good enough so we got out and crouched in front of the headlights, which were so strong I could see the lines quite well. They were few in number, uncomplicated, clear-cut, with a cross between Head and Heart.

I interpreted it, and while we remained crouched in the bright patch of white light, which in a strange way seemed to isolate us from the rest of the world, he spoke of Victor Neuburg and said, 'I think he is a very advanced soul.'

He had nevertheless, he told me, been much shaken by the gravity of

the problem Mr Neuburg had confided to him. He had been sub-
jected to wrong teaching, when young. As a result, his physical frame
was very seriously weakened. 'He asked me if I could prescribe for
him some exercises.' The difficulty was, that for one in a condition so
grave, almost any exercise that he could think of would be too much
of a strain. He dared not risk making things worse, yet did not want
to fail him by saying there was nothing he could do. He had tried to
make spiritual contact with his guru, mentally laying before him the
problem that he found, asking advice what he should do. 'I recom-
mended to him something - almost nothing - which he could do, and
it eased him.'

I did not think Heim ever met Rai.

Heim continued to invite me to tea at the Club but began to speak
about some books at his place in Chelsea which he wanted to show
me. I had begun to wonder why he seemed to have no address save
the Devonshire but I did not want to find myself alone with him in his
'place' either. I had an irrational fear of him amounting almost to
panic. It was because of the way he kept talking about 'the path' I
must follow; he said he wanted to be my spiritual teacher, but I did
not feel the confidence in him which would make such a relationship
possible. And my resistance was only increased when he interpreted
it as fear of the 'surrender of the Ego' which was the precondition of
Initiation; I was, I felt, not a coward, and disliked being made to
appear one. I agreed to meet him at the Victoria and Albert Museum
to be shown the Buddhas.

He led me into a gallery which had cases of them all round it. We
stopped before each case and he waited for me to say something. At
first the rows of cross-legged figures all looked much alike; but contemplation revealed differences. Some were crude; others ornate;
some were seraphic; others austere. I commented upon them with
gradually increasing confidence. 'You like the Kmer', said Heim at
last. 'It's the classic period. But I'm afraid you also like the soft,
smiling ones of South East Asia. Yes, they are very lovely, but it's the
stern-faced ones of the North whom we must follow.'

I shrank from the conjunctive 'we'.

He said, 'Next week, we shall go to the British Museum, to see the big
one with the long ears.'

Because it was a Saturday and I was going on to Vicky's afterwards, I was wearing the green ensemble. Heim had complimented me on it earlier; but over tea, he said, 'That colour is just exactly the vernal colour. It is connected with fertility rituals in certain cults. Rituals which were performed in the spring. You should be careful in whose company you wear it because it can be inciting.'

I was embarrassed. It was true I had sought the colour of just-unfurling horse-chestnut leaves but not with such a thought. Vicky had commented on it but only in a way that was charming; he would never say anything that could offend.

I had not expected to see Heim again until we met the following week at the British Museum. But that evening, in the conservatory, just as the meeting was breaking up, Heim, who never came to the Zoists, appeared in the door. He exchanged a few words with Vicky and Runia and then said to me 'May I give you a lift?' That he had come only for me was so apparent that I was embarrassed.

I met Heim at the British Museum. But I said to him, on the steps, 'I know this Museum well already'.

'Not as I shall show it to you,' he said. And he took me up the stairs to the big Buddha. We stood before it in dramatic silence. 'Look at its long ears,' he said. 'See its expression. It is stern, almost forbidding. *That* is what you must face!'

'You speak as though it were alive,' I said.

'It is alive! With the breath of all the pilgrims who have come before it. It is sacrilege it should be exposed to public view!'(1)

I said it must have been seen by the pilgrims.

'They came with reverence, not idle curiosity like every gaping Tom, Dick and Harry. Tibet is the only land where the people are kept in their place!' I began to see why the young Communist had taxed him with 'spiritual fascism.'

By now things were working to a crisis. He persisted in asking me to his place to see his books and the matter became increasingly an issue. He pulled up the car to face the Serpentine and said, 'You don't trust me!'

I could only say, 'No, I don't'

'And you trust Neuburg?' he said.

'Yes.'

It was not immediately following this bare exchange of words, but probably because he was galled by the recollection of it that, as we were moving in the car down Grosvenor Street, he said, 'Neuburg is riddled with sex. Neuburg is totally impotent as the result of homosexual excesses.'

His words took me completely by surprise. He continued speaking in the same vein. 'Neuburg is a wreck and a ruin.'

I thought he spoke in malice and did not believe him. I said Vicky appeared to have Runia as his companion. Heim dismissed this, saying there was nothing in it.

He drew his car into a mews, to be out of the traffic and so that he could stop in order to speak with greater concentration.

'Neuburg was the associate of a man called Aleister Crowley,' he said.

It was as though something had struck me in the stomach. I knew this was the name of a man who had been involved in a very unpleasant court case. I had not read it. What I remembered was the expressions and comments of some people in a hotel lounge as they looked at each other over the tops of their morning papers. I had the impression some exceptional depravities had been brought to light. I hoped desperately that it was untrue Vicky had been associated with this man.

'Neuburg was Crowley's lover,' said Heim. 'It was the great relationship of Neuburg's life and it lasted for years.'

I told myself Heim was jealous because I preferred Vicky and his motive was to destroy my picture of him. He could be making this up. Yet, a real person's name having been mentioned it had already begun to seem more circumstantial. I wanted to ask Heim how he knew. Instead, I asked what the court case had been about.

Heim said there had been many articles in the press in which Crowley had been accused of Black Magic. 'At last it got so bad he had to do something about it.' He brought an action for libel, over a book and lost it. That had, however, nothing to do with Neuburg, whose association with him has terminated years before.

It seemed to be getting more circumstantial all the time.

Neuburg and Crowley had practised a form of homosexual sex-magic, said Heim. It played upon the subtle currents in the spine and was therefore very dangerous. Either because there was something wrong in the way they did it, or because they weren't ready for it spiritually, it cost Crowley his reason and Neuburg his physical ability.

I could have wondered whether I was standing on my head or on my heels. Most of the malice had now left Heim's voice and he was speaking seriously, as though this was something necessary to understand. Yet it sounded so extraordinary.

'That love should not have been consummated', said Heim. 'And yet, they were so near...so near...' He meant so near to a magic goal.

They were in the desert together, Heim said. But curiously, Neuburg was alone when his revelation came to him. Crowley had gone, leaving him in the desert, when a miracle occurred. '"Words formed themselves in the sand, as though they were being traced by an invisible stick," he told me.'

I realized now that Vicky himself was the source of the story.

'There isn't an hour of the day or night he doesn't think of Crowley,' Heim declared. 'He told me so.'

It came to me that if Vicky had talked to Heim as a friend, in confidence, Heim was breaking the confidence. I said this. Heim said he wasn't breaking a confidence because it was practically public knowledge.

I was considerably upset. I had not been three years on the stage without hearing some reference to homosexuality; people would refer to some actor and say, 'He's a queer' but one never knew and I was sure people often spoke lightly. I thought real homosexuality was probably something very outré, like the physical hermaphrodite immortalized by a sculptor in the reclining figure in a discreet recess of the Villa Borghese in Rome, which I had seen with my mother when I was sixteen.

My regard for Vicky remained the same. It was too deep for alteration. But I was possessed by the desire to know whether this extraordinary thing was true. I thought of his steady, deep, unflinching gaze and knew that whatever he had done must have seemed right to him when he did it. If what I had been told was true it would make no difference to my estimation of him. But it would make a difference to my way of understanding him. He had always been very sweet to me, and I knew he liked me, but if he was really a homosexual I supposed femininity would be negative to him and I must not presume on a friendliness of a very spiritual order.

Yet the whole thing seemed so fantastic. If I could see him alone, I believed I could find the courage to tell him the story Heim had told me and I was sure he would tell me the truth. But it would be necessary to ask for a private interview; Runia would hear me and would ask why I wanted to see Vicky by himself.

Sheer social timidity and convention defeated me. I wanted to speak to Vicky about this but I did not know how to extract him from the circle in order to do so.

This was locked in me like the grave. I didn't even tell my mother.

On Saturday I went to the conservatory as usual. Perhaps because I did not feel like general conversation I turned my attention to the bookcases behind my chair. Taking out a few volumes I perceived that behind them lay another which had been hidden. Putting my hand to the back of those which obscured it I drew it out. It proved to be a volume of poems which opened to disclose beautiful paper and printing. Even before I had found the title sheet, Herbert Corby, who had come up from behind leaned over my shoulder and exclaimed, 'Oh, that must be one of Vicky's own! I wonder what Vicky's poetry is like. Very Swinburnian, I expect.'

I wanted to read my find in solitude. Vicky entered at that moment and I said to him, 'Could I borrow this book to read at home?'

'Yes, of course,' he said, pleased. Then, as though struck by a thought giving him pause, he said diffidently, 'May I see which one it is?' I showed him. He saw that it was *The Triumph of Pan*. This seemed to confirm his misgiving for he said, 'Oh! It's got some funny stuff in it.' He looked at me anxiously and said, 'I don't know what you'll make of it.' I felt sure he was divided between fear lest something in it offend me and willingness that I should, in fact, read and make my own judgment.

Runia joined us and he referred to her. 'Can this little lady borrow this book?'

'No,' she said. 'I'm sorry, we can't lend any of Vicky's books.'

'She'll bring it back!' He said. 'I know she will!'

'We've had to make a rule,' she said.

'Rules were made to be broken!' he exclaimed.

'That's just what they're not!' she said; and to me she explained, 'It's the only copy of that one we've got.'

I felt sure neither of them had known this copy existed before I extracted it from the place of neglect into which it must have been pushed or fallen; but I said I quite understood and she passed on.

Vicky said, 'Would you really like to read something I've written? I'll get you something I wrote last night, straight out of a dream. Wait here a moment.' He went to his room, and returned with some paper almost concealed with his hand. He explained that he had not as yet read it himself. He had woken, precipitated upon the paper nearest his bed the lines of verse which formed part of the dream and gone back to sleep again. When in the morning, he woke properly he saw the paper and remembered that he had dreamed but not the substance of the dream. He had then felt almost afraid to discover what he had written. 'I folded it and pushed it into a drawer, so that I shouldn't be able to read it. It's the first thing I've written in years and I'm so afraid of finding it isn't any good.'

I felt that to be offered the unedited substance of a dream was an immense privilege; I wondered if I should decline it but did not wish to.

'Don't let anybody see,' he said. He slipped the folded paper into my hands with a quick movement which I knew was meant to escape the observation of the others. If it had been anybody but Vicky I should have thought I was being given a *billet doux*.

'Bring it back,' he said, relieved the transfer had been made. 'Because I *shall* read it.'

I plunged it straight into my handbag and did not open it out until I was alone in my bedroom at the hotel. Though folded into so small a compass I found that there were several sheets, covered with a thin, spidery writing. To my dismay, it appeared to me that it was in Arabic. Strange dots and flying curves were all about it. But as I looked closer, the letters resolved themselves into those of the Roman script. He wrote a very odd hand, but words and phrases began to emerge:

> *The Master heard with his remembering hand*
> *He scrawled a message in the wrinkled sand,*

With a shock I recognized something of the story Heim had told me.

> *And straightway from the foamiment [?] of sea*
> *There came the Lady of the Laurel Tree,*

There was much reference to water: rivers that wash where once Thalassians [Thessalians? Thalassius?] built an architrave to guard a moat; singing in the Seine [the river in Paris?] where dolphins struggled to release the foam-flung murmur of enduring peace; the silver ford of Atreus, unparted by the sword which dismembers time upon the Solar way...

I had to remember this was something written before the logic of day replaced the logic of dream. There were two lines that worried me:

> *Weighed in the Libra-mart, the warlock weighed*
> *His vision with his voice, triumph with trade*

Who was the warlock? Crowley? Or Vicky, himself? It was unbelievable to me that he had introduced into anything the spirit of trade. I thought the word had been happened upon because it rhymed with 'weighed' and alliterated with 'Triumph'. But as the scales of Libra could weigh in every sense I wondered if it did not mean he had weighed his vision against the voice of reason; this interpretation seemed the more possible in the light of a following line in which he cried that one should weigh not her songs against the mouths of air.

> *Reveal me nothing to the outer ken,*
> *Who sang between the ranks of gods and men;*

In a reference to physical passion and to Pan, occurred the passage:

> *...the overwhelming Lord*
> *Stripped the sun naked of divine pretence,*
> *Stripped truth from time, rent ecstasy from sense.*

There followed stanzas which seemed to have more to do with eternity than story, the world of soul memory. 'Unspun to web of weariness' and the 'rime that echoes in the surf-begotten shell' I thought of Botticelli's picture, which I had seen in Florence, of Venus standing in a shell on the sea.

The long poem ended in strains of the most unutterable desolation:

> *Wake in my music, hover; sink to strewn*
> *Webs of appeased desire, my Aflatun.*
> *No music and no memory is this;*
> *Nothing at all; a new-begotten kiss*
> *From aureate lips; and trembling eyes revoke*
> *The memory of him who once awoke.*
> *Forget. Ah, far they cry; the ways are known*
> *To one who dreams in autumn, and alone,*
> *Wandering unknowingly the secret way*
> *That lies beyond the moon-track to the bay*
> *Where flowers pass forgetting in the stream*
> *Where Plato lies, the mirage of a dream.*

This final picture of bleak loneliness was at once revealing to me and infinitely distressing. I thought of him as mature, not 'in autumn.' Why 'alone'? Though no name was mentioned, it seemed to me that he had given me a love-poem addressed to Crowley.

Yet, if he had given it to me without reading I felt he must have had a unconscious memory of the substance. Why had he put it into my hands? I would like to think it was because he felt some link, and decided that it represented a deep confidence.

The next morning I made a typed copy. I had undertaken to go up there in the afternoon, as had Herbert Corby, to help clear off an accumulation of entries to the *Poet's Corner* which should long since have been put into their SAEs and posted back to the senders. I took the poem in my bag. I could not give it back in the view of Runia and Corby, and it was still in my bag as we were preparing out leave. Then as Runia and Corby became engaged in conversation with each other for a moment, Vicky said to me, 'You won't lose that poem I gave you, will you..'

'I've got it here,' I said.

'You can keep it as long as you like,' he said. 'It was foolish of me to ask. It's just that I'm nervous, not having read it.'

But I thought it better to give it back to him. Standing so that the others could not see I was opening my bag, I drew it out and passed it to him. He took it and put it in his pocket with the same celerity of movement with which he had given it to me. 'Don't say anything about it,' he said.

The Drama

It was, I believe, the following Saturday (occult dramas move fast) that Runia said that a very old friend of Vicky's whom he had not seen for years was coming to see him 'tomorrow afternoon.' I took this to mean that the rest of us should stay away so as not to disturb them. However, as I was leaving, Cyril Moore asked me if I would be coming, and said, 'She is supposed to be one of the very few Buddhist initiates. I'm very much looking forward to seeing her.'

I said I thought we weren't meant to come. Moore said he had not understood it that way at all. There was an understanding all Vicky's friends could come and see him on a Sunday. As he saw me hesitate, he said, 'I'll tell you what. I'll ask you to tea. If it proves to be a general party, we'll join it. If not, well! You're having tea with me!' He suggested I came early, about two o'clock or two thirty. It was August 4, 1935.

When I arrived a number of people were already milling about in the conservatory. Runia joined us and seemed nervously tense. She said, 'You may find her rather frightening. She is very downright. This is her seventieth birthday and she hasn't been out of her own house and grounds for ten years.'

A young man whom I had not seen before, but who was apparently a reporter on the *Sunday Graphic*, said, 'Do you think I could ask her to give me a story about Jack the Ripper?'

'You can't do that!' cried Runia horrified. 'She's here as Vicky's guest!'

He said it was Hayter Preston who had givien him this address and told him that if he came here he could get a story about Jack the Ripper. Referring to this, Runia said aside to Vicky, what sounded like 'It was naughty of Teddy to send Donald.'

I wondered what a Buddhist initiate could have had to do with Jack the Ripper. Vicky came out from the inner room with his guest, whom he introduced as Cremers, without any Mrs or Miss.

She was dressed in black, and had white hair which she wore cut short. There was in her such an authority that all of us were awed, excepting Vicky. Her eyes drove into each one of us, and as she turned her head to look at first one face and then another there was something eagle-like in the swift, abrupt movements of the neck.

Runia tried to make the right kind of conversation for a hostess and asked her about her garden; but small talk foundered upon the power that was in Cremers and our awareness of it. Vicky brought her over to sit by me, saying, 'This is a little lady I would like you to talk to, Cremers.'

I was immensely flattered but could hardly find my tongue.

Vicky said to Cremers, 'It's strange not to have seen you all these years. The last time I saw Crowley he cursed me. Did you know that?'

It was the first time he had spoken the name. So it was true.

'No, I didn't know,' she said.

'Just before he left for America. It was done with full ritual. In that room. You remember that room with all those things in it?'

She nodded but said, 'You knew a thing or two yourself! You would have taken measures to protect yourself.'

'I didn't,' he said. 'I was too miserable. So I was completely open.' He meant that it had every chance to work. The whole ritual had occupied a long time. He had just stood there. 'It was such a foul curse. He cursed me to die. Of all the most loathsome, obscene and painful diseases he could think of.'

Cremers gave a brusque laugh and said, 'Well, you're still here! Crowley couldn't curse! He hadn't the power!'

Vicky said that by that time, perhaps he supposed not. When he decided to make the break he had ceased to believe in the authenticity of Crowley's claim to be a Master. But he had been terribly upset by the curse all the same. 'It was nervous and emotional.' It wasn't, really, that he expected the curse to materialize in its exact terms. 'I felt rather funny for some months to be living under a ritual curse. It still does when I think about it.'

She said, 'You're reasonably all right, aren't you?'

He nodded and said, 'I've had things, of course. This trouble here.' He put his hand over the lower part of his chest, or upper part of his stomach: I was not sure which. 'But none of the things he thought of for me. It was the malice!' he said. 'I couldn't have believed he could bear me so much hate as to wish such things upon me! After all we'd been through together.'

The Drama

Cremers seemed to think he had been naive if he hadn't realized that Crowley, being a vengeful personality, would turn nasty on being left.

Vicky said he hadn't expected him to be pleased; he had been prepared to face anger. He had not been prepared for such vindictiveness. He couldn't have believed they could have parted as badly as all *that*. 'I had a nervous breakdown,' he said. 'I was completely dazed. I went down into the country...'

Runia joined us and the conversation stopped.

Cyril Moore came to talk to me and suggested I come down to his room to look at his new Paul Nash print which the artist had signed specially for him.

While we were still looking at the picture, Vicky and Cremers appeared at the French windows.

'Would you like us to go out?' Moore asked, tactfully. 'Jean and I can walk in the garden.'

Vicky protested against this extraordinary greeting. 'We didn't come down in the hope of finding the room empty!' Turning to his companion and laughing he said, 'They think we're a spooning couple, Cremers! They think we want to be alone!'

I could not help sharing Moore's evident feeling that they had, in fact, sought sanctuary, but since they motioned us to keep our seats we did so. Vicky pulled a chair between Moore's and mine and Cremers took one facing us. Almost at once Crowley's name was again on their lips. Despite Vicky's words, I felt they had come down here in order to be able to talk about Crowley without being disturbed. I thought Moore and I should feel complimented that our presence was felt to be of such an unobtrusive quality that it did not matter; and indeed, neither of us said another word.

Speaking with immense force, Cremers said, 'Crowley wasn't a magician, Victor.' It was the first time I had heard his name used in its proper form. 'He wasn't White. He wasn't Black. Half-way in everything Crowley. He had enough knowledge to raise a current he couldn't control. Couldn't get it up. Couldn't get it down. So it went round and round.' She made a circular motion with her hand over her abdominal region. 'It drove him mad. He wasn't a magician, he was a maniac!' At moments she slapped her knee or made lightning passes in the air with her hands which, though thin and bony, seemed animated by a power almost electrical.

Vicky, flinching, murmured, 'I know...I know...'

'All those books!' she said. 'Pseudo-scientific piffle.'

'They took a long time to write,' he said, as though to moderate what she had said. 'It's a tragedy. His brain had disintegrated....'

'He never had one!' she said roughly. 'He had only megalomania.'

Vicky said he had been reconsidering some of Crowley's poetry. 'It's just verse,' he said sadly. It was a term he used to designate that which had the form but not the inspiration of poetry. He said he had made the experiment of reading some of it to two of the young poets whom he had launched. 'You wouldn't know them. But they're good'. I knew he was referring to Pamela and Dylan. Neither of them thought it was any good. 'They're moderns,' he said; but he thought they would have sufficient objectivity to be capable of recognizing the quality of something written in an earlier style. It was obvious neither of them thought it was anything at all. That had been a revelation to him.

As though in mitigation of Crowley's offence he kept saying it was 'as though his mind had gone.'

Cremers said, 'It was sex that rotted him. It was sex, sex, sex, sex, all the way with Crowley. He was a sex-maniac.'

Vicky, who had been wincing continually, said, 'You're not telling me anything I don't know, Cremers. Why do you find it necessary to say all this to me?'

He was like a naked nerve. I wanted to protect him. In this strange encounter I felt that nothing was accidental: since I was there, I was meant to be there. I tried, by my thoughts, to give him support.

She said she had not met Crowley before he came to America. In answer to a puzzled query from Vicky, she said she meant on his first visit, in 1901. He had travelled in Asia but he had not learned from a real Guru. 'He learned from white faces. I learned from brown faces.' She had heard of this man, Crowley, and thought that if he was genuine she might help him. 'If not, I would break him. I came to see.' What she saw, she did not like. 'I set myself to break him,' she said.

In the only sarcastic tone I have ever heard him use Vicky said, very bitterly, 'You must have succeeded, then!'

'I killed Crowley!' she said. Though I suspected a metaphor I was not sure.

Vicky's eyes closed, as though he were in terrible pain. 'You are a beast, Cremers,' he said. All his muscles had contracted as though he would shrink out of existence and his head was drawn down to his chest.

I felt a touch on the shoulder. It was Cyril Moore, motioning to me that we should leave. I rose and, passing behind Vicky's chair, followed him out into the garden. As I turned to close the French windows I saw that Vicky was gazing straight at Cremers now, an expression of terrible agony on his face. Moore and I walked side by side through the bushes, breaking through the spider webs. Moore said, 'When two or three are gathered together, there is Crowley in the midst of them.'

'What...What....?' I began, but hardly knew what question I wished to ask.

'I know very little about it,' he said. 'Only the little Vicky has told me himself. And I don't know how much of that is meant to be public.'

Both too subdued for conversation, we must have made the circuit of the garden a couple of times when the conservatory door opened above and Runia called down to us, telling us to ask Vicky and Cremers if they would care to come up as it was time for tea. I was not eager to disturb them but it was not possible for either of us to explain why, so, taking care to tread with noise, we approached the French windows and opened them. Vicky and Cremers were still there. We delivered the message, each of us repeating a phrase of it, literally. To my relief they both rose without demur.

The young man from the *Sunday Graphic* came down the steps and said to Cremers, 'Might I have a few words conversation with you alone, before you go?'

Astonished, she asked, 'Why do you wish to speak with me alone?'

He murmured something about 'Jack the Ripper.'

She drew herself up to her full height, looking even more imperious and threatening, and said, 'Why do you wish to speak with me about

Jack the Ripper?'

He faltered something about 'an interesting story.'

In a tone of inconceivable disgust, she asked, 'Are you a newspaper reporter?' One could have thought she had said sewer-rat.

Vicky had at first looked as puzzled as Cremers, but as he took in the situation a smile of delicious mischief broke out upon his face. He said, 'Dear Cremers, you're at the mercy of the press!'

He left her to it; and to my surprise she stepped back into Cyril Moore's room with her pursuer.

Vicky and I were left to climb the iron staircase together. With amazement, I realized he was no longer in agony. He was light as air, as though the sun had come out. It was a brief moment in which we were alone. Standing there on the iron staircase he paused for a moment and said, 'This little lady has had a strange afternoon.' He looked at me searchingly and said, 'We've been talking about someone whom you never knew. I don't know how much you've understood.' I did not know how to answer him, being so moved.

'It's been the great drama of my life,' he told me. In simple words, he described Crowley to me as he had seen him in the early days: his build, his walk and deportment, which was very dignified and had something leonine in it, his feature, his broad brow. 'I thought he was a noble person. I think you would have thought so too.' He said this searching my eyes, his own puzzled and wide open, as though I could explain to him this thing which he was still unable to understand.

I had no words, being too deeply affected. I was grateful and honoured that he told me, as though I had a right to know because of a kinship of the spirit which he recognized.

'Later it was all different,' he said. 'You have heard what was said below. You have heard Cremers. But I want you to know how he seemed to me when I first knew him. And as I prefer to remember him.'

I was overcome, and still had not said a word.

'We shall have to join the others,' he said, to my regret. 'Or they will come to look for us.'

We went into the conservatory; and he was at once engulfed in the social whirl, only to be glimpsed between the heads of other people carrying plates of cakes and other things. I found a chair. He reached me at last and said, 'Have a macaroon.'

Macaroons! After all that had passed below it seemed to me incredible he could so quickly adapt himself out the role of host. I took a macaroon.

Cremers came in and joined us. And, for the third time, Vicky tried to get her and me to talk to each other. 'I'm afraid we really have been very inconsiderate of you,' he said to me. When he said something to mitigate what had been said about Crowley, she turned away and helped herself from the cake-stand. Then more people joined us and we were separated, finally. Vicky and Cremers and Runia withdrew into the inner room. So far as I was concerned the afternoon was over now, and as soon as I decently could I rose to leave. I would simply have gone but Cyril Moore, who was now sitting next to me, said, 'You must go through to say good-bye.'

With some reluctance I knocked on the door of the inner room, and said timidly, 'I've come to say good-bye.'

I had seen Cremers lacerate Vicky and was not sure whether she was to be regarded as his friend or foe. But the atmosphere within the room was friendly so I supposed she was a pal of his and that he was used to her violence and, so to speak, accommodated it. Yet though I had come to say good-bye, I would, by a curious quirk, have gone without shaking Cremers' hand had Runia not jogged my elbow.

I was afraid Cremers would have noticed the near omission; but when I gave her my hand, she held it for a moment in her hard grasp, looking at me intently. I maintained her gaze and felt her eyes going deep into mine, trying to fathom me, while I tried to read in hers her real being. If she was a friend of Vicky she might be a protection to him.

'Ha! Child,' she said. 'How old are you?'

'Twenty.'

She continued to examine my face for a moment. Then she smiled as she said, 'Good-bye', and released my hand.

The next afternoon Heim called for some reason at the Pembridge, and for the first time encountered my mother, in the hall. After exchanging a few words he drove off with me, and asked in the car, 'Who was at Neuburg's yesterday?'

I mentioned Cremers' name and instantly regretted it. 'She is a witch!' he said with violence. 'Didn't you notice her hands? They are like claws. Did you notice the way she looks at each person in turn? She is a Black Magician. You must not go to her house.'

I said she had not asked me. I was not sure if he was right about her.

She was intensely fierce and my feelings had risen against her because she caused pain to Vicky; yet it was obvious Vicky bore her no ill will.

I was puzzled by the relations between all these people. Vicky, Crowley, Cremers and Heim seemed all to have known, or known of, each other. All believed in magic, all spoke of 'currents' and all, used the peculiar word, 'skry'. I asked Heim, 'Was there some organization to which you all belonged?'

'You want to know too much!' he said, and his eyes glinted, I thought like a pig's.

I took my novel to show Vicky. Runia said, 'It's very naughty of you!' meaning, to impose on his time. Heim said he would like to read it and perhaps he could find a publisher for it. We could go through it at the same time as looking at his books. I agreed at last to be shown them and he gave me the address. It was in Beaufort Street, Chelsea.

I had not realized how serious was the library Heim wished to show me. What he let me into was not a flat but a single room, entirely filled with cases of books, which divided it into lanes and reached to the ceiling. It was stuffy from the smell of them and almost dark. This was because a curtain was pulled across the single, small window. 'To keep out the sun,' he explained, 'otherwise it would perish the books.' He drew it slightly. There was only one piece of furniture in the room and that was a school-child's desk, just in front of the window. He told me to sit in it and laid before me a massive volume which, to my astonishment was all in Tibetan writing richly illuminated in glowing ruby reds, emerald greens and sapphire blues. The paint was so thick that as I felt it with my finger it seemed almost to stand up from the stiff pages. These were made of something that was not paper: Heim said it was parchment, and I believed him. The binding was in vellum. There were full page illustrations showing Tibetan deities with their shaktis. I was not shocked, for I knew that these embracing couples represented cosmological principles although their ruby lips made them look lascivious. I was the more discomforted by Heim's breathing, which I could hear behind me and the strangeness of this secret seeming room.

'Are these insured?' I asked, not because I wanted to know but because I was fighting against the fear that I was the only person who had ever been inside this room, from which I could see the street only through the chink he had made in the curtain. I had the irrational feeling I could vanish here and my mother would never be able to discover where or how I had disappeared.

He confirmed my worst fears by saying he had disclosed the secret of this library to nobody but me. 'It's magic,' he said, 'Everything in this room is magic.'

'Where did this come from?' I asked.

'You want to know too much. Some of these books are missing from a monastery in Tibet.'

The volume he had first placed before me was his chief treasure, but when I had turned all the leaves he took it away and brought down another. This I liked less for it contained people being tortured. When I protested, he reminded me that many Christian churches had panels which showed the damned being forked into Hell. The writing in this looked less like Tibetan than the Indian script called, I believe, devanagari.

He now began to demand secrecy concerning what I had seen. 'The secret is in two halves now. You could give me away.' I disliked this, as it was not by my wish I had come here. He said, 'It worries me your having met that woman. I don't know what I have done in bringing you to this room. You must promise me never to breathe a word of this at Neuburg's.'

'Not even to Vicky!'

'Of *all* people not Neuburg!' Tight voiced, he said, 'There are four conditions of attainment, to know, to dare, to will and to be silent.' It was in this stifling room, from Heim's lips, that I heard for the first time Eliphas Levi's famous words; and they seemed to me to be charged with menace. 'Neuburg knows,' he said. 'And he has willed, and he has dared. But he is not silent! He spills sacred knowledge before fools, pearls before swine...' What was really worrying Heim was that through Vicky knowledge of the library should get back to Cremers, of whom he seemed to be in mortal fear.

At the end of the afternoon we still had not looked at my novel, which remained in the brief-case against the desk. As I was picking it up he said, 'Leave it! We'll look at it next time.'

I had not meant there to be a next time; but although it had been a rather overpowering afternoon he had not attempted to touch me, and I began to think my apprehensions on that score were ground-less. And so I agreed.

I had resisted the pressure to give a pledge of secrecy, but in fact I told no one about the books. I wondered how this strange business would end.

It ended when, in that room again, things came to the pass I had feared all along. He had been hoping I would become his magical partner. He said, 'Neuburg and Crowley were very near! Where they failed we shall succeed!'

I said I should like to leave.

He placed himself between me and the door, impeding my exit. I thought he was going to try to embrace me. I asked him to stand aside. He did not do so, and our eyes met in a contest of will. I prayed, inwardly, that he would move aside and at last he did so. I went through the doors and his curses, but not his footsteps, followed me down the stairs.

When I gained the street, I walked, with measured step, until I had reached the corner and turned into King's Road out of sight from his window. Then I ran.

---

(1) It is no longer on view, though I believe it is stored in the basement.

4
Comment Magazine

Meanwhile, the affairs of the *Poets' Corner* continued. Since I became part of the circle, I had only sent in one poem; it received an Honourable Mention in the week that Dylan's poem, 'Incarnate devil in a talking snake', was the chief prize winner. In another column, conducted by Templar, I saw a competition for a translation of a passage from Dante's *Inferno*. I tried my hand at it, and on October 13 read that I had won a prize. Although it was not in his column, Vicky noticed and congratulated me on it. In early October, Pamela looked in at the Zoists again. On October 20, Vicky, perturbed about the preoccupation with the dark side of things for which he believed the Surrealist movement was becoming a channel, wrote in the *Sunday Referee:*

Delirium is the evil aspect of ecstasy, and much modern art is inspired by the lower forces that normally lurk in subjection in the human mind...It is time to check the black introspection that is a threat to civilization and all that it has won in centuries of painful effort. It is dreadfully easy to fall back into primal barbarism, as these modernists who are parleying with the mind's depths know.

Though he did not know when he wrote it, it was his last article for the *Sunday Referee*. October 27, 1935, was the day of a catastrophe. My mother who was at breakfast before me, greeted me with the words, 'Something dreadful has happened to the *Sunday Referee*. It's all different. I can't find the *Poet's Corner*'.

In fact, every familiar feature had vanished. Headlines were splashy. The effect was as though one had opened the *Observer* and found oneself reading the *People*. 'Poor little *Poets' Corner*,' said my mother. 'I wonder what Vicky and all of you will do now.'

Immediately after lunch I hurried to Vicky's; in the conservatory I found almost everybody. Only Vicky and Runia were not there; but presently they came in from the outside. Vicky said, 'The first thing we knew about it was when we saw the paper this morning. The type was set up last night, all ready to go to press as usual.' They had been to see first the Literary Editor, Hayter Preston, and then the Editor, Mark Goulden. The position was this: the proprietors of the paper had wished to switch to a policy they believed would increase its circulation. As this must lower its tone, Goulden had resigned and so had Preston. 'Almost the whole staff is out.'

This seemed final and we all stood very glum. 'There is just one possibility we've been thinking of,' said Vicky. He looked at Runia and said, 'May I tell them? As they're *here*!' Receiving her assent, he said, 'We haven't got a lot of money but we have a little. We've been wondering whether we couldn't bring out a paper of our own, carrying the *Poets' Corner*, and perhaps articles and stories. We shouldn't be able to pay contributors. But if ever there should be any profits, that would be a first use to which we would put them.' They had not meant to tell us until they had had time to go into figures. 'We've been in buses all the morning. The idea was born in a bus.' But they didn't want us to go away thinking this was necessarily the end.

Geoffrey Pollett spoke. 'Vicky! Both of you! You're being very gallant and I don't want to be damping. But if you put money into this you're likely to lose it. If there are no writers with known names contributing who's going to buy it? And if the circulation isn't wide enough to attract advertisers how will you meet the costs of production?'

Vicky said, 'Very pertinent questions, Geoffrey. I'm quite unable to answer them. We can only put it on the market and see what happens.'

'But Dylan Thomas and Pamela Hansford Johnson are known names!' Runia declared.

Vicky cried out, 'There you've hit it! That's it! He's independent now and so is Pamela. They can stand on their own feet. That thrills me. It means the *Poets' Corner* has been an effective shop window.'

Vicky's generosity showed in that he could rejoice that those whom he had launched had achieved independence of him. The great difficulty, he said, was for young and unknown people to get their first work published. What usually happened was that they sent a poem to the *London Mercury* and it came back with a rejection slip. Then they sent it to *New Verse* and it came back with a rejection slip. After accumulating a certain number they became discouraged, and perhaps wrote no more. Some of the words he spoke are still printed on my memory. 'What is needed is more encouragement for young writers during the time they're still producing their relatively immature stuff. People laughed at the *Poets' Corner* because there seemed something childish in the system of giving Honourable Mentions. I realized that but I liked it because it enabled me to give encouragement to more people than I had space to print. Somebody would send in and perhaps find that he had got an Honourable Mention. He would feel encouraged and send in again. He would get better and perhaps after a time win a prize and appear in print.'

The funny thing, he said, was that after they had been printed in the *Poets' Corner* they found other periodicals willing to accept their work where they had not done so before. Notably, a number of those who had started in the *Poets' Corner* were now published in *New Verse*. That meant the *Poets' Corner* was read by Editors who did not trust their own judgment. 'They let us do the seeding for them,' was another of his indelible phrases. 'In two and a half years, the *Poets' Corner* has proved itself a service, and if this Lady and I can keep it going we shall consider it more worthwhile than anything we've ever done.'

He said this with great emotion and it amazed me. He was an oak tree, weathered and proved by the storms of time; but we, saplings that had grown up beneath the shelter of his boughs, were yet of untried worth.

We kept thanking him. He wanted us to share our thanks with Runia. 'You will owe it all to this good Lady,' he said. 'Now, if you'll forgive us, she and I will go and do sums.' (I believe it was partly Runia's money which made the project possible.)

The next Saturday when we reassembled it had all been settled. *Comment* would appear on Saturdays, price 3d. It would be a few weeks before the first number could appear but we could begin sending in contributions; and there was clerical work to be done in the way of circularizing all the three thousand people who had sent in to the *Poets' Corner* to tell them that although it had disappeared from the *Sunday Referee* it would reappear in *Comment*. Volunteers were asked for. I volunteered. So did Herbert Corby. It was arranged we should come on Friday evenings and in this way we became intimates of the inner circle.

We not only sent out the circulars. We found an accumulation of poems which had been sent in by people who had ignored the request that a stamped addressed envelope should be sent with entries but which Vicky had not had the heart to destroy. We addressed envelopes in which we sent these back, clearing the pile gradually. Vicky in his armchair was re-reading the newly received manuscripts. 'Can you see anywhere that poem by Symons I want to print?' he asked Runia. 'Is that it under the butter-dish?'

Runia lifted the butter-dish and peeled from underneath it a paper covered with writing which she scrutinized. 'No,' she said. 'It's one of Dylan's. It's the one he asked us to send back to him.'

'Oh but it's good we've found it!' exclaimed Vicky. 'He won't mind it a bit buttery.'

Walking to the bus with me, Herbert said he hoped Vicky was not counting too much on Dylan to send poems for *Comment*. 'They aren't paying, and Dylan can sell his stuff now. He doesn't produce much because he writes very slowly, and I know definitely that he counts the shillings.' He talked to me about how Vicky had persuaded the *Sunday Referee* to publish the book of Dylan's poems and how he had gone through them with Dylan and helped him to choose the best of them. 'Dylan had the whole of the money on the sales of that. Vicky didn't take anything. Dylan has every reason to be grateful to Vicky.' His voice sounded anxious, and I knew he was afraid lest Vicky should be hurt. 'There's another thing,' he said. 'They seem to be rather counting on a story from Pamela. With Pamela it wouldn't be a question of money. But she has a contract with an agent now which doesn't allow her to sell her work under a certain figure. I don't know whether they'll let her give it away!'

On the following Friday while we were there, the late evening post brought a bulging envelope from Wales. Vicky's joy as he pulled the enclosures from the packet was such that I realized he must have been subconsciously anxious. 'Oh, the good child! He *is* a good child! He *is*!' He began unfolding the sheets. Besides a letter, there was a story and several poems. 'What's he sent me? "Grief thief of time crawls off..."'

Runia tried to prepare him for a disappointment with regard to Pamela, mentioning the agent.

Vicky exploded. 'What! If they won't let her give a story to her old Editor...I'm her *father*!' It was the only time I ever saw him show possessive feeling about any of his 'children'. He was fond and proud of Pamela. Once he had read me a line from something she had written - 'His clothes were new and nervous' - and exclaimed, 'Such style! Such economy!' For conciseness, he declared, she could be compared with Jane Austen.

A story from Pamela was contained in the first number. This appeared on December 7, 1935. Its editors appeared as Sheila Macleod and Victor B. Neuburg. I took Sheila Macleod to be Runia, though I also sometimes heard her called Mrs Tharp. As the pile of gleaming numbers was revealed on the floor and we each took one, I think my excitement equalled Vicky's and Runia's. 'Keep your first numbers,' they said to us. 'They may some day be worth something!'

Corby and I still came on the Fridays. Our job was to send out the issues of *Comment* to the subscribers who received them through the post. We took it in turns to address wrappers and to lick them while Vicky read manuscripts in his chair and Runia busied herself with something else.

I enjoyed these Fridays at Vicky's even more than the Saturdays because of the greater intimacy. Vicky, reading the contributions, was in heaven. He loved the good poems because they were good; and the bad poems because their infelicity was endearing; the in-between ones he could not bring himself to say were bad. As he read them he put them down into one of two piles; those he wanted to keep and print on one side of him, and those which were to go back to sender on our table.

Once Herbert committed a sin. He read aloud in tones which made it sound ridiculous, a rejected poem about a goldfish swimming around inside a bowl. Vicky cried out in pain. 'That's not funny! That's tragic! That's a poor little old lady, with nothing else to love. Can't you see her? You're a little beast, Herbert! Give it back to me. I must write something nice on the slip.'

Some of the entries were not printed because they were ostrobogulous. This was a wonderful word of Vicky's. It was used in the place of indecent or pornographic, and had the advantage over these words that it implied no moral attitude towards the subject. He would speak of an ostrobogulous tale or a passage in the classics.

Morton was the only person to whom I ever saw Vicky show a poem before it was published. He did the judging entirely by himself, in silence. He took Morton's opinion on ostrobogulosity.

'This man is a good poet!' he said to me. 'He's got a pile of stuff - he shows me things and then won't let me print them!!' He said that Morton's work was superior to much that was sent in. As a result of this conversation two of Morton's poems did appear in *Comment*, not in the *Poets' Corner*, but, like Dylan's, separately.

About eleven we would have a snack, little chipolata sausages, sausage rolls or sardines, with tea. Runia would put Sanatogen in Vicky's tea. He did not like it because it spoiled the flavour and gave it a peculiar consistency. I realized with dismay that this was their evening meal.

One evening Cyril Moore came in bringing a bottle of Chianti.

Runia allowed him to pour it out and to pass glasses to me and to Herbert but said, 'Not for Vicky!'

Vicky protested, 'Mustn't drink! Mustn't smoke! Mustn't umph! What a life! What I've come to in the end!'

Living without defences, transparent before everyone, he remained undiminished in his mystery. He was a creature of volatile flame; a flame that sometimes flickered but always returned to the vertical, smokeless and true.

And yet because he was, for me, the mystic way, I asked him if he had been born under Pisces.

'No, Aries,' he said. 'My hair used to have a hint of red. That would have given you the clue,' he said kindly, lessening my mistake. I don't suppose you can see it now. But I've always been Mars. I danced down Mars, and I was Mars when I skryed,' he said. I was sure he was giving me information, and was pleased by his communicativeness but the terms he used were strange to me; I was too timid to ask their meaning yet stored them in my memory.

He seemed to me more deeply rested during these evenings; I felt it in his voice. Though in his spasmodic laughter it could touch a falsetto note, it was, when he was relaxed, low though with almost no voice in it. Despite the absence of resonance it had a quality which was pleasant to hear and the articulation was distinct; I had never to ask him to repeat anything.

The Saturday evening meetings of the Zoists still continued, but in Cyril Moore's room as the conservatory had become too cold and no electricity had yet been installed. At our request Vicky gave a talk on Swinburne. He opened by reading a passage from the 'Sapphics'. Then he read 'The Hounds of Spring', his voice rising until he was almost out of himself in the lines:

The ivy falls with the Bacchanal's hair
Over her eyebrows hiding her eyes
The wild vine slipping down leaves bare
Her bright breast shortening into sighs;
The wild vine slips with the weight of its leaves,
But the berried ivy clutches and cleaves
To the limbs that glitter..

'And that,' he cried, flinging the book down and picking up another, 'is by the man who later wrote this!' He read a letter by Swinburne deploring that George Eliot was living with a man to whom she was not married. He could not forgive Swinburne for having been in his later years captured by respectability.

Arthur Leslie Morton said when he came to see me many years later, with reference to Victor's relationship with Runia, 'Could one say she was his Watts Dunton?'

In fact, Victor obviously felt he was threatened by Swinburne's fate. Speaking of the throttling Victorian household in which he had been brought up by 'three mothers', chief of whom was an apparently ghastly aunt whom he called 'Fraub', he said. 'They talked about one's getting ideas as they might about getting the measles. As though they were something catching. And they were, too!' He said they always watched him to be sure he was doing nothing wrong. He added, unexpectedly, 'The same situation seems to be catching up on me again, now!'

Runia cried in hurt reproach, 'I hope you don't feel like that about me!'

He said, 'Even in *this* house there's growing up an atmosphere of "see what Vicky's doing and tell him he mustn't".'

But he had that in him which could never be made tame, except in a superficial manner. He was unshockable, except by misuse of words. Once, as I was speaking, he pointed a finger at me, looking at me with such an expression as one might at a dear one caught in an unfortunate situation. 'You split an infinitive', he said.

Runia said she was going to give us all a talk. And she warned us the week beforehand and on the night, 'I'm going to shock you all.'

Her title was 'The New Morality', her theme was the battle her generation had fought for, freedom from conventional codes with regard to sex. It seemed to me needless for an audience composed of us and I think all of us were embarrassed, even Vicky. This was obviously the propaganda of some 'advanced' movement preceding the world war during which I was born. I wondered if Runia had been associated with the Suffragette movement. (Much later I learned that this was the case).

Vicky's attitude to the New Woman was everything she could desire. He had an exceptional degree of courtesy to women, and when he had occasion to pronounce the name of a woman author it was with a kind of purposive deference to her opinion which I felt was meant to show the honour in which he held the sex. When he referred to anything in which Runia had assisted him he always put her name first.

Vicky was forward looking. He believed in continuing evolution, not merely of species but of the soul. He felt that everybody must, from incarnation to incarnation, progress in wisdom, despite apparent lapses. One Saturday he came into the room with a copy of the *Daily Express* and exhibited in distress the front page. The main news item was concerned with Mussolini's aggression in Abyssinia; others with murders, robberies, accidents, etc. He read out the headlines, column by column, and said, 'There isn't a single item which by any stretch of imagination could be considered good, happy, or hopeful news. Why is this?' He walked over to me, as though I could tell him, and I said, 'Because people don't believe in anything. They've lost conventional religion and haven't found one in which they can have faith.' He was dismayed.

All scientific discoveries interested him but particularly in the field of astronomy, this partly because of the idea that globes and galaxies were in evolution, but also because he felt that with so many other worlds there must surely be some with inhabitants superior to ours whom the development of interplanetary, and even interstellar, travel must one day enable us to meet.

Runia had a gruesome Wellsian theory of the future in which, woman having learned to procreate without assistance, the male would linger on only as a neuter, 'Like the worker bee'. Thus would be created a new kind of slave population perhaps with a single Queen. I used to wonder if the idea was derived from an early film called *Metropolis* in which, if hazy memory serves me, there was a population of robots ruled over by a kind of Queen. Many years later, I realized it could equally be a variant of the universal esoteric tradition concerning the eventual re-creation of the androgyne.

Sometimes a tall but tired elderly man called. He was the artist, Julian Tharp. I was told he was Runia's husband; they were not divorced. Once when he came she was not in the room. He sat making conversation with Vicky and Corby and me until Vicky said, 'If you want Runia she's up in her room.'

'May I go up?' said the husband, 'I'd like to speak to her about something.'

'Yes do,' said Vicky.

Another time while Corby and I were working at the table Runia said, 'I wonder what's happened to Heim? He hasn't been here for weeks.'

'There's a reason,' said Vicky, from his armchair.

'Oh, What is it?'

'I don't know. I didn't mean I knew. But at one moment he was here continually, and now he isn't. Something has happened.'

I thought it had to do with me. I would have liked to tell Vicky, but not before others.(1)

There was another Friday evening when Corby, exceptionally, was not there. Vicky left the room for a moment and Runia asked me suddenly:

'How long is it since you've seen Gussy?'

I made a quick calculation, 'Seven weeks.'

'What is your opinion of him?' she asked intently.

'I don't like him. I think he's a bad friend to Vicky. To you and Vicky.'

'Thank you. If Vicky asks you will you tell him frankly?'

'Yes, but he wouldn't. I'm so much younger, he wouldn't ask my opinion about a man of his own age.'

'He might do. He would pay attention to your intuition. He likes you. I know what I'm saying.' The sound of a chain being pulled announced his imminent return.

'Ssh!' she said. 'Give me your permission to repeat what you've said to me.'

The Magical Dilemma of Victor Neuburg

I nodded assent and in a moment he was with us again. Runia did not refer to the subject of which we had spoken and I was too timid to initiate it, because of the 'Ssh!'. And so I let slip my golden opportunity.

But that night when I left Runia saw me to the door and gave me a kiss.

One Saturday evening, Walter Ford said to me, with the slight formality he affected, 'I wonder if you'd care to dine with me one evening. I'm inviting Mr and Mrs Neuburg.' (It was the first time I had heard them called that. The name under which Runia appeared in *Comment*, Sheila MacLeod, was, so she told me, one she had taken by deed poll, and we never used it; neither did it seem suitable to call her by her husband's name; her baptismal names she did not like, and we called her by the invented first name she preferred.) I accepted because Vicky would be there.

We found ourselves, an artificial four, seated around a chromium and glass table in Ford's jade green flat. As we were leaving Runia wanting to show her 'advanced' ideas, tried to leave me behind.

I had no intention of being left behind, insisted on leaving and walked with them in the direction of the nearest Underground. Runia, who walked between Vicky and me, seemed annoyed. But looking across her I saw that Vicky was shaking with silent mirth, ribs convulsing, lips parted and drawn up a the corner almost to the ears.

On another occasion, Walter Ford invited me to a party saying, 'Pamela Hansford Johnson will be coming.' The publication of her first novel, *This Bed Thy Centre*, had made her a literary lion.

I shall always remember that party. Ford told an unpleasant sounding story of how Vicky had been invited to give a lecture at Oxford and all they wanted to hear about was 'That camel'. (I have, in this summary, watered it down; besides being, as I know now, factually incorrect, he had given it a twist which made it most offensive.(2)

Pamela turned on Ford flushing with fury and distress. 'It's a very unkind story if it's true. It's too bad for any one of us who have been helped by Vicky to repeat such a story. Nobody can come into Vicky's circle without being told foul stories about him and it's so unfair. We don't know *who* Vicky is! We only know how kind he is!'

She told us with simplicity how much she owed to Vicky, and said she was sure it was his publication of her poems which had made other publishers interested in her work. One would have to go a long way to find anybody else so disinterestedly interested in helping one. 'All we know about him is how much he has helped us. We don't know his past. We don't understand about these other things...I talked with Dylan about it on Clapham Common.' She had been very relieved to find Dylan felt the same way and they had agreed they should defend Vicky by refusing to listen to ugly stories.

I had not understood why Vicky's name should be associated with a camel, but some sixth sense told me it had to do with his relations with Crowley. I had not known how to speak without revealing what I knew. My gratitude to Pamela was the more.

I had always wanted to read Vicky's hands and one Friday evening found the courage to tell him so. At once he held them out to me. Thinking they might bear a line associated in the books with sexual abnormality I said, hesitatingly, 'This is not really a thing to do in public.'

Catching my meaning instantly, Vicky said, 'Haven't you got the gift of euphemistic expressions?' Then, kindly, as if he knew my awkward candour, he said, 'No, perhaps you haven't. Well, try to express it in a way that's fit for public entertainment. If you can't, I give you leave to take me out into the conservatory.'

I had never been alone with Vicky; my instant hopes were dashed when Runia said, 'There's no light in the conservatory. She can't see your hand without light.'

Vicky, confused and blushing at his own boldness, said, 'You can make your examination here and then take me out into the dark to tell me the worst. You can take me down into the bushes at the bottom of the garden and whisper it into my ear under the cover of the darkness of the night.'

I had not the hardihood to rise and put on my coat; partly because I was afraid Runia would be offended, and partly because the marking was not present and I could not see anything sufficiently 'bad' or embarrassing to justify my insisting upon privacy in which to say it. I thought he would think me foolish if, having got him outside, I had nothing of sufficient import to say to him.

His fingers were short in relation to the palm, compared to mine, but exceedingly flexible and could be bent back to an unusual degree or separated very widely from each other, and the thumb could stand away from the fingers so as to create over a right angle; from all this I deduced an extraordinary degree of openness of mind. All the mounts were full. The palm was covered with a scramble of fine lines showing the nervousness of his temperament, but all the main lines were in their right places. A good Heart line swept down from the base of the first finger in a generous curve; the Head line had a slight, but not exaggerated, slope towards the mount of the Moon; but the most remarkable thing was the line of Destiny. Rising from the wrist, after a break just above the Headline, it swept over to end on the mount of the Sun, in a three-pronged fork or Neptune trident. I have never seen such a marking on any other person's hand.

When I had said all that I could think of - Vicky was enjoying it - I mentioned Rai's hand, and that it had the Mystic Cross.

'Hasn't Vicky got the Mystic cross?' said Runia reproachfully.

Today I am not sure that this mark has special significance, but I said that on a hand showing so many criss-crossing lines it was difficult to tell but, if one could be picked out, it cut the lines of Head, Heart, and Destiny. Vicky said, 'I know what it means,' and was instantly asleep. I was surprised; then I thought it was not an ordinary kind of sleep. He had 'gone' somewhere.

'Poor Vicky,' said Runia.

One evening, after referring to her, as he often did, as 'this good lady', he added 'She is a good lady, you know. She saved my life! When she found me I was buried in the country. I thought my life was over.'

He had been staying with his cousin in Sussex, at a place called the Sanctuary, and it was as they emerged from deep bracken that they encountered her and a woman friend she was with. Later, when he was staying at his cousin's house, she came to visit them and talked about his future with Stanley, as though he were an absent third party. In the end, she had brought him to London with her and insisted on his re-entering the swim.

Then he had been offered the unexpected post on the *Sunday Referee*. 'A whole new life started,' he said wonderingly, 'I liked going to the office every day.' For him, the very ordinariness of the routine had the charm of novelty. 'Teddy Preston, the Literary Editor, is a friend of mine,' he said with pride and affection. 'At eleven o'clock we would go across the road together to have morning coffee at a little place on the other side.'

What I did not know was what he had been doing down in the country. About that he said only 'I was in a dazed state.'

I told him my mother and I had lived in Brighton where I was at school.

He exclaimed with emotion, 'We might have met! I lived for years of my life in a little village called Steyning, which is no distance at all from Brighton. We could have met years earlier!' He said it almost with reproach.

I, too, felt self-reproach. With Arthur Overton, I had in 1928 climbed to the top of Chanctonbury Ring which I was convinced had had to do with the Druids, and afterwards we had descended into Steyning. To think I could have found Vicky if only I had known!

One Friday evening, Cyril Moore came in carrying a small book, which he held out to Vicky saying, 'I found this in a second-hand bookshop.' His tone was oddly significant.

Vicky looked at it, almost as if a snake had been tendered for his inspection, and instead of taking it asked, 'What is it?' 'There's an inscription in it,' said Moore.

Vicky was regarding the book as though he were connected to it by invisible live wires. Raising his eyes to meet Moore's, he asked, in a low voice, 'A.C.?'

Moore's silence was an assent, his nod almost imperceptible. He said, 'It was lying where anybody could have picked it up. I thought the best thing I could do was to buy it and bring it to you.'

I wondered whether it contained something compromising to Vicky or just Crowley's signature.

At last Vicky took it; without opening it to look at whatever the inscription was he put it in his breast pocket, and was at once asleep. I thought of that other occasion on which I had seen him cede to sudden sleep. I had no doubt that he had gone straight into that realm of consciousness which he and Crowley had shared. If he wanted to repudiate the relationship, he could have put the book down on the table, or anywhere, not next to his heart. I felt that a passion which had so lasted commanded respect.

When he woke he looked across at Herbert and me and said, as though nothing had happened, 'You two will get gumboils from licking all that gum. Let me do some.'

One Saturday evening instead of a talk we had a competition for the best original definition of poetry, Vicky to be the judge. Slips of paper were passed round. I declined, saying, 'I don't know enough about it.'

Vicky, visibly disappointed, said, 'Oh, but you must have a go! Do try!'

I shook my head. I wanted to make no impression on him save the best, and was not sure enough I knew what poetry was to risk writing something he would not think very good.

So far from profiting from what he could, as a poetry editor, have done for me, I resisted all his attempts to draw me out - even to such a point as must, as on this occasion, have seemed churlish, if he could not divine the reason for it.

Vicky, unable to know these convolutions of my mind, did not understand what was the matter. He would ask me to write poetry. He would say, he said that evening 'Because I feel you can, I feel it's in you. But it's locked up, in some way.' (He was right, but he did not know in what way.)

That night, however, feeling that my refusal to produce anything caused Vicky disappointment, I found what at the moment seemed a solution. I could write a short story! I wrote one, using as a basis my tiny adventure with the photographer in Dean Street, but turning it round to give it drama, and sent it to him under the title *Many are Called.*

---

(1) Looking through my file of *Comments*, I see that the issue for December 14 carries a review of the Chinese Art Exhibition at Burlington House by 'Chela'. This was Heim; and I was present when Vicky, having received it, ragged him gently for the modesty of the pseudonym; this puzzles me because I had thought Heim had disappeared from the scene before the appearance of *Comment*. I have left the order of events as they stand in my spontaneous memory; nothing hangs on it. Vicky may have had the article long before he printed it.

(2) Nevertheless there is an absurd legend, of which this was a variant, that Crowley changed Neuburg into a camel!

5
The Last Days

It appeared on January 18, 1936. Vicky had told me, 'It's rather long. I may have to split it over two numbers.' Yet it was all in the one. He said, 'I couldn't find a place to split it so I've left something else out.'

Herbert Corby congratulated me and I sat down with him at the table to do the wrappers, for it was a Friday evening. Leslie Daiken came in with a couple of others. Vicky showed them my story and they too, congratulated me.

I thanked them while going on with the wrappers. There was an explosion from Runia. 'I do believe you're less excited than Vicky and me! I had expected you to be beside yourself with excitement at seeing your name in print and occupying two whole pages!'

Desperately anxious lest Vicky also should think me unappreciative, I exclaimed, 'But I am! I am excited!' It was true, but now that the words had been wrung from me in this way, they sounded forced. On an evening when I should have been in a happy glow, I was terribly distressed.

When I got home and examined my copy more carefully I saw what Vicky had left out in order to make room for me, an instalment of his own serial, The Perfect Stranger, which he wrote under the pseudonym M Broyle. It told the story of a small boy called Frankie and the curious thing was that it began before he was born. It started with him as a grown man, descended from a star, Aldebaran; as he alighted by the side of a wood, in the district that was to be his home, a grey figure came to meet him and they exchanged communications through coloured flashes before he entered the womb from which he was to be born.

Frankie was eight when he had his first important experience; he was on the way to the store to get something for this mother when he and the sky became one. After some moments he stopped being the sky and became Frankie again but he never forgot. It was after this, passing by the edge of the wood, that he met again the grey figure, who now seemed to him very tall. Although he had forgotten the manner of his arrival he recognized his friend.

Vicky delighted in writing under pseudonyms. As *Alfricobas* he commented on world affairs, as *Benjie* he wrote an occasional poem himself in a disguised style, and as *Richard Byrde* he did the book reviews. Reviewing a biography of Heine by Antonia Valentin on January 25, 1936, he wrote:

...the poet's genius deprived him of every trace of commonsense. Once again was a great artist a complete fool: divine possession is no guarantee of ordinary intelligence.

Opening the issue for January 25, I found the centre pages given to 'The Atys of Catullus', a translation by Vicky, this time beneath his own initials, VBN. From remarks by Corby and others, I got the impression this was creating a stir. Runia, half embarrassed, was saying 'There, children! There's a classical translation for you!'

I found an out-of-the-way chair, near the window and began to read:
> *From over the towering sea-trave his impetuous shallop bore*
> *Atys fierce-footed; heart-flaming, the Phrygian forest-shore*
> *He prest; the heavy-gloomed forest of the Goddess he craved, and there,*
> *Urged by inerrant raging, in his ecstasy of despair,*
> *Slit with jagged flint-cutter the globy tokens of man,*
> *And feeling his thews grow nerveless as his manhood's fire outran,*
> *And the soil was yet newly-streaked with trickling gouts of gore*
> *With swift and snowy fingers at the slender drum she tore,*
> *The horn, the drum, Cybele, our Mother, that are thine own;*
> *And swinging in rhythmic cadence the bull-hide hollow-blown,*
> *In thunder vibrations of fury to her feres was her song begun:*

I could have read no further than this when Vicky came up and seated himself on the inside ledge of the window-sill, just behind me, so that he was reading it over my shoulder. 'It's not a new thing,' he said. I did it years ago and never did anything with it, so I thought I might as well print it.'

It was a peculiar poem to be reading with the translator looking over one's shoulder. I saw that through seven stanzas of slowly writhing hexameters the poor creature, having castrated himself and symbolically changed sex, agonized and regretted the deed, thereby incurring the wrath of Her for whom it had been done. It ended:
> *Cybele, vast Goddess, sole Goddess of Dindymous Hill,*
> *Far from thy dwelling, O Mistress, stay all thy fury still;*
> *To others be granted thy frenzies, to others thy raging Will.*

The Last Days

I wondered what had made Vicky write this and, uncertain what to say, looked at the head which had come over my shoulder.

'I've got lots of translations in trunks,' he said.

It seemed to me that he was almost trying to dissociate himself from this piece of work, or at any rate to take away any feeling that I might have that it was Masochistic or of personal significance; so I, too, treated it impersonally, and agreed it would have been a pity to leave a translation of this quality in a trunk.

Some people were worried by Vicky's use of hyphens; it was the corollary to his way when speaking of breaking words into their semantically significant parts; he would by this means secure a meaning within a meaning. Hearing Vicky use the word e-ducate, one would not miss the meaning that the purpose of education was to lead or bring out of the pupil the capacities which were innate in him, rather than to impose a clutter of alien information.

One day we learned that a new periodical called *Janus* was coming in to the field and would be a rival to *Comment*. Its chief man had contacted Vicky when he lost his space on the *Sunday Referee* and proposed a joint enterprise for which he would put up money. But Vicky had declined the offered partnership because the other man's idea was to accept payment from the unknown poets whose work they published, a thing repugnant to Vicky. Then Vicky received a phone call from one of his children who was also an artist, and who had done a sketch of him, saying that, being hard up, he had accepted an offer of a few guineas for the sketch; he was uneasy, because the purchaser was the *Janus* man. The first issue of *Janus* carried the portrait of Vicky over the words *VBN reading Swinburne*.

Runia wanted Vicky to get an injunction to restrain. 'You can call their whole first edition in!'

'That would hit the young people,' said Vicky. 'If it were only *him*, I wouldn't mind. But they're doing the same thing as us, publishing unknowns, although in a way we don't like. He said he would require a statement to be inserted in their following issue that, contrary to any impression the reproduction of his picture might convey, he was unconnected with *Janus*. 'That I can enforce', he said.

It was my experience that Vicky had a good sense of the law. With regard to copyright, libel, 'ostrobogulosity', he knew exactly where he stood, or what anybody could get away with; and he could help an inexperienced person to read a contract, pointing out any clauses under which they might possibly lose.

His own values were not of the world but where the interest of any of the young people who looked to him for guidance was concerned he was shrewd as a pin.

Janus failed after only a few issues.

Comment received a certain number of review tickets, for theatres, cinemas and concerts; these were handled by Runia who would give them to whom she thought. Those for concerts went to Brian Crozier, the rest to other young men of the Zoists. As two tickets were always sent, they would sometimes ask me, and in this way I came in for a certain number of first nights.

Geoffrey Pollett took me to the first night of Auden's *Dog Beneath the Skin*, I was bewildered by it, but to my surprise the house went wild with enthusiasm at the final curtain. 'It's the Communists!' Pollett said. One strident voice, however screeched abuse; we recognized it, and saw 'the only British Nazi' standing up and calling forth. As we were leaving we met Hugo Manning who had also been in the house.

When next we were at Vicky's, Vicky asked, looking at me, 'Was David Gascoyne there?'

I said, 'I don't know what he looks like.'

Pollet answered for him, 'I don't think so. I didn't see him.'

Vicky said to me, 'Have you ever seen Gascoyne? He's a long, pale weedy lad who looks as if he'd grown in a cellar. You know what hyacinths look like if you've started them in a cupboard in the dark and forgotten to take them out. One day you open it and find them there - all long white leaves.'

Runia gave the tickets for the première of H G Wells' film, *The Shape of Things to Come*, to Herbert Corby and as I was sitting beside him he asked me if I would come with him. Vicky from his armchair, suggested I might write a review, too; why shouldn't we both send one in? Runia endorsed this and so after the showing I wrote one separately and posted it. Both of them were printed. There must also have been a first night with Walter Ford; I can remember his producing an orchid for my evening dress, but that is all I can remember.

When, however, there was a performance of *Lysistrata* at the Arts, the tickets were not delegated. Vicky, who seldom went to the theatre, said he was going to see 'a real comedy, written before the Age of Shame!' Runia went with him.

Vicky was asked to give another talk, and having nothing special in mind was put down for February 15 under the vague title of Poetry. What happened was, I believe, entirely impromtu. He began by speaking of the change which had come in the last half-century. When he was a young man, the accepted poets wrote about roses and lilies, with which they associated their young ladies. He quoted from Tennyson, Rossetti, William Morris and others. These concepts belonged to the drawing-room, where there was always a three-tiered cake-stand to be handed round. Some of the younger people felt this represented rather a limited section of life; there was a revolt against the sugary and a search for wider and stronger themes.

Now the pendulum had swung the other way. 'Dylan Thomas writes about worms.' Particularly the sort connected with the corruption of the flesh, as a symbol of death. Dylan had introduced us to 'The long worm of my finger'...'The living worm'...'The worm beneath my nail'...'That same crooked worm'...and, for a change, 'The maggot in my stool'. Only Dylan's genius made this sort of thing bearable; from those without it, it was nauseating.

'I'm afraid he's started a new school,' Vicky said. There were worms in half the entries to the *Poets' Corner*. Julian Symons's poetry had worms in it. He was sorry to see another poet, whom he usually liked, Francis Berry, perceived a worm in the moon. 'Poor Selina!' said Vicky.

For every worm which he let into print, there were many more which were rejected. The cumulative impression engendered by reading so much manuscript with images of one type was disturbing; this preoccupation with decomposition belonged not to the light but to the darkness.

He felt partly responsible because he had launched Dylan Thomas upon the world; if worms were to become the cornerstone of a new school, he would begin to wonder whether he had done a good deed.

'There are fashions in these things. The worm is now the fashion. When I was young it was lilies and roses. Now it's worms and excrements. If one must have set themes I'm not sure roses and lilies weren't the pleasanter conception!'

He said this with a touch of primness, relieved by a humorous consciousness that from him it came oddly. His talk was finished, and there was a hush in the room. It was as if a chastening had taken place.

When at last people began to speak, it was in subdued voices.

At one moment Vicky looked across at me from his low perch. (Though he read manuscripts from his armchair, when addressing a meeting it came natural to him to sit on the floor. Only in the earlier sessions, in the conservatory, had he sat on a chair, in deference to his title as Chairman. In these fireside evenings, in Moore's room, we who accepted chairs had become accustomed to a speaker below our own eye level, cross-legged or legs folded under him.) Speaking to me, he said, 'You've been brought up in a generation already relatively free. I don't suppose its possible for you to realize how stiflingly repressive was the world in which I was brought up. One felt, deep within one, that everything they said was right was wrong, and that everything they said was wrong was right. One felt one had to do everything they said was a sin. It was as simple as that. One had to break the taboo, to prove to oneself that one was free.' I thought he said this in case I should have been puzzled by report of his excesses with Crowley and I was touched.

As we trooped through the passage on the way out, Vicky beckoned to me from inside the doorway of his own room. His manner was conspiratorial, and wondering what secret I was being invited to share, I stepped within. He said, 'What is the Latin or Greek technical name for the study of worms?'

The only time Vicky appealed to me for information, I failed him. 'The Common or Garden Earthworm is *Lumbricus*. I'm afraid I don't remember what the study of worms is. I could look it up.'

'Don't trouble,' he said. 'I can look it up myself. I want to write something amusing in *Comment* so that Dylan will see it, as he wasn't here to hear the talk.'

Soon, afterwards, this paragraph by Vicky appeared in *Comment*, March 21, 1936:

A Note on Helminthology

The distinguished poet and fictionist, Dylan Thomas, whom we are proud to have as a contributor, did a doubtful service to contemporary verse by making worms popular. Many poets think, apparently, that the mention of worms transforms an otherwise mediocre lyric into a thing of surpassing beauty. I do not share this view; and I hope the Vermicular School will not run their worms to death(1)

During one of the Friday evenings, Vicky spoke to me spontaneously of his days with Crowley. He said, 'At any rate we did something which has never been done before! Well, not for hundreds of years anyway. We had no predecessors in the times in which we live.' He told me about the 'Calls' for entering into communication with the Angels transmitted to Queen Elizabeth's astrologer, John Dee. 'It's doubtful whether even Dee himself ever called them. And since his day they have done nothing but lie on dusty shelves. *We* called them. We went out into the desert and called them. We didn't know what would happen.' Some of the consequences, indeed, had been of an order they had not bargained for. But that didn't matter. They had followed their own idea, in the face of all warnings, and taken their fate into their own hands. 'We went to sea in a sieve.'

'And', he said, 'in some things we did we were quite original. At any rate in the form we gave to them, they could never have been done before. We made up our own rituals and thought out everything we would do.' They had tried to resuscitate the tradition of the ancients, but it was not possible to know exactly what the ancients did. Most of the clues were to be found in Roman and Greek texts but they were scanty and needed to be interpreted by the intuition. They had reconstructed and performed a ritual along the lines of that which they believed to have been practised in antiquity; but in this reconstruction, or perhaps one should say construction, they had used their imagination and in this sense one could say that what they had performed was an original creation.

Looking very deeply into my eyes, he said, 'We didn't know.' I knew that when he said this he meant that they had a deficiency of esoteric knowledge. I could feel that he felt, retrospectively, wonderment at their own temerity. 'We had no one to tell us,' he said. 'We were simply groping. We had the courage of our convictions.'

They had adventured, holding nothing of themselves back, into the complete unknown, in defiance of all the teaching of the last two thousand years.

'We got right off the beaten track,' he said, using a more homely phrase, which seemed to satisfy him.

The Magical Dilemma of Victor Neuburg

I realized that despite all the agony through which he had passed, he was at peace with himself and without regret; and I thought he was braver than any person I had ever known.

If only I had had then the knowledge I have now. What I regret today is that I gave Vicky such little answer in response to all that he opened out to me of himself; when he opened to me most completely, I was dumb. It was because, so full of feeling, I feared by an ill-placed word to jar upon his sensibility; and also because of the proximity of other people. I answered solely with my eyes, opened wide into his.

March 7, 1936, was my twenty-first birthday. I had not said anything about it at Vicky's but it fell on a Saturday, and for that reason I missed a meeting there. Normally my attendance was regular. On the following Friday when I went, somebody happened to refer to me as being twenty. I said, 'Twenty-one.'

'Oh! This child's had a twenty-first!' cried Vicky, starting up. 'And she never told us, and we haven't done anything about it. We can't it let go like this! We must do something about it, even if it's late! I'd like to give you a book of my own poetry, if I may.'

'Vicky! All yours is pornographic!' cried Runia in alarm.

'Oh, no it isn't!' he protested. 'It isn't, really! I'll find her something that isn't, anyway. The volume I have in mind hasn't anything in it...I'm sure it won't offend her.'

I wanted to ask him if he would write something specially for me; but I did not know if one could ask a serious poet to write a piece for a twenty-first birthday; and I was timid lest he should think the request presuming, or Runia disapprove.

Vicky spent the rest of the evening searching for the volume, using a chair to climb up and look in the topmost tiers of his bookcases, and going down on his knees to inspect the lower, or look at the piles under tables. He still had not found it at the end of the evening but knew he had it.

During the week I received through the post a poem for my twenty-first birthday from Walter Ford. It was neatly turned, and avoided slushiness.

After this, I wondered if I couldn't dare to ask Vicky for one instead of the book, especially as he could not find the book.

The Last Days

But when I arrived the following Friday, Vicky greeted me in triumph with a slender yellow and black volume, and as I saw he had inscribed it for me I felt it would seem greedy if I asked him to compose a poem for me as well. He gave me the volume, which I saw was called *Songs of the Groves*. On the fly-leaf he had written:

FOR JEAN:

V O Fuller ˙/.

From V B N ˙/.

For her 21st (7.3.36) ˙/.

14:3:36 ˙/.

Vicky ˙/.

I noticed the curious division sign, or dash between two dots, which he used for punctuation; also the slight hesitation as to the degree of familiarity to assume. I was pleased he had written Jean on a line by itself, as though he had at first meant to let it stand so. He had never called me Jean, and I would have liked him to. Perhaps, it occurs to me now, it was my place to have invited him to do so but I was too shy. I realize that he must have had some impediment which made him use the 'This little lady' form of address, as a sort of half-way house.

But that evening was exceptional. Runia, with unexpected warmth, said, 'I don't know what he's given you, and I'm sure it's highly unsuitable, but here's my kiss with it!' She gave me a kiss.

After that, Vicky was able to give me a kiss, too.

When I got back to my bedroom in the hotel, I opened the book he had given me, and almost at once found the poem 'Druids', which still seems to me his greatest. A prologue in prose explained that, it being the Summer Solstice, a sacred victim was slain in order that an omen might be obtained. I had not the slightest doubt that this was on the top of Chanctonbury Ring. The opening lines described how the initiate who was to be the sacrifice having been laid flat upon the altar, beneath the night sky, the white-robed priests gathered round him, staring down, while he prepared himself for immolation:

> Back from my breast I drew the heavy robe,
> Baring the curving belly, the sun's globe,
> The silver knife was over me: I lay

The Magical Dilemma of Victor Neuburg

In ecstasy of life-in-death: away
Faded the silly world: again I knew
The source of living, as they shaved the hair
From breast and belly and all luminous blue
Swathed round me; I was dead, no longer there
Before the knife had split my navel: far
....

He describes how he seems to be at a great distance above the body in which but lately he had been, and watches almost with detachment the gushing of blood. He has a heady and supernal consciousness of glory, as though he were himself a god; he is swimming easily in the air and hears rising like a roar the voices of the priests as they intone their appeal to him; there is a white flash:

I stood before the flame, like living ash
Gifted with speech...
                    now I knew all
The Druid mystery: the festival
Of blood was bared....

Though he is before them, he has not yet uttered. After a silence their voices continue to roar. 'Speak!' they demand. He sees them bend over his entrails, searching their design, then again demanding of his living self, 'A Word':

                .....I saw a chasm
Before the altar, invisible to all
Of flesh. Then flared the thought: The altar's dead
Then came the word: Woe! was the word I said;

There was another poem, called 'Downwood', written in an aetherial metre, which spoke of the same scene, at another period, in another mood:

A light rain falls; the hills have become blurred:

...
Dead leaves go and go,
Slow,
Slow blown by eddies of wind
Playing, playing,
Thinned, thinned,
...
And a single pale star
Shines, and a wing

Flutters in the hedge.
...
The tune
The winds sing
Is an old rune
Or an old rite,
Here,
In some long dead year,
They worshipped.....
Forgotten things
....
Forgotten wings
......
The old lights are dim:
....
I go
To my desire
By the warm fire.
But I know
The dream was true.

But not all the poems were set in Sussex. There was one entitled 'Gold Night', which opened

Above the cupolas,
And wide, white domes
Of coloured stars,
Bubastis smiles
Upon the wide grey sea
.....
The white town
Of queen Bubastis
....lies
Under the dark indigo skies
....
Bubastis is the Grey Cat
Who is the diadem
Of Khem,

...

Vicky was loosening up. It was one evening shortly after this that he began telling me a story which Runia must have recognized, for she cried out in considerable alarm, 'No Vicky! You mustn't! It's impossible!'

Vicky maintained his ground and said with a vital determination that was as new as it was astounding., 'I *will* tell my story! It's not obscene. I insist! She won't be shocked.'

Runia, seeing she could not stop him, said to me, 'Vicky's beginning to feel *at home* in your company. For a long time he was on his best behaviour in your presence. Now you've lost your status as a stranger, I take no responsibility for anything you hear in this house. He's capable of saying *anything*.'

Having won the field, and an expectant silence, Vicky began telling me his story. He was standing facing me, and I was sitting at the table beside Corby. When I thought he was still only at the beginning of the story, he stopped speaking. As I had seen nothing with any point to it so far, I waited for him to continue with it. Then I realized it was apparently complete. I was puzzled. There had been no word in it which I did not know; therefore there must have been one which had a secondary meaning with which I was unacquainted.

'You're *not* shocked, are you?' Vicky asked in pleading tones.

I did not like to own that I did not know what it meant. I felt foolish. It seemed to me too cruel a twist of fate that the first time Vicky had so far unbent with me as to tell me an ostrobogulous story I could not comprehend.

The worst happened. Vicky shrieked with delight. 'She doesn't understand it!' He bent down and peered into my face with prodigious curiosity. 'Don't you really understand it?' Incredulity and glee were written all over his face. I could hear Corby's raillery to add to my embarrassment. I had not answered Vicky's question but he was finally satisfied from the perplexity on my face that I had understood nothing, and his joy was hilarious.

Even Runia was laughing - with relief - and said, 'She's been too well brought up, Vicky!' This made me feel even more foolish.

Needless to say, I didn't have the courage to ask and I wish I knew the meaning of the story Vicky told me.

Morton was asked to give another talk. 'Can I be political?' he asked Vicky.

The Last Days

'I suppose I can't refuse you, Arthur.'

On an impulse Morton said, 'Vicky, I'd like to ask you something. I'm not trying to convert you. I've known you long enough to know it's useless trying. This is simply something which I should like to be able to understand. Why aren't you a Communist?'

'I haven't got the religious temperament. I don't worship according to the Gospel of St Marx.' He suddenly flung up his hands exclaiming, 'I'm just a red, red, red, red, red revolutionary!'

'Well, then?' said Morton, puzzled.

'I'm not against *the* Government. I'm against any possible form of government that ever has been or ever could be. I just don't like being governed!'

'It seems like an inconsistency with the sort of person you are that you should not be a Communist,' said Morton.

'I used to edit a little paper called *Freedom*,' said Vicky, 'But I was too anarchic even for the Anarchists. I'm an anarchist with a small a, not a capital.'

He hadn't wanted to edit the official Anarchist organ but they came to him saying they couldn't find anybody else and he hadn't the heart to refuse. It meant going down to a little press in the country once a week.

'In Essex,' said Runia, in tones of inconceivable disgust.

'It was really very interesting,' Vicky said, including me in the conversation. 'I never realized the utility of the majority vote until I worked with Anarchists. They haven't got it. You have to have unanimous agreement so you have to go on and on talking. You can't say, 'Well, we'd better take a vote', so there's no way to stop. Even when obtained, an agreement was never final. Someone would come up afterwards and say in strong foreign accents, 'Sorry, Vicky, von of us disagree.' The temptation to act on one's own and present them with the *fait accompli* was considerable. 'It was the living proof of Plato's thesis that demagogy gives way to dictatorship!'

When they suggested he resign he was a little hurt because he had given a lot of time to it, yet it was a relief.

It was arranged Morton should give his talk on March 21.-'History'

Vicky had more than once suggested I should bring my mother to see them. I was hesitant about bringing my two worlds together in case they clashed, yet I realized Vicky's curiosity was real; so I mentioned it to her. The Saturday she chose was March 21.

I brought Mother down into Cyril Moore's room where a group was already crouched around the fire, Runia in the most ancient red shawl. I introduced Mother to her and to Vicky; and Mother, knowing *Comment* was an altruistic venture, asked Vicky, 'Why do you do all this?'

Vicky said, 'I've failed at everything I've tried to do on my own account, and it seems to me the best thing I can do is try to be useful to the younger ones. I've got two, already, who are beginning to make names for themselves, and I have my eye on one or two more who seem to be coming up. If some of these young ones can make something of themselves it will be a kind of compensation. Anyway, we get a lot of fun out of them!'

It was time for the talk to begin. Morton, seating himself almost in the fire-grate, crouched on his haunches, with his back to the blaze, in order to address the semi-circle of listeners. He did not at first mention Communism, and I began to hope that Vicky, sensitive to the apprehensions I had not voiced, had tipped him off that my mother was coming and asked him not to say anything that could upset her, but gradually Morton began to get on to the emerging consciousness of the workers as a class. 'They knew they had something to kick about. And they had a pretty good idea whom to kick.' After developing this he rounded on my mother and brought his argument to a conclusion by saying, directly to her, 'And then we shall oppress you!'

'But will that be any better?' she asked, appreciating his glint of humour.

In the discussion which followed everyone seemed to take for granted 'the progress of humanity'.

Mother asked dubiously, 'Does humanity progress?'

Vicky exclaimed, looking at her very earnestly, 'Oh, but one must believe it does! Otherwise there would be no point in living! But perhaps I see your point. If one is reading Plato, one may think that since the fifth century BC no greater mind than that of Socrates, or Plato's own, has manifested itself.' He hesitated, and then, almost inaudibly, because what he was about to say touched his deepest beliefs which might not be accepted, he suggested that the reason why one did not meet in the world today persons superior even to Plato and Socrates was that, with the attainment of a certain stage of evolution, the need for a physical body was transcended. There was no reappearance in the world, or only voluntary reappearances at very rare intervals. 'Those who are in the van pass from among us, having blazed the way,' he said.

Turning to bring in Morton, with the courtesy that typified him, Vicky continued, 'To make a point which our speaker might appreciate, though the lamp in Greece burned very bright, its light was confined within a small circle.' One was, Vicky developed his exposition, so delighted by the Socratic dialogues that one was 'apt to think one could have dropped in to supper at any house in Athens and the conversation one would have heard would have been of the quality of that in the 'Symposium'. In fact, it was probably very rare. Unless one had the good fortune to be introduced into Socrates' circle 'one might have felt as much out of place there as one does here.' The small, unconscious give-away produced sympathetic smiles all round, which caused him only a slight confusion. Today, he went one, one had not got Socrates, but there was printing, and the dialogues could be read in cheap editions. Turning back to my mother, he said, 'If you will look at it in that way, you will see that humanity has progressed. The illumination has worked its way down through more layers, and is permeating the mass of the people.'

We all climbed the stairs to the ground floor, and were trooping through the hall towards the front door when Vicky detained my mother and me, saying, 'Won't you stay to supper?'

We ate tiny little sausages, of the sort sometimes served with cocktails, but with tea. Or perhaps they were little sausage rolls. I cannot recall the conversation, but it must have gone well for we stayed long enough to have missed the last bus and had to get home by a circuitous route.

Because Morton had done the speaking, Mother was the more vividly impressed by him; this was a tribute to his striking appearance and personal charm, not his politics. The other thing which left an indelible impression on her memory was that we had eaten off a table laid with newspaper.

It had been the *Daily Worker*, at that! I said I didn't think it was Vicky's own paper. Someone must have brought it in. I believed Vicky's regular paper was the *Daily Herald*. I then made the discovery that Mother didn't know there was any difference in the degree of their redness. Our paper, of course, was the *Daily Telegraph*.

Of Vicky, Mother seemed chiefly to have noticed his pallor and emaciation; she thought he was suffering from malnutrition or some wasting illness.

Mother asked, 'Is that all they have to eat in the evenings?'

Defending them I said I supposed they ate a really big meal in the middle of the day, stoking up to last until 11 pm supper. But I did not know.

Mother's rejoinder was, 'Is he a strict Jew? I mean, could you take slices of cold ham? Or I believe one can buy other kinds of cold meat by the slice now. You can say you've had so many meals that you feel you ought to make a contribution. But try to make sure most of it is eaten by *him*. And fruit. You can take lots of fruit.'

She said once or twice she supposed she should invite Runia and Vicky to dinner at the hotel, and she never did. I think if it had been a question of Vicky alone, she would have.

Vicky's great subject was Blake. It was Runia who told us he had lectured on Blake at the Poetry Society at Oxford. The Zoists wanted him to talk on Blake; he said, if he did he would have to split it over two Saturdays and it was arranged he should talk on March 28 and April 25.

Vicky started with 'The Marriage of Heaven and Hell', and read aloud in their entirety the famous maxims of the devil. After each one of the great indelible phrases, he looked up, and his eyes sent their meaning deep into me:

Man hath no body distinct from his soul...Energy is eternal delight...The road of excess leads to the palace of wisdom...Prudence is a rich, ugly old maid courted by incapacity...Sooner murder an infant in its cradle than nurse unacted desires.....

Daiken said, 'Taken literally, it's anti-social.'

I said, 'Considering he says, "Man has no body", it can't be meant to be taken literally.' But it was really Vicky whom I was answering. Although I had always loved these maxims I felt, suddenly, that they were extremely dangerous, or were so for Vicky who had lived by them. Surprised by my temerity, I launched into a thesis that they were a revolt against exaggerated repression; a series of illuminated half-truths which required to be interpreted by a kind of rectifying intuition because words were used with inversion of their usual meaning.

Vicky must have realized how personal was my anxiety, for he did not argue. He simply said, 'Of course.'

It was Herbert Corby who was our epistolary link with Dylan Thomas. Corby wrote poems to a girl called Beryl and, in a letter which he passed around for u all to see, Dylan said 'Lucky Beryl to have such an exciting poem written for her.' Dylan's writing was very small, yet though he had used a foolscap sheet of paper, and the letter consisted of only four or five lines, these were all crowded together close to the top. I wondered what psychological characteristic was betrayed by this eccentric spacing.

On Friday evening Corby showed us a postcard from Dylan saying he was coming to London to give a lecture and hoped we would be there. Pollett dropped in and was shown it. Somehow, it came about that they were both teasing me over my refusal to be kissed. My way of saying good-night after an evening out was with a firm handshake, which I always found effective in daunting my escort. They said, 'We'll have to bring her up against Dylan!'

I was surprised because when I had met him Dylan had been well behaved.

They told me I hadn't seen him 'On a wild night out with the boys!'

Corby said, 'First, we'll all take him out for a coffee.' This was because the pubs would be closed by the time his lecture finished. 'Then we'll see to it that it's *he* who sees Jean home!'

'But then we shan't see any of the fun!' protested Pollett. 'We don't want just to hand him over.'

'That's true,' said Corby. 'He wouldn't tell us...either way. We'll have to think of something better than that.'

Vicky, pretending to read manuscripts, in his armchair, was obviously listening to this. I caught his eye with a look of mute appeal.

The Magical Dilemma of Victor Neuburg

Seeing that I wanted him to come to my rescue, he said, 'It isn't fair! Two to one isn't fair. Let her be, boys! I don't want her frightened away. I'm always fearing one day she won't come any more.'

Before I left, Vicky said to me, as though fearing I might stay away from the lecture, 'You *will go* to hear Dylan? I want you to tell me what kind of a platform presence he's got It's important of have a good platform presence.' He would not be able to attend as he had been invited to speak at a dinner.

I was escorted to Dylan's lecture by Herbert Corby, Geoffrey Pollett, Idris Davies and Walter Ford. It was at a hall in Tavistock Place. We filed in and occupied the front row, left-hand side, the right being occupied by a contingent from *New Verse*. There was apparently some coolness between the two groups for they contrived to avoid seeing each other, and there was whispered consultation between our lot. 'They didn't acknowledge us', Pollet said, 'We didn't acknowledge them. We ought to have done. If Vicky had been here he would have greeted them so naturally we should all have become one party.'

Dylan came on the platform and I could hardly believe he was the young man I had known at Vicky's, then he had been civilized, now he was a tough with rumpled hair. 'He's been drinking!' murmured our lot in dismay.

After the lecture was over Dylan was surrounded by a crowd of people. Julian Symons was suddenly beside me, and after congratulating me on the poem I had had in *Comment* on May 2, asked, 'Where's Vicky tonight? This boy's his star child!'

The star child was still surrounded, and the crowd filled the staircase on to which he had moved. 'Let's shout for him,' said Pollett. 'I'm tired of hanging around.' We gave three calls: Dylan! Dylan! Dylan!' As if to mock us the door at the head of the stairs closed, separating him from us. Pollett suddenly lost patience and dragged us away to Lyons Corner House.

A few days later Corby showed me a reproachful letter he had received from Dylan, already back in Swansea, saying he had got free as quickly as he could and could hardly believe we hadn't waited for him.

Vicky asked me, 'Was he good?'

'He gave a very energetic lecture,' I said.

'Does that mean he wasn't any good?' he asked quickly apprehensive. 'Does he come over?'

I remember not knowing how to reply. And I felt, as all of us did, that Vicky, although he did not say it, was disappointed that Dylan had returned to Wales without coming to see him.

Vicky must have seen something - or been told something by the others - about anterior fits of Dylan's drinking, for one evening, when only a few of us were crouched about the fire, he expressed his foreboding. 'He's got a death wish,' he said, 'It's in his worm symbolism.' He thought that perhaps many of the Welsh, due to their isolation, were inbred. 'It's the mixed product of incest and Revivalism.'(2) He feared that the morbidity was deep and was working out into this way of living. Gazing seeingly into the glowing embers he said, 'He's got four things against him. Too little sleep. Too little food. Too much alcohol. And too much sexual intercourse.'

He thought that Dylan was killing himself deliberately because he craved the grave.

Runia exclaimed, 'But can't you do anything about it? Can't you talk to him about it? You're the only person he might listen to!'

Vicky reacted with exasperation. 'I refuse to turn into an old woman in my old age! One must leave other people free to choose their own course. There isn't anything that anybody can do. He knows that he can get a bath, a meal and a bed here any time he wants it.' Apparently, there had been an occasion when Dylan had arrived very early in the morning to ask if Vicky and Runia could give him breakfast, a bit of Hampstead Heath in his hair betraying where he had slept. If he didn't choose to come, said Vicky, there was nothing they could do about it. 'If he feels he has to face a moral lecture when he does come, he'll stop coming altogether,' he added to Runia, 'It's the surest way to discourage him.'

Continuing in the present way, Vicky said, Dylan could not be expected to live beyond the middle of his natural life-span. Only, one hoped he was going to be a considerable poet. 'It means he hasn't got very *long*. He'll have to make his mark *quickly*.'

This sombre prophecy left us all sitting very silent.

Vicky's specific reference to a bath may have been prompted by something I was told though not by him. On one of his visits to

London, Dylan had been invited by another editor to spend the night at his home, and was asked if he would like a bath. Dylan found himself followed into the bathroom by his host who remained the whole time he was bathing, alternately walking and standing about talking about poetry and looking as it seemed to Dylan, too fixedly. Embarrassed by this survey, Dylan completed his bath as rapidly as possible and redressed. Later he told the story to Vicky, and asked him whether, perhaps, in London literary and unconventional circles, this behaviour would be taken as quite ordinary, or whether he would be justified in thinking it signified the hope of a relationship?

Vicky shrieked, and half in tears with laughter, said, 'I don't know, Dylan, I'm sure. But if you want a bath at any time, you can use the bathroom here, without my coming in and walking about in it.'

To celebrate the third anniversary of the *Poets' Corner*, on May 9, a dinner was to be held at the Rendezvous restaurant in Dean Street.

It would be the first occasion for Vicky to see me in evening dress so I wanted of make the most of it. I had a dress I prized above all others, which I had worn as Lady Cattering in *While Parents Sleep*, the most alluring and daring role I had played. It was a slinky sheath dress in a shade between sky blue and smoke turquoise. I went and found Mother in her room to ask her opinion. She thought it was perhaps a bit outré for a Zoist dinner.

'I could cover up some of the décolleté if you would let me borrow your white fox fur,' I suggested.

Mother looked doubtful and she thought any dinner presided over by Vicky and Runia would be extremely informal. From her glimpse of the Zoists she would not be surprised if one or two of the girls turned up in trousers and sweaters.

'It's in a proper restaurant!' I said. 'We can't be going to eat off newspapers!'

Mother looked only half convinced. She brought out a gold lamé evening blouse and said, 'Put that on over the top.' When I had done so she said, 'It's still an elegant silhouette and won't be quite so eye-catching.'

At the restaurant I found we had the first floor. I immediately caught sight of Vicky, in evening dress, which made me wish I had been firm in my audacity.

The Last Days

Most of the faces were strange, being those of contributors who had come up from the provinces specially. There were also friends of Vicky's from other spheres, Bayard Simmons from the *Freethinker* and from *Freedom*, an anarchist couple with Slavonic accents. Neither Dylan nor Pamela were there though affectionate messages from them were read. As we were taking our seats somebody asked me to make one of the after-dinner speeches. I was both honoured and alarmed, never having spoken at a dinner before. I asked Ford how to begin.

'Unaccustomed as I am to public speaking,' Ford said facetiously.

He was going to be no help. I tried conversation with the man on the other side of me; but he disclosed that he had recently been discharged from a lunatic asylum. A note was passed under the table. It came from the Dinner Secretary and explained that he had miscalculated the cost of the tickets, which he had intended should cover the second helping of chicken for every person. We had eaten more than we had paid for; what should be done? I passed it on and saw the wave of sobering faces go up the table with it, until it reached Vicky and Runia. Their heads bent in conference. Then she smiled and wrote a cheque.

Everybody relaxed.

The awful moment came for me to speak, and I found myself on my feet. Everybody else had spoken about poetry and the services rendered to it by the *Poets' Corner*. Feeling that I was floating out upon a void I said, 'What I want to say is how much affection we have for Vicky and Runia as persons...'

It was very short, but I resisted pressure to get me back on to my feet.

Vicky spoke last, and told us of the genesis of the *Poets' Corner*, when he had been invited by his friend Hayter Preston to edit a column on the *Sunday Referee*, and of its subsequent history, and launching of *Comment*. He read 'The Jumblies' from beginning to end and when he came to the line: 'Our sieve ain't big', we all knew that we were its passengers.

When he sat down, amidst applause, I realized there was a fringe audience; the waiters were all standing, spellbound. Somebody came to tell them they were neglecting the diners below. A woman none of us knew stood up and sang Schubert's *Heidenröslein*, without music and perfectly in tune. More songs and recitations followed by the

Russian Anarchist woman, Leslie Daiken, Idris Davies (in Welsh), Brian Crozier, Walter Ford and others. The waiters had all crept back to listen.

After we rose from the table, and were moving towards the door, the Russian Anarchist couple found their way to me. The woman said to me, radiantly warm, 'I vant to thank you. For Vicky. It is not often one sees such a sincere emotion. Ve are very old friends of Vicky.'

'Ve know Vicky all our lives,' said her husband beaming with sentiment. They both embraced me.

While I was recovering from my happy confusion, Vicky was suddenly before me taking my hand. 'Your speech nearly undid us,' he said. 'You nearly achieved my reduction to tears. In public. Which would have shamed me. But thank you!'

The Saturday meetings of the Zoists had not run for a year when Walter Ford began issuing invitations to gramophone recitals at his place. The first time he did this I thought he could not have noticed that the day was Saturday. When he continued to do it I knew it could not be by accident, and thought it was too bad to try to draw Vicky's people away. Not that they all deserted in a flock, but the certainty of finding everybody at Vicky's on a Saturday being broken, the thing dwindled away. Herbert Corby and I still went on Fridays to address and send out *Comment*.

One evening Heim came in. It was a shock to me. Fortunately, he had with him a girl, an actress, who called him 'Sun Lion'. This was a protection for he would not be able to attempt to see me home. Yet his presence caused an odd fear. To gain a moment's respite from his proximity, I went to the lavatory. As I returned I realized this had been a bad move for he was standing in the passage, waiting to intercept me. 'I have something to say to you,' he said, seizing my wrist, and trying to prevent me from opening the door of Vicky's room.

'Let me go or I shall scream!' I said at the top of my voice, hoping it would carry through the door to Vicky's ears.

'Damnation on you!' he said as I swung the door open and reentered the room.

The Last Days

I looked at Vicky's face but it gave nothing away.

Heim after only a minute or two said he must be leaving. After he and his companion had gone I breathed again, yet it had unnerved me.

Shortly after this, Runia said one evening that it was a pity Herbert and I should waste our time addressing wrappers when this could be done by anybody. She could get the woman who came in to do the cleaning to do it for a small fee. We need not come any more on Fridays.

This sounded to me like a knell. I looked at Vicky hoping he would say, 'But you must keep coming to do the wrappers!'

He did not say it. He could not realize we would not meet again. Neither did I. We didn't even say good-bye. We parted as on any other night.

On May 30 and June 6, no *Comment* reached me. I wondered if something had gone wrong with the despatching. On June 13, however, one came, and it was number 26. That for May 23 had been No 25, so the numbering was consecutive.

No more numbers reached me.

Three years passed; for me a whole cycle of life. During that time I became engaged to be married and in order to be near my fiancé lived in Oxford, in an academic milieu. What had become a deeply unhappy love affair had now broken down. The beginning of the war found me in London again, on my own. My mind turned once more to Vicky. I wished, very much, to see him and I went to Springfield Road. The house had been pulled down. Disconsolate, I went away.

Months passed. He grew in my mind continually. I turned over every detail of his story and wrote down everything I could remember concerning my meetings and conversations with him. For some reason it seemed important I should do this: I had the feeling the record should be preserved. This took me some weeks and during all the time I was concentrating upon it his image and the sense of his personality became stronger and stronger in my mind, until it mounted to the feeling of a kind of possession by his spirit.

One evening in May 1940 this so overwhelmed me that I went out into the street and started walking towards the place where I had known him. As I walked I said to myself, 'This is madness. I am walking to a house which is no more.' His reflection could not stop me. I went on like the wind, in great strides.

I reached Springfield Road and the place where the house had been. I stood not knowing what to do. As though I drew it in on the air, the idea came to me that I must go into one of the other streets near by in order to feel something that spoke to me of Vicky. I thought, if a feeling of this order can be called thought, there must be a street near here which is more likely to have him in it. I retraced my steps to Loudoun Road, walked along it and found myself at the intersection with Boundary Road. I turned into that. I walked down it very fast, with unreasoningly mounting hope. I saw a house with a glass canopy covering the steps and path between the front door and garden gate. I had a curious feeling that this was the house he and Runia lived in, almost an illusion that it was the same house in which I had known them. I exerted my reason and said to myself, 'It's because that one had a glass conservatory and this has a glass canopy. It's the glass which is the only connection.'

I stood for some time before it on the opposite side; then I crossed over. I had a strong desire to go up the steps and ring the bell. Yet if somebody answered it I should feel foolish in having to confess I was looking for someone I had no reason to connect with this address. I crossed back to the other side yet could not tear myself away.

How long I stood thus, rooted in indecision and contemplation, I do now know. It had been light. Now it was dusk and turning chill. At last, with a feeling of unbearable loneliness, I walked away.

I had not kept in touch with any of the Zoists, but I had a recently published book by Dylan Thomas and wrote to him, c/o the publisher, asking if he knew the address to which Vicky had moved. After a fortnight I received a reply:

Laugharne,

Carmarthenshire,

Wales

19 June 1940

Dear Miss Fuller

I haven't heard anything from Vicky and Runia for years, until about a fortnight ago.

The Last Days

Then Pamela Johnson wrote to tell me that Vicky had just died. I was very grieved to hear it; he was a sweet, wise man. Runia's address is 84, Boundary Road, NW8. At least, I suppose she is still there. I wrote her a letter, but I haven't had a reply yet; probably she's too sad to write.

Yours sincerely

Dylan Thomas

Joined with sickening depair was the certain knowledge of what had happened. I went to Boundary Road and saw that 84 was the house with the glass canopy.

(1) Recently I have checked through Dylan Thomas's *18 Poems, Twenty-Five Poems, The Map of Love* and *Collected Poems* in search of the word 'worm'. I find it in ten of the *18 Poems*, in only two of the *Twenty-Five Poems*, in only one of *The Map of Love* poems, and not at all in the whole of the rest of his work. I have since read Ralph Maud's *Entrances to Dylan Thomas's Poetry* and find that he gives the same count (p63). The interesting thing is, as he points out on p 122, 'About half the poems in Thomas's two middle volumes *Twenty-five Poems* (1936) and *The Map of Love* (1939) had their origin in the amazing burst of creativity in the two years prior to *18 Poems* (1934.)' Now, the two worm poems in *Twenty-Five* are 'Here in this spring' and No III in the 'Altarwise by Owl-Light, sonnet-series and one in *The Map of Love* is 'If my head hurt a hair's foot'. Turning to the 'Chronology of Compositions' in Mr Maud's book, I see (pp 130, 129 and 132) that 'Here in this spring', according to the dating in Dylan Thomas's own notebook, was first written on July 9, 1933, though revised in January 1936, that the 'Altarwise by Owl-light' sonnets I-VII were probably written in summer 1935, while 'If my head hurt a hair's foot' was 'finished March 1939', which leaves open that it, too, was an earlier poem. It seems obvious that Dylan, at a certain moment, laid off worms, after previously being obsessed with them. Mr Maud notices (p 65) that after the early preoccupation with the word, 'Thomas apparently shied away from the use of "worm"'. But he seems to be groping in the search for an explanation in terms of Dylan Thomas's internal psychological evolution.

I am sure the real explanation is simply that having read Vicky's 'Note on Helminthology', he took the hint. Though he used up some of his old poems in subsequent volumes, he did not write any more with the word 'worm' in them. That he accepted this criticism from Vicky shows the regard in which he held him.

(2) I do not think this is to be taken literally.

6
After twenty years

Twenty further years had passed. A life-time. One filled with strange events. After the war, during which I had been an Examiner at the Postal Censorship and had taken an Honours degree at the University of London (English), I used a letter of introduction given me by Vilayat Inayat Khan to the *ashram* in Paris of the Frenchman, Vivian, who was in contact with other silent and unknown philosophers. It was also because of having known Vilayat, and his sister Noor that when in 1949 the George Cross was posthumously awarded to her I began to investigate the fate of the SOE network to which she had belonged. As readers of my three war books will know I was plunged, almost before I was aware of it, into such a world of sinister mysteries that I became engrossed for more than a decade in unravelling them. I travelled continually to France and Germany and even to Tunisia, to speak with agents, double agents and smugglers and there was a time when half my acquaintances seemed to belong to this shadow world.

It occurred to me that all the major developments of my life could be traced back to Vicky. Two main branches I owed to Vilayat; but I had met Vilayat through Basil Mitchell. I had met Basil (and all my friends) at Oxford University through Harold, to whom I had been engaged. I had met Harold at Vicky's. Vicky was the bole from which the tree of my life had grown.

When at intervals my thought returned to Vicky it was always emotional and in the moment when I became possessed by the idea, in July 1961, that I might become his biographer, I saw him before me with such clarity that the most minor details of his appearance re-emerged before the inward eye as on a photographic plate. He seemed to me immensely gay, gayer than I had ever known him in life, even in his moments of extreme hilarity; it was as if his vitality suffused me. When I asked myself how I would handle the 'ostrobogulous' side of his story, it was his grin which I found on my own lips. For days I could hear his laugh. Wherever I went it seemed that he was with me.

After Twenty Years

But each time I thought of Runia the laugh died. It would be no laughing matter with her. When I had spoken with her some months after Vicky's death she had said Crowley was a Black Magician and that his name must never be mentioned, except by the initials, as to speak it aloud set up a vibratory connection which he could use to get one into his power. I think she may have got this idea not from Vicky but from Betty May. Runia denied vigorously that there was any homosexual connection between Crowley and Vicky. I thought he had told me in his own way there had been. I thought he thought I knew and that everything he said was to explain it to me and to communicate the kind of quality it had had in order to lessen my revulsion. I had got over the shock, but I thought that, for Runia, it would impair the image she lived by.

Yet if I wrote about Vicky, what I would want to write would be the deep story of his life. Experience had taught me that when I started a serious research into a subject I always acquired a mass of information and I knew that I must learn everything possible about Vicky's relations with Crowley. When I was young I was frightened of anything to do with Crowley and would have shrunk from a research that would bring me into contact with his world. It came to me now that while I was young the fear had been protective; but I was of age, and the time had come for me to scrape the bottom of this barrel and see what lay on it.

While I was meditating on these things, I read in the *Aylesford Review* a notice of an Exhibition of Private Presses which contained a reference to 'books printed at the Vine Press, Steyning, by Victor B Neuburg - 'a figure who surely cries out for a biographer.' I am not a Catholic but I had done occasional reviewing for this periodical and knew Father Brocard Sewell, the Editor. It was he who had written the notice and I wrote to him, telling him I had known Victor Neuburg and was more than minded to become his biographer, though there were problems connected with homosexuality. He replied:

I think the whole subject could be treated in such a way as to keep the unpleasant matters in the right proportion and yet be perfectly frank. Truth if told with right intent will not do harm and will, without any moralizing, sound a useful warning to the curious. It seems to me that you are unquestionably the right person for this biography - and that it is needed.

He gave me the names and addresses of Mr Gerald Yorke, Mr Louis Wilkinson, Mr Charles Cammell, Mrs Wieland (Ethel Archer) and Anthony d'Offay, a dealer in rare books.

I realized at once that I had struck an exceptionally rich vein. Besides these people, I wrote also to my namesake, General Fuller, whose address was in *Who's Who* and, c/o their respective publishers, to Arthur Calder-Marshall and John Symonds. From every one of these people I had a reply.

Yet, years of research having taught me it was preferable to exhaust public sources before seeing private individuals, I made my first call at Somerset House. As I knew the year in which Vicky died I had no difficulty in tracing and obtaining a copy of the death certificate. On this I read that death had taken place on May 31, 1940, at 84 Boundary Road at the age of 57 years, in the presence of Mrs Tharp (Runia), of tubercular pneumonia, and chronic phthisis. Subtracting 57 from 1940 gave me the year of his birth and I put in for the birth certificate. He had, I found, been born on May 6, 1883, so he had Sun in Taurus 15.

I obtained a copy of his Will and saw that he had left his entire estate, real and personal, to Runia who was his sole Executrix. The will was dated December 16, 1937, and the estate was valued after death at £4448 3s 9d.

I was puzzled because Father Brocard had mentioned a son living, which presumed a wife at some time and I wondered why neither had been mentioned. I traced the son through the telephone directory. When he came to see me he told me his parents had never been divorced or even legally separated. His mother Kathleen was alive until about 1960. He gave me the approximate date of their marriage, which I subsequently verified by drawing the marriage certificate from Somerset House.

Other certificates which I obtained from Somerset House as my research proceeded were the birth certificates of the son and of the wife; the birth and death certificates and Will of Vicky's mother, the Will of his grandmother; the birth certificate and Will of his Auntie Ti; the marriage and death certificates of Jeanne Merton; and the birth certificate and Will of Aleister Crowley, whose literary executors were Louis Umfraville Wilkinson and John Symonds. I applied to them for access to his papers and so on, and I should like to put on record that they were most helpful.

I had had no communication with Runia for twenty years but now I traced her, too, through the telephone directory. Her position was this: subject to the condition that I would submit the entire manuscript for her approval she would place her papers at my disposal and introduce me to her Executor, Brian Crozier. (Someone had shown me leaflets sent out in her name and Crozier's announcing their hopes of re-starting *Comment* after its interruption by the death of Victor B Neuburg. The phrase had nettled me because it suggested that Vicky was replaceable.)

I would have been willing to let Runia see any use I made of any material which she herself confided to me, but I could not bind myself to submit the whole book, most of the material for which would come from quite other sources. I decided I should have to do without her co-operation. A pity, but at least I should be free to write my own book.

I communicated my decision to her in writing. Then I sent a letter to the Editor of the *Daily Telegraph*:

Dear Sir,

I am considering writing a biography of the late Mr Victor Benjamin Neuburg, editor of the *Poets' Corner, Comment*, etc, and should be grateful if any of your readers could send me useful information.

Yours faithfully

Jean Overton Fuller

Its appearance in print occasioned one further communication from Runia. She telephoned me and said in tones of the most intense anger, 'He's incorrectly described. You have described him as editor of the *Poets Corner* and *Comment*. He was editor of the *Poets' Corner* on the *Sunday Referee* and on *Comment*. He was not the editor of *Comment* as a whole. If you will look at the front page of *Comment* you will see that he was *co*-editor with *me*.' She addressed me in terms of such personal accusation that I did not feel I had to listen and I said that if she had anything further to communicate to me she should do it in writing. I heard no more from her.

I had thought of her as having a devotional attitude towards Vicky. It appeared to me now that her concern was not quite of the order I had supposed and this realization altered my own attitude.

About the homosexual angle I consulted the son, Victor E Neuburg. He said, 'There's only one person who has a right to mind, and that's me. I don't. I can tell you what my father would have said. Put it all in!'

I inserted similar letters in the *Daily Herald* and *The Times Literary Supplement*. Having seen the latter the book dealer, Anthony d'Offay, wrote to me that he had at one time thought of writing a book on Victor Neuburg and that he had been collecting Neuburgiana with that in mind. I had been buying Neuburg's books from him one at a time. He would sell me the remainder of his Neuburg collection for sixty guineas. I bought.

Almost to my surprise, I had a reply from General Fuller. It was hardly possible to correspond with a namesake without comment on the coincidence of name and exploring the possibility of relationship. The Fullers from whom I descended came all from Surrey and Sussex. I sent him a copy of the family-tree. He said he had not got his, but he was born in Chichester and thought it was probable we were 'distantly related.' I had heard he was a Fascist, and thought he might have been one of those locked up during the war under 18b. He was not, therefore, altogether the sort of relative I wanted to claim. When I went down for the day, I was wary. He and his wife received me very well. They were both on Crowborough station platform to meet me, took me to a hotel for lunch and then back to their home. I felt they were living very isolated, and that they were in fact lonely and glad to have someone to talk to, though he was certainly very 'browned off' with Crowley and disillusioned with the esoteric.

The d'Offay collection included all Vicky's books except the first, *The Green Garland*. Passing The Times Bookshop in Wigmore Street, a thought took me inside, to the antiquarian corner. I was looking through some volumes on a counter when a voice asked, 'Can I help you?'

'I'm looking for *The Green Garland* by Victor B Neuburg.'

'So am I!'

It was Timothy d'Arch Smith, whom I had previously only glimpsed at a Conversazione given by Brocard Sewell on May 2, 1960. He told me he was the manager of the Rare Books Department at The Times. It was so that I became friends with Tim, since 1968 my partner in Fuller d'Arch Smith Ltd, dealers in Rare Books.

Book Two

Vicky's Story

...if anyone favours another, believing him to be virtuous, for the sake of becoming better through the intercourse and affection for his lover, and is deceived; his lover turning out to be worthless, and far from the possession of virtue; yet it is honourable to have been deceived.

Plato
The Symposium 185a
(Shelley's translation)

1
Beginnings

Victor Benjamin Neuburg was born on May 6, 1883, at 129 Highbury Hill, Islington, London. His mother was Janette Jacobs, daughter of Moses Jacobs, Cane Merchant, and his wife Rebecca, formerly Levy. The marriage of Janette had been arranged by her parents in an exchange of letters with the Neuburg family in Vienna. The young people had never met before Carl Neuburg, aged 26, General Importer, son of Moritz Neuburg, Gentleman, arrived in London to be introduced to his bride. The marriage was solemnized with Jewish rites, at her home, 123 Highbury New Park, on July 29, 1882, and she gave her age in the register as 23. As she was born at 90 Suffolk Street, on March 30, 1855, she was actually just over 27.

The result was not an advertisement for arranged marriages. Of Carl's character nothing is known, save that he is reputed to have had an inclination to art or the company of artists. He appears not to have liked London or the family into which he married for he returned almost immediately to Vienna, leaving Janette with the child whose coming (as she confessed to him in after years), she tried by every means to stop.

As if to compensate for having tried to get rid of him she greatly coddled him once he had arrived, and his earliest memories were of spoonfuls of rice pudding being pressed against his closed lips, and platefuls of meat he was equally reluctant to eat. His childhood was a resistance against too much food and being weighed down with clothing. He was wrapped up even in summer. They lived at Highbury Park with the grandmother, Rebecca. She was described by Cyril Davis, Vicky's only surviving cousin, whom I contacted through the family firm, as "a grand old lady, deeply religious and a strict disciplinarian".

I find it difficult to get much impression of Vicky's mother. It is said that she was sweet natured and graceful when dancing; later she became a Christian Scientist after being cured of an arthritic hip. I have a much clearer picture of the two sisters: Aunti Ti (Theresa, later Mrs Royce), who had red hair, a lively temperament and seemed to

99

like Vicky more genuinely than did any other member of his family; and Aunt Hannah (Mrs Barnett), whom he called Frau B, until he shortened it to Fraub, which later became his generic name for any woman of the type of an overbearing Mrs Grundy. She always knew what was 'right' to do in any circumstance and she would say, 'in my opinion,' in a way that maddened Vicky, for everything pronounced following these words was held to be incontrovertible. She was a woman of invincible propriety. It would be impossible to over-estimate her influence; his whole life was a rebellion against her.

There was also a fourth sister, Fanny, who became Mrs Davis, and four brothers, of whom the most important were Uncle Ben, after whom he had been named, and Uncle Edward, who shared a flat at the Savoy. It was Uncle Edward who had the bulk of the family money. He was, according to Cyril Davis, 'most excellent company as well as a first class business man, an outstanding bridge player and one of the finest fly fishers in the country having one of the best beats on the River Dun in Hampshire.' It was he who paid for Vicky's education but, oddly, nobody could tell me where Vicky went to school.

All I knew from Vicky was that he had been no good at any branch of mathematics but later wished he had made more effort while at school to understand geometry, since its principles underlay so much occult doctrine.

In a reply to my letter in the *Daily Telegraph* a Mr Oswald Carlton Smith said that his brother Fred, who was at the City of London told him of a classmate called Victor Neuburg who drank ink from his inkwell! He put me in contact with his elder brother who wrote to me:

Victor was the chief of the three school chums I had at the City of London School, Victoria Embankment. I remember him for his generosity, his interest in poetry and other literature, his sense of fun and his fearless thinking. He was, as a schoolboy, already a vegetarian. I had very little money. When Victor bought sweets he shared them with me. Sometimes after school we browsed together amongst second-hand books in and around Paternoster Row. He would treat me to a ginger beer with ice cream in it. We used to amuse ourselves looking at books, and occasionally Victor would buy one. I noticed a book with some such title as *The Awful Adventures of Maria Monk*. Victor said if I should be interested to read it he would purchase it for me, and he did. There was one bookseller whose opinions were evidentally what are miscalled Fundamentalist and exhibited scathing written posters at which we both smiled, with sorrow for the narrowness of the writer of them.

The other chum in our trio was the ward of an Anglo-Catholic clergyman. He and Victor sometimes sandwiched me between them and while walking homewards they

Beginnings

tested my Puritanism (as I was a young Baptist) by antiphonally saying, "Damn, damn, damn; aren't you shocked, Smith?" But they gave this up when they found I was not very easily shocked, although I did not repeat the word myself.

Although rather a free thinking youngster, Victor already had a poet's sensitiveness. He told me that he felt indelicacy and irreverence in anyone's pulling up a flower and looking at its slender, naked root. He admired Shelley and Swinburne, poets who combined beauty of language with thoughts challenging ideas regarded as orthodox. Victor was the first to introduce to me, while we were schoolboys, Dickens's *Christmas Carol* and Jane Austen's novels.

...It is true that Victor, as a schoolboy, had no dislike for the taste of ink, and used sometimes to get his fingers inky. He certainly liked to *épater les bourgeois*, and I think he did once take a little ink from his inkwell, either to add to the surprise of his school-fellows or to confirm that he did not dislike the taste of his inky fingers.

I went to dine with him and his mother, when they resided in Highbury New Park, Canonbury. Half a century ago well-to-do people lived in that residential road and for the first time in my life, the door was opened to me by a butler. At dinner Mrs Neuburg congratulated me on being prepared to eat meat like a sensible boy, and on not being, as her son was, a vegetarian. She said that rabbits, for example, were so numerous that they seemed to be intended for us to eat. Victor said, 'Oh! my dear Mother, your argument is so primitive. Human babies are very numerous!'

As he reached the age of reason and argument, Victor was increasingly in rebellion against the stuffiness of his family. If he queried an opinion he was told it came from 'someone older than you.' The final authority was always 'common sense'.

He left school at the age of sixteen and a half (the school register shows him as having been there from September 1896 to December 1899); then he was put into the family business of Jacobs, Young and Westbury, Ltd, 109 Borough High Street, SE1. The firm imported canes, fibres and rattans. Victor was bored to distraction.

In 1903, on August 27 his grandmother, Rebecca Jacobs, died at her home. She left £21,105 7s 1d. After some small, particular bequests the Residuary Estate, about £20,000 was left in trust for her children, the interest to be divided between them equally, and on the death of any daughter with issue 'as to both capital and income in trust for all or any of her issue in such manner and form in every respect as she shall by Deed or Will or Codicil appoint.'

I went into this to discover Vicky's financial position. As his mother was one of eight children she would have received the income on just over two and a half thousand pounds. One must remember that the purchasing power of money was enormously greater in 1903 than now; she would have been reasonably well off. Victor, just over twenty when this happened, had nothing but knew that this must come to him eventually.

The matriarchal home at New Highbury Park was now dissolved. Auntie Ti took a flat in Victoria Street and her brother Edward bought Vine Cottage, in Steyning, Sussex, which he gave her as a present so she really had two residences.

Victor's mother moved to Hove where she took a flat. Victor, though he still came up to the office every day, went to live there with her. In considering such a life as Victor's most people would ask what his mother was like. It is difficult to get a picture of her, for even those who met her found it hard to name any characteristic. She cannot have had a personality which impressed itself. The most I could get out of anybody was that she seemed quite nice and under stress gave way to tears. The word 'sweet' has been used, and I think it possible she may have been cloying. Victor never spoke of his childhood and adolescence except with utter horror, yet it does not appear, and indeed he never alleged, that anybody was purposefully unkind to him. What does appear is that their lack of imagination and incapacity to understand the continual questions arising in an imaginative mind was so complete as to constitute a torment. To them it seemed silly to ask any question except of a practical order; Vicky's far-ranging questions about life and death were always met with a platitude.

Even in his middle forties when he was walking with someone (1) in Hove and they passed Albany Villas, he quickened his pace and explained that his mother lived there and he used to do so, and that he could never pass it without a shudder.

(1) Mrs Baker.

2
The Mystic of the *Agnostic Journal*

I remember Vicky's saying once, as we sat in the garden at Springfield Road, that it was 'while walking down a dusty road in South London' that he saw in the window of a shop 'a little paper that changed my entire life.' I thought he was going to say something occult, but his next words were 'The *Freethinker.*'

After all these years I myself stood in that 'dusty road in South London.' It was the Borough High Street. The shop was at 103 and there were still copies of the *Freethinker* in the window. It was only a few yards from Jacobs, Young and Westbury, in the same road. Vicky must have stopped and looked in this window on the way to or from the detested office. Here he had found metal more attractive! To understand what Freethought had meant to Vicky, I had to realize that in the stifling atmosphere in which he had been brought up anything which he did spontaneously or that was any fun was displeasing to God. God was not merely the God of Vengeance; he was Fraub, argus-eyed. The discovery that there existed people who did not believe in the existence of this ogre was electrifying and liberating.

It was with a sense of retracing his steps in history that I pushed open the door, as he must have done, and went inside. Elderly Mr Cutner, who could still remember him, led me up a flight of narrow stairs to a room filled with dusty volumes. 'These are our files,' he said. 'I knew him only from 1930, but you should be able to find his contributions from the beginning of the century. I'm sorry there's no heating.' He left me there and I began the research which later I continued under conditions of greater comfort in the Newspaper Library of the British Museum at Colindale.

Turning the pages of a weekly, one by one, issue by issue, is a long job. I had likewise the *Agnostic Journal* to go through, and it was in this that I found the earliest reference to his name. This was in the issue for September 5, 1903, in the column devoted to the Editor's reply to correspondents, and read: 'V.B.N. At your age you promise well.' Victor must have sent in a poem for criticism. It was also in the *Agnostic Journal* of October 10, 1903, that I found his first poem: about an unwed mother who jumped into the river with her baby.

His first contribution to the *Freethinker* which I found, was in the issue for October 25, 1903. It was a poem, entitled:

> Vale Jehovah!
> *What if to the Race I was born?*
> *To me that's no reason why I*
> *Should cling to a faith that I scorn,*
> *When my birthright's the infinite sky!*
> ...
> *Thy yoke I for ever throw over!*

It was a declaration. And he never went back on it.

In the *Agnostic Journal* there was more correspondence with the Editor, another poem on October 31, and another on February 13, 1904. February 27 saw his longest poem to date. Called 'Strong-heart', it is addressed to a companion whom he has never seen but whose presence he has sensed at different time:

> *All nature sings a passion song that echoes my desire:*
> *You come to me, Strong-heart, in wind and rain and sea and fire.*
> ...
> *Strong-heart, strong-heart, I have not sought for you, I know, in vain,*
> ...
> *Your voice comes to me softly from the days of long ago.*

There is a note in the correspondence column of the same issue:

'V.B.N Kindly correct proofs in normal way. See *First Steps In English Composition* which our publishers would send you post free.'

There are more poems in the *Agnostic Journal* for March 12 and March 19, and on April 23, there is one, 'To Count Tolstoy', which must be the reply to some diatribe on chastity. This, says Victor, may be all right when one is ninety-one, but he is only twenty now and means to have some fun!

> *I will not crush my nature 'neath my heel*
> *To please a problematic, tyrant God.*
> *Great Caesar! Tolstoy! I'm a man,*

The Mystic of the *Agnostic Journal*

He had another poem in the same journal on May 14, and on August 21 a curious one in the *Freethinker*, in which, having fallen asleep in a girl's arms he glides, as it were, into a country of sky and stars.

> *...Oh, many lands did pass.*
> *Leaving earth, I know no fear,*
> *Feel no bridge, 'twixt here and there.*

This is followed by another poem in the *Agnostic Journal*, on October 8: 'Between the Spheres'. He slips out of his body and although still warm from the habitation he has left, feels his ghostly self expand in the aether as he floats through it. He senses that he has travelled far from the earth and when he turns to look he sees our globe spinning, like a small green ball:

> ....
> *I am among the ones I knew...*
> *I have forgotten...I am afraid...A voice calls to me from the wide.*
> *I cannot stir...What is it I fear?...The sphere widens: here is the one I know.*
> *He takes me forth gently...I am by his side.*

There are further contributions in the journal on December 24 and, starting the year 1905, January 14, January 21, March 4, May 6, May 13, May 20, June 10, June 13, July 8, September 30 and January 27 of 1906. Some of these are translations from the French of Hugo and the German of Heine.

On February 17, 1906, another of his unearthly poems, 'The Dream', appears. While lying down he feels himself rise out of his body and go walking, a now familiar companion beside him; it is only as they talk that he realises, with a start, that this is something which happens only after one is dead. Wide-eyed, he asserts, 'I am not dead!' Instantly, he is jerked back to his body, and wakes.

He had another poem in the journal on May 2, and four on June 2. June 30 saw the publication of his first article, 'Freethought' in which he wrote:

While the religionist is made, the Freethinker becomes...Dogmatic religions teach us to satisfy a problematic God by denying certain nature. Free-thought teaches us to satisfy nature by complying with her demands.

Victor was becoming increasingly one of the supports of the paper. The Rev Arthur Peacock, replying to my letter in the *Daily Herald*, tells me he understood from Guy Aldred that Victor Neuburg was, in fact, Sub-Editor of the *Agnostic Journal*. He has more poems in it on August 8 (four sonnets to William Blake), August 25, September 15 and 22 including two translations from Heine.

These were his last contributions before going up to Cambridge. His Uncle Edward paid for him to go, appreciating that he was not cut out for business and that his gifts were of a different order.

I wrote to the Clerk of Trinity College who replied after consultation of the records that Victor Neuburg, after passing a compulsory examination in Latin and Greek, went up in the Michaelmas term of 1906 and read for a Tripos in Modern Languages. (At twenty-three he was late in starting, but he had left behind him a literary reputation other students might envy.)

Ironically, his life might have been brighter had he never gone. Not only would he probably not have met Aleister Crowley, but he might have been asked to succeed to the editorship of the *Agnostic Journal* when, on November 30 the Editor, Stewart Ross, alias Saladin, died. The issue for December 16, 1906, carries Victor's tribute, 'Saladin: In Memoriam', occupying almost a whole page:

Saladin's creed was one that underlies every great religion in the world...Saladin slashed and hewed at the grossly materialized symbols that form the idols of the unthinking...In happier times, Saladin would have been a revered and happy member of some more positive school of thought than that with which he identified himself, and whose acknowledged chief he was. Such a man as he, born in our superstition-cursed day, could but be a leader out of the paths of falsity. The work was necessary, but I, for one, cannot help regretting that he, who possessed a mind at once reverent and critical, a heart both fiery and tender, a wide and thorough academic knowledge, and, above all, the artist's love of perfection of form, should not have been devoted to some more constructive system than that to which his life was given...For me... a light has gone out of life; and there is sadness in my heart when I recollect that I shall never again hold that firm hand in my own, shall never again, in the flesh, see the brave eyes flash their indignation or their humour...

There are also poems by Victor in the same number. In the next there is an acknowledgement to him and his mother for a contribution to a fund for Mrs Ross.

On January 5, 1907, there is a poem by Victor, 'De Morte', occupying almost an entire page, in which he pictures Saladin, the shell which was his body burst, passing into a higher state of being, free. Beneath this poem appears Richter's dictum: 'Never does a man portray his own character more vividly than in his manner of portraying the character of another.' A thought for a biographer!

On January 18, 1907, there is a long article by Victor, a page and a half, 'Paganism and the Sense of Song'. He says his quarrel is not with the spiritual reality underlying all religions, but with the gross materialisation of symbols which were meant to teach truth in the language of poetry, which causes the seeming contradiction between religion and science. The most important authors for the present seem to him: Spencer, Darwin, Swinburne and Walt Whitman. The materialization of symbols has made organised religions useless, and inspiration may be received more truly through listening to music, or to the sounds of nature. If one makes one's inner ear sensitive, intimations of a mystical order can reach one:

Cosmic consciousness is obtained only after repeated manifestation on the physical plane...is unexplainable in words; but to those who have experienced it, it is so real that ever afterwards ordinary life and thought take on a more or less unreal appearance. To the orthodox secularist, all this will be the greatest heresy; but, none the less, the present writer must, in honesty, say, that the only times he has really lived here have been when this new Consciousness has manifested itself.

One sees that Victor, at twenty-three, was not an atheist, but what might be called an agnostic platonist. One reader protested, and Victor replied on February 9:

As to god I am quite agnostic; indeed I call myself an Atheist, which I claim to be in the real connotation for that term: I am, so far as I know, without a personal God. An impersonal God is inconceivable to me; but I do not - because I cannot - deny the possibility of His or Its existence. On that particular point I am Agnostic.

On March 2 there is another of his mystical poems, 'The Recall'. He is ill in bed and sees at his side an angel in a dark robe, who beckons him to rise. He does so, still in his night-clothes, and floats with him, as it seems out of the window. They pass over the gardens and over many cities. At length the angel turns and takes Victor's hands, and at the same moment the sun comes up over the horizon; the angel drops Victor's hands again, surveys the dawn, lingers a moment longer, looking into his eyes, then unfurls the mighty wings which Victor has only just noticed, and flies away. Victor wakes in bed, and the song of a thrush is carried in from the garden.

He had another poem in on March 20 and on April 6 another long article:

It is simply egotism...to describe a man as converted when you have merely made him think as you think. Real conversion can only be affected by awakening the Man in an individual, and inducing him to think for himself. Whether he agrees with you or not is

a matter of relatively small importance...for as soon as his intellect has been awakened, a man will find a path for himself...he who is truly free will never encroach upon
the freedom of others.

Here is a pure and evolved viewpoint, from a young man not yet
twenty-four. In a footnote, he says:

...on this particular plane of being on which we find ourselves, much must remain
forever unknown...But there is a possibility, and, in my opinion, a probability of the
existence of other planes of being. And on these planes, now almost inconceivable to
us, a degree of Gnosticism may be possible.

His last contribution, on May 18, was 'The Ballad of the Daisy',
translated from the Old French of Froissart. Then the *Agnostic Journal*
closed down because, as Mrs Stewart Ross explained in the final
issue, it had been impossible to find anybody to take over the editorship.

3
Crowley and the History of The Golden Dawn

Before bringing Crowley into Victor's story, I must say something about him. He was born on October 12, 1875, at Leamington Spa, Warwickshire, and registered and baptised in the names Edward Alexander. It was because he disliked being called Alec or Sandy that he later converted Alexander into Aleister, a form which did not lend itself to such familiarities. His father was a rich brewer and a Plymouth Brother. The doctrine of the Plymouth Brethren is Calvinistic and Fundamentalist. Christmas was not celebrated in the household, being regarded as a pagan festival, and the child was not allowed even to have toys. He used to listen often to his father's intent, fanatical preaching, for which he never entirely overcame a retrospective, reluctant admiration, though his desire was to reverse the sense of it.

As a start he had relations with the maid on his mother's bed. His mother was so horrified that she compared him to the Beast 'having seven heads and ten horns...and upon his heads the name of blasphemy', mentioned in Revelations xiii. Though he was later to refer to his mother in print as 'an ignorant bigot' he thought she was, in this, inspired, and that she had told him unknowingly his destiny and his mission which was to 'make war on the saints' of meek, self-denying Christendom, and to bring in a religion for the strong. The chapter in Revelations ends: 'it is the number of a man; and his number is six hundred three score and six.' To the end of his life, he was to analyze the occult properties of this number.

Every book on Crowley states that he went to Trinity College, Cambridge. I came, eventually, to wonder what he did there, ie, what subjects he read and with what results in the examinations, informa-

tion incredibly not given by any of his biographers. In the end I wrote
to the Clerk of Trinity College, who had already furnished me with
information about Victor. He replied:

According to my records, Edward Aleister Crowley matriculated in 1895. He passed
the second part of the General Examination in the Michaelmas Term 1896, the first
part in Easter Term 1897 and took the Special Examination in Chemistry in the
Michaelmas term, 1897, obtaining a second class. He did not graduate. He was in
residence from the Michaelmas Term 1895 until the Easter Term 1898.

Crowley was, by this time, already interested in magic, and reading
everything on it that he could find. I should explain that, to the
esoteric student, magic is not the pretension of making impossible
things happen. The occultist or mage is not a man who believes
natural law can be upset; he says there are natural laws not suspected
by our present science and that they can be brought into operation.

The term Black Magic is never used by occultists except to define the
abuse of magic; it is magic practised with evil, selfish, wrong intent.
When performed with good, unselfish and right intent, it is called
White Magic, though the neutral term, Magic, is more often used for
brevity where no confusion is likely. I hope it is unnecessary to add,
in these days of hypersensitive race consciousness, that these ancient
terms have nothing to do with the colour of the skin of the practitio-
ner but the colour of his heart. Similarly the term, the Left Hand Path,
meaning the path of Black Magic, has no reference to politics. The
origin of these, the proper terms of the study, are lost in the night of
time and though they may be confusing to moderns it seems useless
to try to change them.

Crowley with his Nietzsche-like philosophy, was precariously balanced, as on the edge of a razor. It was another chemist, George Cecil
Jones, who introduced him to a magical society, The Hermetic Order
of the Golden Dawn. In this Jones was Frater Volo Noscere. On November 18, 1898, in a hall in Queen Square, London, Crowley was initiated as a probationer and became Frater Perdurabo.

The Golden Dawn was a Rosicrucian Order with an odd history. As
Gerald Yorke told it to me, Dr Woodman, head of the Societas Ros-
icruciana in Anglia, found amongst some old books the texts of some
rites which seemed to be those of a Rosicrucian Order other than their
own. He consulted with two of his colleagues, Dr Wynn Westcott, the
Coroner for Hoxton, and Samuel Liddell Mathers, brother-in-law of
the French philosopher, Bergson. At Mathers' suggestion he commu-

nicated with the Rosicrucians of Nuremberg and received a reply from a Miss Anna Sprengel or Sprengeler (the name is differently given) otherwise Soror Sapiens Dominabitur Astris, who was the head or Imperatrix. She recognised the rituals as being those of the Licht, Liebe, Leben temple in Nuremberg, and issued the three English Brothers a charter authorizing them to constitute themselves as an English Order to be known as The Golden Dawn.

Modern scholarship, however, has challenged this. Even the existence of Anna Sprengel is doubted. The grounds are set out in *The Magicians of the Golden Dawn*, Ellic Howe (Routledge, 1972). If Howe is right, Westcott forged both documents and charter, with or without the help of Woodman, and Mathers, at first deceived, kept silent after he realized. One has to do, then, with an English Rosicrucian foundation, though the line of communication to the gods of ancient Egypt would have been none the less real to those who believed the Order's claim historically true. As I see it, if someone thinks he is invoking Horus, he is.

Narrowly speaking Golden Dawn was the title of the Outer Order, for there was an Inner Order, the Rosae Rubeae et Aureae Crucis. A system of grades was established:

The Inner Order or Rosae Rubeae et Aureae Crucis

7=4   Adeptus Exemptus

6=5   Adeptus Major

5=6   Adeptus Minor

The Outer Order or Golden Dawn

4=7   Philosophus

3=8   Practicus

2=9   Zelator

1=10 Neophyte

0=0   Probationer

It will be noticed that there are eleven grades, and that each of the numerical equations adds up to eleven, the right-hand numeral decreasing and the left hand increasing as they mounted from below.

Too much attention need not be paid to the titles of the grades, some of which were from time to time altered or reshuffled; it is the numerical equations which constitute the unalterable structure of the system and contain the meaning.(1)

Nevertheless, it is interesting to note that the titles of the grades, from the 3=8 upwards, are those of the Golden Rosicrucians (supposed to be the most mystical) of the Rosicrucian lines - and this ties up with the fact that Nuremberg is known to have been a centre of Golden Rosicrucians from the fourteenth century, and suggests to my mind that the word Golden was incorporated in the title of The Golden Dawn to indicate the descent for those who knew.

Some people have the idea that The Golden Dawn rose out of, or was part of, The Theosophical Society. This is false. The Theosophical Society was founded in 1875 - the year of Crowley's birth, a coincidence to which he liked to draw attention - under the inspiration of Madame Blavatsky and of two Indian Masters mainly resident in Tibet who showed her sacred books and interpreted them to her; it is their teaching which forms the basis of her monumental classic, *The Secret Doctrine*, which is in a sense the work of the three of them. The Headquarters of the Theosophical Society is at Adyar, in India.

The mystic tradition is universal and in this sense Theosophy and Rosicrucianism are one. But in the narrow sense, Theosophy is a movement inspired from Tibet, while Rosicrucianism was organized in Europe in the Middle Ages and drew its inspiration from Egypt, even as, in the infancy of European history, Pythagoras and Numa Pompilius had drawn it. Rosicrucianism was the secret religion in Europe for those who had found the Christian Church unacceptable; and Rosicrucians claim as forerunners, or lines collateral to that of their own ancestral tree, the Templars on the one hand and the Cathars, Waldenses and Albigenses on the other.

Between all esoteric schools there is a basic linkage. If one has graduated in one, so to speak, one can find one's bearings in another. It is as though, being familiar with a book in one's own language, one should happen upon a foreign edition; thumbing through one can find in what manner a particular passage has been translated. There is no doctrinal difference between Rosicrucianism and Theosophy but there is a difference of language and of approach. The Theosophists taught that each individual evolves through successive incarnations until he transcends the human state when various options open to him, one of which is to become one of the Masters of Wisdom who remain in touch with the human race, to help it from behind the scenes. Memory of previous incarnations, like other kinds of transcendental knowledge, comes with the vivification of the pineal gland.

The Rosicrucians had always taught reincarnation, but only under seal of secrecy, to their initiates. They had presented a corpus of teaching descended from the mystery schools of antiquity, despite constant oppression by a Church hostile to it, their very terminology at times disguised in that of the Bible so as to afford them some protection should their papers be seized. They were the inheritors of a way of thinking and feeling which came from having tended the flame and kept it alight, *sub rosa*, which here means under the rose, through nearly two thousand years of Christian persecution; but though this had by the end of the nineteenth century, dwindled to very little, and though they recognised the initiation of Madame Blavatsky, they were not sure whether the time was ripe, even now, for so much of the secret doctrine to be given out publicly to a world grown alien to its reception.(2)

Moreover, some of those whose interest in occultism was kindled by the Theosophical books were irritated by the Oriental terms. They felt that there should be a Western occult tradition which had been lost to sight, and began thinking about Druids. The amount of information available concerning Druidic culture being limited both Irish and Scottish folklore were tapped. It is significant of this trend that both Mathers and Crowley used MacGregor as an additional name, and appeared on occasions in kilts. It was the seekers for a Western tradition who tended to The Golden Dawn. This might not seem exactly Western for the Gods it invoked were those of ancient Egypt, and it claimed, however fictitiously, that its rituals descended from the Egypt of remote antiquity. But there is a tradition that Egypt, like the Celtic lands, was in part colonized from the lost Western continent of Atlantis. The feel of this idea can be obtained from Lewis Spence's books, *The Mysteries of Britain, The Problem of Atlantis*, etc. Theosophical literature treats the Pyramids and Stonehenge in a manner which relates them; and indeed, the ring of monoliths at Karnac in Brittany, if it is the twin of Stonehenge by its form, is that of the temple in Egypt by its name.

It was in the reading-room of the British Museum that, a decade before Crowley entered The Golden Dawn, the poet, W.B. Yeats met Mathers. Mathers was by this time already a 7=4, and the head of the Order, in which his name was Deo Duce Comite Ferro. Yeats had some years earlier been co-founder in Dublin of a small esoteric society called The Hermetic Students, and in London he had become Frater Daemon Est Deus Inversus, shortened in his signature to D.E.D.I.

The Order by now had branches in Weston-super-Mare, Bradford and Edinburgh, the Imperator of the Edinburgh Temple of The Golden Dawn was Peck, the Astronomer Royal for Scotland. I mention this because it shows of the doctrine was not repugnant to scientific people. Indeed part of the reason why the Theosophical and Rosicrucian schools of teaching appealed to many was that science had made such inroads on conventional religion that people who did not wish to be left with a bleakly materialistic position turned to something which offered a spiritual conception of the universe capable of comprehending in its symbols scientific as well as psychological truth.

Others in the Order in London included Arthur Machen, Brodie-Innes, A.E. Waite and Annie Horniman, who later financed the Gate Theatre. Algernon Blackwood was on the fringe. A serious member was Allan Bennett, Iehi Aour, with whom Crowley shared a flat in Chancery Lane and, in parenthesis, the only person from whom Crowley is known to have acknowledge having learned anything. Florence Farr, Soror Sapientia Sapienti Dona Data (S.S.D.D.) was, when Mathers transferred his headquarters to Paris, left as his representative in London, although it seems that Yeats took over from her progressively and effectively before he did so formally.

My feeling is that too many people were initiated and too quickly. Gerald Yorke suggested to me that one of the reasons people came down was the pledge taken at the 5=6, 'that with divine aid I may at length attain to be more than human... and that in that event I will not abuse the great power entrusted to me.' To aspire to transcend the failings which characterize humanity is one thing; but the phrase 'more than human' seems to make an appeal to ambition and is therefore unfortunate, being inflationary.

My other thought concerns the candidates. They were taken in on such short acquaintance it was impossible their character should be known, and even more impossible they should appreciate the seriousness of what they were doing.

Crowley was allowed to ascend the earlier grades rapidly. Having gained the 4=7 early in 1900 he applied for the 5=6 to Yeats, who was then 7=4, Adeptus Exemptus and Imperator of the London Temple of Isis-Urania. He perceived Crowley's ambition and instability and refused him the promotion.

The refusal at this stage was bitter for a special reason. Yeats would not allow members of the Order to practise magic or make invocations until they had attained the 5=6. Crowley wanted more than anything to practise magic and make invocations; that was the reason he had joined. Convinced that Yeats was jealous of his 'superiority' as a poet, and potential superiority as a magician, he went to Paris to tell Mathers. Now Mathers, in Paris, had done something very wrong. Intoxicated by the beauty of the rituals, he had had part of them performed on the stage of a theatre to which the public were admitted for a fee. This was a betrayal from the top of the pledge taken by every Probationer on entry of the Order to keep its secrets. Nevertheless, Mathers gave Crowley his ear. He initiated him in his Temple of Horus in Paris. Then he told him to go back to London and ask Yeats for the papers that went with the grade.

Yeats held the same grade as Mathers and was his equal in the Order, and while somebody had to be administrative chief of the whole, if the thing were to hang together, he had power to cut the London Temple adrift from that in Paris. Between the two Imperators there was already dissention; Mathers wanted the expulsion of Annie Horniman for what seemed to Yeats inadequate reason. Yeats refused absolutely to hand over to Aleister Crowley papers containing instructions for the practice of magic. In session with his committee, which included Florence Farr, A.E.Hunter and P.W.Bullock, he resolved no longer to recognise Mathers' authority.

Crowley went back to Mathers. He returned from Mathers, this time as his 'envoy plenipotentiary' in a kilt, and for melodrama (I cannot think of any other reason) a black mask and tried to take possession of the properties and papers in Yeats's custody. Yeats threw him out. In letters written during these fateful few weeks, Yeats refers to Crowley twice as 'an unspeakable person', three times as an 'unspeakable mad person,' and also to his 'unspeakable life.'

In some way Crowley was able to threaten Yeats with a legal action;

The Magical Dilemma of Victor Neuburg

on April 25, 1900, Yeats wrote to Lady Gregory:

..even if I lost the case, it will not occasion confusion, though it will give one Crowley, a person of unspeakable life, the means to carry on a mystical society, which will give him control of the conscience of many.

Though Crowley did not proceed with the threatened suit, Yeats found the position too difficult and resigned his connection with the Order. The English section then came under A. E. Waite - who Christianized it with the aid of two parsons. Those who did not like this, split away and called themselves the Stella Matutina, which Violet Firth, alias Dion Fortune, later took over.

I obtained this story from questioning Gerald Yorke. Some of it appears in Symonds's biography of Crowley, and some of it in Allan Wade's footnotes to Yeats's *Letters* (Macmillan) but both Wade and Symonds got their information from Gerald Yorke; I therefore went to the primary source - and drew out more, in particular Yeats' grade and title, and the grade for which Crowley applied to him. Yeats in his autobiography, *The Trembling of the Veil,* is very discreet and gives no indication either of his position in the Order or the reason for his withdrawal from it, save that this was occasioned by quarrels over personalities. But Gerald Yorke told me Yeats burned all The Golden Dawn papers in his keeping.

In helping Crowley, Mathers had done a bad day's work for himself. It was his own position Crowley coveted. He was one of those who use people as ladders; ingratitude was his hallmark. However, he did not immediately show his hand. For the time being satisfied with putting a curse on Yeats, he set off for New York, Mexico, and ultimately Ceylon, to visit Allan Bennett who had become a Buddhist monk.

It was on a brief return to this country that in 1903 he married Rose, the sister of Sir Gerald Kelly, later to become president of the Royal Academy. I often wondered what so conventional a person as Sir Gerald made of his extraordinary brother-in-law, but when I spoke with him almost the first thing he said was, 'When I first knew him he was an utterly delightful person. I met him at Cambridge during his last term there. We just overlapped. I didn't feel anything in the slightest degree sinister.'

The portrait Sir Gerald gave me was of an almost extrovert type: sunny, humorous, athletic, good at everything, good looking. 'He was very well read, and he wrote verses which he didn't pretend were poetry. He was a very rich man. The only thing was -' here, Sir Gerald caught himself, hesitated, and then took the plunge - 'this dates me, but I'll say it - he was not a *gentleman*. He had certain vulgarisms. But he was very good company. When he invited me to his house in Scotland, Boleskine, I enjoyed every minute of it! I thought he was a quite wonderful personality. My sister married him and for about two years I believe they were wonderfully happy. Then he began turning so peculiar she had to get rid of him.'

While it was obvious to me that Sir Gerald had at no time even an inkling of Crowley's inner life, I have quoted him at this length because his words prove that Vicky was not of singular blindness in seeing Crowley, in the beginning, as a fine man.

It was through Sir Gerald Kelly that Crowley came to know a number of distinguished men, Augustus John, Jacob Epstein, Auguste Rodin, Somerset Maugham and Arnold Bennett. I believe it is because they confuse him with Allan Bennett that several authors, probably copying from one another, have put Arnold Bennett into The Golden Dawn; Gerald Yorke, who seemed to know more about the history of The Golden Dawn than any then person living, had never heard of Arnold Bennett as being in it. I wrote to Mr Somerset Maugham and he replied, 'I was not connected with The Golden Dawn, and my acquaintance with Crowley was purely social.'

By the spring of 1904, Crowley was with Rose in Cairo. Here, he said, she told him Horus was waiting for him. If she really did, I can only think she picked up telepathically what he wanted to hear and relayed it back to him. On April 8, at noon, he sat down with a pen and waited. A voice began to speak from over his left shoulder; the speaker was a dark man about his own age, 'with the face of a savage king'. He said he was Aiwass, the Minister of Horus, and what Crowley took down at his dictation he called the *Liber Legis* or Book of the Law. Its key phrases were, There is no law beyond 'Do what thou wilt' and 'The word of the law is *Thelema* '. The Equinox of the Gods was come (this was a reference to the doctrine that every two thousand years brings a new dispensation or teaching): the Aeons of Isis and Osiris were passed away and the Aeon of Horus was begun.

I should say at once that I do not believe one word of the *Liber Legis*. That is to say, I do not believe, as Crowley did, that it was dictated to him by a supernal Intelligence.

The Magical Dilemma of Victor Neuburg

I have had a good deal of experience of 'communications', published and unpublished, claiming as their source inspiration, and my opinion is that the only useful criterion lies in the internal evidence or quality of the writing. I discredit the *Liber Legis*, not because of what I know of Aleister Crowley, nor yet because of the blasphemies against Jesus and the Virgin Mary, but because it is written in such an abominable style, half out of Revelations and half out of Rabelais. When I read a passage beginning, 'O blessed Beast, and thou Scarlet Woman of his desire,' I am unable to credit that this proceeded from a superior Intelligence, either heavenly or infernal. Similarly with the 'shocking' things. I can conceive of words which could cause deep shock to Christian and even to other conventionally minded people, but which because of the insight behind them would arrest attention and forbid facile dismissal. That is not the case with the blasphemies of the *Liber Legis*, which seem to me of a character so puerile that they could only have proceeded from a mind in some way immature. In fact the style is Crowley's which (alas) I have come to know well.

I do not doubt that Crowley saw and heard what he said he did. Where I criticize him is in his failure to consider the possibility that the phenomena emanated from within himself. He was not without criteria. The fact that the voice came to him over his left shoulder should have warned him. It is impossible that the symbolism of this should not be apparent to anybody who had read as much occultism as he had, save that he chose to close his eyes to it. So anxious was he to give the communication credence that he managed not to think of this. In my view, he entered a world of delusion from the moment he mistook a subjective psychic phenomenon for an objective one.

His very insistence that it was so external to him he did not at first welcome it, that so far was he from regarding the *Liber Legis* as a treasure that he almost at once lost the manuscript and was for years without it, increases my feeling that he was placing upon an external authority the responsibility for the formulations of a disowned part of himself.

In fact, he had it both ways, for he decided the experience constituted his initiation as a 6=5 and wrote Mathers a letter saying it had been revealed to him that he, not Mathers, was the real head of the Order.

At the same time he began a new system of dating, starting from 1904 as the first year of the Aeon of Horus; when using dates in the ordinary calendar he distinguished them by adding, not AD but EV,

118

standing for Era Vulgaris.

He now went to India. Cremers was factually incorrect when she said he had not learned from 'brown faces'. He met teachers with brown faces; though whether somebody who presented himself as the Logos of the Aeon of Horus (and as one who respects the Egyptian Gods part of Crowley's offence, in my eyes, is that he took in vain the name of the hawk-headed deity) could sufficiently subdue himself to listen, is another matter. Via Shanghai and New York he returned to London in 1906.

In rivalry to Mathers (who refused to abdicate) he now set up the *Argentinum Astrum*. He kept the name and the rituals of The Golden Dawn for the Outer Order, but added dangerously:

A:gentinum Astrum

10=1   Ipsissimus

 9=2   Magus

 8=3   Magister Templi

These are the supernal figures. Ipsissmus is absolute spirit.

It may be pertinent to ask whether Crowley had even the documents of the 5=6, which Yeats had refused him. Had Mathers, or not, a set in Paris? Gerald Yorke suggested that Allan Bennett who was a 5=6, may have allowed him to copy his set. He certainly had not those of the 6=5, which he 'gave' himself in Cairo. He had not, as yet, even claimed the 7=4.

It is important to realize that this inside story was not available to the disciples whom Crowley now attracted. General J.F.C.Fuller, then a junior officer, saw his advertisement for a prize of £100 for the best essay on his published works to date; it seemed to him that Crowley's books offered such a freedom from the shackles of cant as the world had never seen and, completely carried away, Fuller wrote in his *Star in the West*: 'It has taken 100,000,000 years to produce Aleister Crowley.' He was notified that his essay had won the prize and after this he met Crowley, only a few months before Victor did so.

---

(1) What I think these equations mean is:

10=1 Malkuth = Kether or in other words: Physical Manifestation = Absolute Spirit

The Magical Dilemma of Victor Neuburg

9=2	Yesod = Chokmah	Moon = Whole Zodiac
8=3	Hod = Binah	Mercury = Saturn
7=4	Netzach = Chesed	Venus = Jupiter
6=5	Tiphereth = Geburah	Sun = Mars
5=6	Geburah = Tiphereth	Mars = Sun
4=7	Chesed = Netzach	Jupiter = Venus
3=8	Binah = Hod	Saturn = Mercury
2=9	Chokmah = Yesod	Whole zodiac = Moon
1=10	Kether = Malkuth	Absolute spirit = physical manifestation
0=0	-	-

The = sign means 'balances', or 'is balanced by'; and it will be obvious the propositions are to be taken in a symbolic and psychological sense, since in the physical sense they are false. They are all equal to one another in value, despite that they are lived in a different order. The Hebrew terms are from the Kabalistic Tree of life. In each of the equations, it is the term on the right-hand side which gives the level of the focus of the candidate, or perhaps I should say, initiate. The descending numbers on the left probably correspond to the out-breathing of the universe, and all the equations add to 11 because that is the number of the Great Work to be achieved; Kether, the Crown, 1, reflected in Malkuth, the physical form, 10.

(2) It is believed that there has never been a papal encyclical against belief in reincarnation.

Although it has sometimes been thought that the Catholic Church was involved in the anathemas pronounced at the Second Council of Constantinople, otherwise called the Fifth Ecumenical of the Undivided Church, which opened on May 5, 553, the Church of Rome was not represented on this Council and the Pope disapproved of its convocation. The anathemas, moreover, were not pronounced during the council but by an extra-conciliary session of the Oriental Bishops, held a few days before it opened. They ratified the anathema which the Emperor Justinian had pronounced. This was: 'if anyone assert the fabulous pre-existence of souls, and shall assert the monstrous restoration which follows from it; let him be anathema.'

The terms in which they ratified it were as follows: 'Whosoever says or thinks that human souls pre-existed, ie that they had previously been spirits and holy powers but that satiated with the vision of God, they had turned to evil, and in this way the divine love in them had died out and they had therefore become souls and had been condemned to punishment in bodies, shall be anathema.'

It is believed that this extraordinary document, which by its evident mis-understanding of the doctrine bedevils the issue, was at no time offered to the Pope for his approval.

4

The Initiation of Victor Neuburg

General J.F.C.Fuller replied to my letter, saying:

I first met Victor Neuburg in 1906 at the house of Mr William Stewart Ross in Brixton...At that time Neuburg was an undergraduate at Cambridge, and Crowley, who was also a Cambridge man, was, from time to time, in the habit of visiting the university as he knew some of the undergraduates, I mentioned this to Neuburg...Personally I did not introduce him but indirectly it was through me that he introduced himself.

General Fuller was mistaken only in one particular; the responsibility for Victor's having met Crowley was not his. As Victor related it to a number of people, Crowley just walked into his room in college one day and introduced *himself*. As Crowley was a former student of Trinity it was perfectly in order for him to visit his old college and to walk up any of the staircases. He explained his call on Victor, saying that he had read some of his poems in the *Agnostic Journal* and that they interested him because they showed experience of astral travel.

Some of Victor's secularist friends have told me they find it difficult to reconcile his acceptance of Crowley's magical doctrine with his scepticism as a freethinker. I find no inconsistency in his position. Let me try to remove the appearance of it. Most people think the concept of immortality implies belief in God and that the two go together. In fact, the ideas are perfectly separable. From the earliest days he could remember, Victor had felt that he existed prior to his birth and that his new body and surroundings were strange to him. He had no feeling that he had ever begun or would ever end. The idea of metempsychosis was innate with him. A mystic from childhood, he had never felt this world to be more than the rind of the real; but the religion his family tried to teach him seemed to him sham, as did all conventional religion. It seemed to him nothing but a series of prohibitions, deriving superstitious authority from a sky-seated tyrant he was sure was non-existent.

This conviction carried him into the ranks of Freethought. Yet the character of the *Agnostic Journal* was really very open. Turning the pages of the files from 1900-7 in search of contributions from Victor, I took note of the character of the paper. I was impressed by the sense of forward movement into what was to be a new and truer world which characterized progressive thought in the first decade of the century. The new century was to usher in a world cleared of cant. There was to be no more unfairness, no more class distinction, and women were to emerge from their subjection. Equal sex morality was urged with the same sense of right as equality in public affairs. Women must, absolutely, be given the vote. Women distinguished in any field were made much of. References to Madame Blavatsky in the pages of the *Agnostic Journal* are always respectful; and to Annie Besant, by this time President of the Theosophical Society, it extended hospitality of its columns to the extent of lengthy discussions in print between herself and the Editor.

Stuart Ross was not hostile to mysticism so long as it was not dogmatic. He was dismayed only by Mrs Besant's apparent new willingness to compromise with Christianity as shown in her statements that, beneath the face of the childish superstitions, there was perhaps a mystical reality which she would not wish to deride. Ross retorted that this was not apparent in any presentation of the Christian religion he had ever encountered. And so they went on, through issue after issue, each explaining in turn to the other what they had meant when they had said this or that. If they never reached unity of viewpoint it was yet a dialogue between friends, seekers for truth.

Victor, subbing, would have read all this and was to some extent acquainted with the esoteric standpoint before he met Crowley. He had his own experiences of ecstasy. He was, in fact, prepared to 'take' a mystical doctrine so long as it was neither Judaic or Christian before Crowley walked into his room. He had read about Masters. Here was somebody who said he was one. He took him at his word and jumped at the offer of being accepted as a pupil.

So far from implying a reversal of his previous position the step was a natural one. What he found unacceptable was a creator pre-existent to the universe of his creation; the idea was not only philosophically but emotionally repugnant to him because it suggested a supreme tyrant; but he had no objection against hierarchies of Masters and Gods evolved from within the universe. This would imply not a child-to-parent but a brother-to-brother relationship in which the difference was only between elder and younger. He did not think it improper to submit to the tutelage of one more advanced. His mistake was in taking at its face value Crowley's claim to be a Master. He was bluffed.

One must remember that Crowley had behind him not only a mysterious Order into which he promised eventual initiation. He was a man of wide and recondite reading, much exceeding Victor's at that time, and must have seemed to Victor an inexhaustible fountain of information upon every arcane question. Victor did not have the sense of being asked to give up his freedom of judgment, for Crowley, too, professed a Freethinking position. The *Agnostic Journal* had brought them together. The reading list which Crowley drew up for his pupils included the *Essays* of David Hume, the *First Principles* of Herbert Spencer, *The Age of Reason* by Thomas Paine, and the *Essays* of Thomas Henry Huxley, Rationalist works which were given equality of importance with the more speculative *Three Dialogues* of Bishop Berkeley and *Prolegomena* of Kant and the definitely esoteric works.

The books on Crowley's list were not 'mumbo-jumbo'. The five works named above would form part of the proper studies of a student reading Philosophy at Cambridge or any other university (though not of a student reading Modern Languages, French and German). Crowley's list included some books on magic, but it also included odd literary classics such as *The Golden Ass* of Apuleius; Cicero's *Dream of Scipio*; The *Satyricon* of Petronius Arbiter; Pope's *Rape of the Lock*; Burton's *Arabian Nights*; Rabelais's *Complete Works*; Carroll's *Alice's Adventures in Wonderland, Through the Looking Glass* and *The Hunting of the Snark*; Malory's *Morte d'Arthur*; Edwin Arnold's *Light of Asia* and *Song Celestial*; Walter Scott's *Redgauntlet*; Huysmans' *Là-Bas* and *En Route*; de la Motte Fouqué's *Undine*; Balzac's *Le Peau de Chagrin*; Hewlett's *Lore of Prosperine*; Shakespeare's *Macbeth, Midsummer Night's Dream* and *The Tempest*. As well as Sufi poetry generally.

With regard to esoteric and mystical works proper, I will not copy Crowley's list exactly as it includes one or two things (such as the *I Ching* and *Scrutinium Chymicum*) which I have not studied and of which I cannot know the quality; on the other hand I have added some works which do not feature on the list but which Crowley and Victor certainly studied. I have put on the list only those of the works they read which I have, myself, read in their entirety:

Eliphas Levi (Magical name of the French Rosicrucian, Kabbalist, yet

Roman Catholic, Alphonse Louis Constant, Crowley's favourite author): *Transcendental Magic* (*Dogme de la Haute Magie*, 1855, and *Rituel de la Haute Magie*, 1856) bound in a single volume, 438 pages; *History of Magic (Histoire de la Magie*, 1860) 384 pages; *Key to the Mysteries (Clef des Grands Mystères*, 1861, 215 pages; all issued in English by Rider, the first two translated and annotated by Waite and the last by Crowley.

H P Blavatsky: *Isis Unveiled*, 1877, 2 vols, totalling 1321 pages; *The Secret Doctrine*, 1888, 6 vols, totalling 2653 pages; *The Voice of the Silence*, 1889, 289 small pages; *Key to Theosophy*, 1890, 370 pages; the first named from the Theosophical University Press and all the rest from the Theosophical Publishing House.

Mabel Collins: *The Blossom and the Fruit* (it was perceptive of Crowley to put down her little-known novel, but why not her more famous short classics, *Light on the Path*, *A Cry from Afar* and *The Idyll of the White Lotus*?) all Theosophical Publishing House.(1)

S L Mathers: *The Kabbalah Unveiled*, Routledge; 360 pages.

Hermes Trismegistus: *The Divine Pymander*. I do not know in what edition they studied this, but I have one published by Watkins under the title *Thrice Greatest Hermes*, translated and annotated by G R Mead, 3 vols totalling 1295 pages.

Pistis Sophia, translated and annotated by G R Mead; 1896, Watkins, 325 pages.

The Book of the Dead; again, I do not know what edition they had. I have one with translation and annotations by Budge, produced by the Medici Society in 1913, 2 vols, totally 704 pages, plus facsimile reproduction of Papyrus of Ani on folding sheets.

Plato's Complete Works, except, perhaps *The Laws* which is so unlike the rest, not least in being so dull! (2)

The Tao Teh King

The Shiva Samhita

The Bhagavad Gita.

This reading list may surprise those who think of Crowley purely as a buffoon; but unless his ability to direct the intellectual studies of those whom he attracted to him is recognized the picture remains a dimen-

The Initiation of Victor Neuburg

sion short. If he was mad it was in the way only possible to a man of much learning. If his recommendations were to some extent idiosyncratic, the list nevertheless constituted in itself a liberal course in the humanities, cutting across the ground of many university courses though following the lines of none. No person could read all the works on this list without having his mind greatly expanded thereby. Crowley may have seduced his pupils, but at least he cultivated them. What was unfortunate for Victor was that this vast world of reading was opened up to him just when he was supposed to be reading for a degree in a much narrower field.

Crowley, though he had a sentiment for his old university and habitually came to it to recruit for his Order - Mudd, Pinsent, Merton and Gerald Yorke, were all Cambridge men - did not regard degrees and did not care two pins whether Victor got his. Victor, trying to pursue both Crowley's and his proper tutors' prescribed courses of reading was never able to take his eyes out of books.

I was unable to trace any of Victor's tutors at Cambridge; indeed they must be dead. But an outside glimpse came from the younger Carlton Smith, Oswald who was now at St John's. When I went to see him at his home in Bognor Regis he showed me entries from his diaries for 1907-8 from which it appeared that he and Victor met, sometimes at Trinity and sometimes at St John's, five times, others sometimes present including Pinsent and Mudd. There was nothing conspicuous in Victor's behaviour which he could recall. On one occasion he mentioned that Crowley had been with him and that they had been smoking some weed and gone out in the astral, which Carlton Smith did not take very seriously.

In 1908 Victor's first book appeared, *The Green Garland* (now very rare.) Mr Oswald Carlton Smith communicated on my behalf with another John's man, C.N.Raad, who wrote that it was a wealthy undergraduate named Schmiechen, also of Trinity, who helped Victor finance the publication through Probsthain & Co. It contained most of the poems which appeared in the *Agnostic Journal* and received excellent reviews in the *Morning Post* and in *The Times.*

Norman Mudd, a Mathematics student of Trinity, had become, like Victor, a disciple of Crowley and also Secretary of the Cambridge University Freethought Association. In this capacity he was summoned by the Dean, who showed him a letter received by the college authorities in which Crowley was accused of paederasty.

The Magical Dilemma of Victor Neuburg

The Dean asked Mudd to refrain from distributing Crowley's books and to cancel an invitation sent to him to speak to the C.U.F.A. As Crowley was a Trinity man I cannot help feeling the Dean might have handled this situation in some braver way than by showing this communication to Mudd, the weakest personality amongst those involved. With surprising toughness the C.U.F.A., of which I imagine Victor must have been President (it is defunct and I have been unable to obtain a list of its officers) sent the Dean a written reply saying they declined to comply with his request.

What was Victor's knowledge of Crowley at that time? In the summer of 1908 they had been together for a walking tour in Spain. Victor's *Triumph of Pan* (not published until later) contains a section of this date, headed puzzlingly:

The Romance of Olivia Vane

To Olivia Vane

and her other lover

Paris March 1909.

For a long time I looked for two persons in this poem-series; now I am convinced there is only one. No II begins:

Sweet Wizard, in whose footsteps I have trod
Unto the shrine of the most obscene god,

The 'sweet wizard', a masculine term though qualified by a lover like adjective, is obviously Crowley. The god would be Pan, or Priapus, but I was at first puzzled that Vicky should refer to what he would think of as the sacred relationship as obscene. Later I realized that this reflected Crowley's idea of combining the heights and the depths, as though they balanced each other; this produced a revelling in lewd terms, as though they were in some way healthy. On Victor's style it was a temporary graft.

No III has an interchange of masculine and feminine terms which are in apposition, not opposition:

O thou who hast sucked my soul, lord of my nights and days,
My body, pure and whole is merged within the ways
That lead to thee, my queen,

No VIII is a powerful sonnet showing the freshness of the emotion, the pride, the feelings with which he looked back to what must have been the first incident:

The Initiation of Victor Neuburg

I think that never in my loneliness
May I forget my glory and my shame,
Nor the swift lightning flash that 'twixt us came
...

After some purple patches, it ends:
Let me once more feel thy strong hand to be
Making the magic signs upon me! Stand,
Stand in the light, and let mine eyes drink in
The glorious vision of the death of sin!

However much one might regret the object was Crowley, I think it impossible not to feel how superb is the love shown in this passage. No XI is another proud and strong poem in which he keeps a firm texture throughout. He pictures a time when he shall be old and younger men shall ask him what his beloved was really like, his miracles, his dress, his manner. Then he will smile, as old men do to the young, and recreate the appearance of the great one for them:

And they shall know how once I gave my breath,
My hand, my lyre, to thee, and said, 'Till death
The image of this man shall not depart
Out of the inmost shrine within my heart.'

Reading these lines written in such a noble confidence, I remembered how Vicky really had spoken of Crowley in his later days; the ghastly conversation with Cremers, in which he admitted all her charges and could find nothing to say in palliation of his former friend's offence but that 'his mind had gone'. Yet it was true that his image had not departed from the innermost shrine within his heart; I remembered also the words he had spoken to me afterwards on the iron staircase, when he tried to draw for me the picture of the man he had loved, as the noble figure he had first seen 'and as I prefer to remember him.'

The text contains the occasional completely plain line:
Take thou my body, now hermaphrodite.

He believes that, in very truth, as the beloved says, Horus has been reborn. Having gone ahead in France, he walks idly in the Jardins du Luxembourg and the streets of Paris, waiting for the reunion that there will be when the beloved arrives in a few days from England, to join him.

How far had Crowley led Victor in this development of their relations? I am inclined to think Victor must have had at least some latent homosexuality, otherwise he could never have been aroused to so great a passion. On the other hand, it is evident from the emotion in the poems that what had happened between them was without precedence in his experience and constituted a complete revelation and ecstasy. Like a girl who has just experienced the delight of love for the first time, he is at once bashful, and on a summit.

While I am sure Crowley led him in the physical initiation - he was eight years the elder and had prior experience - I have no doubt that Victor, having renounced the Judaic Law, had already turned his face towards the Greek, via Swinburne, Whitman and Edward Carpenter. It should not be forgotten that the latter's classic, *The Intermediate Sex*, by which Victor was much influenced, appeared in the previous year, 1908, just when his relationship with Crowley was in the making.

Carpenter, who shows a debt to both Platonic and Oriental doctrine, asks for recognition of the homosexual as a natural and valuable variant, and suggests that as the normal union has for its fruit children, the homosexual, (or as he prefers to say, homogenic or Uranian)(3) might give back to the community through consecration to such occupations as are unsuitable for the family man because the renumeration from them is small, irregular or subject to hazards: poetry and the arts and crusades requiring the heroic character.

Carpenter says we do not know what nature is deriving at in producing this type and suggests that we may be in for a new phase of evolution. Nothing seems to me likelier than that Victor put this together in his mind, with hints found in the Kabalah, *The Secret Doctrine* and elsewhere that man, prior to the Fall, was androgyne, and that androgyny is destined to be recaptured in the far future when physical transformations have made possible the reproduction of the species in a manner different from that known at present.

While it would be difficult to see how physical homosexual practices could forward such an evolution in a precise manner, my feeling is that Victor thought that anything conducive to a hermaphrodite state of consciousness must be in line with the ultimate purpose. This was my first reading of his mind; but I shall later show evidence that this was exactly what he did think.

Then there is the esoteric doctrine concerned with the precession of the Equinoxes and the new dispensation of teaching every two thousand years. According to this, Jesus was the teacher of the Piscean age; and about the turn of the century there was a strong feeling abroad that the Teacher of the Aquarian age was already due. Aquarius is the sign to which the majority of astrologers assign Uranus; there is, however no direct evidence that either Crowley or Victor pursued a line of reasoning which might proceed from the association of Uranus with Urania. For the Theosophists, Krishnamurti was the vehicle whom the world Teacher would inspire. (4)

In the context, it may be noted that his beginnings were clouded by the scandals touching Leadbeater.

There was also Inayat Khan: when he came from India in 1910, teaching a broad form of Sufism, some of those who gathered around him thought he was the Messenger, and the hot-house cult which built up around him was a source of acute embarrassment to his children.

Crowley, of course, thought that this divinely appointed instrument was himself. Elaborating the original words of the *Liber Legis*, he explained that the Aeon of Isis had been Matriarchy; the Aeon of Osiris, Patriarchy; the Aeon of Horus, which was initiated by his own advent, two sexes in one person. He said the male magician must, without losing his virility, cultivate his female side.

I go into this because, unless it is understood, Victor's dalliance with the man he claimed as his spiritual teacher might seem to show insincerity. It was not that; quite the contrary. He really believed Crowley to be the Messiah of the new Age and thought that in being allowed so close his position was one of singular privilege.

Daily life with such a being must have constituted rather a strain; though a more casual note was introduced by Crowley's teasing. When they went into a restaurant in Paris together Crowley taunted him because, although he was studying Modern Languages at Cambridge, he had difficulty in ordering the meal. When they got their meal Crowley said, 'How illogical you are! You won't eat meat for humanitarian reasons, and yet you eat *pommes soufflées*.' As Victor looked puzzled, Crowley went on, 'Are you not aware that the potatoes must actually be on burning charcoal while being blown out, and that the men employed, *souffleurs* as they are called, rarely live more than three years after taking the job.'

Poor Victor dropped his fork with a clatter and went ashen. When he recovered the power of speech, he was ready to devote his life to getting a law passed to prohibit the making of *pommes soufflées*. Crowley then said he had only played this trick on him in order to demonstrate Victor's lack of judgment when his emotions were aroused.(5)

Victor returned to Cambridge for his last term in a state of exhilaration though this wore off because of difficulties with finances and family, and the need to catch up with his studies. Three weeks before his finals he came to London for the day to be initiated into the *Argentinum Astrum*, of which the parvois was still called The Golden Dawn.

Probably in an ante-room to that in which the initiation was to take place, a black robe was put upon him. This was almost certainly the same one that had been worn by Crowley at his admission as a Probationer, and Victor would have been told this for his fortification. It was like a cloak except for wide sleeves edged with gold, and had a hood with eye-holes which could be brought up right over the head. Once robed, the Brother who had been made responsible for his initiation into the Order, and who would also have been wearing a robe, would have taken him through to the hall where, stationed amidst strange symbols, an assembled company awaited him. In the midst was Crowley, garbed as Osiris. The ritual was extremely long and must have taken at least an hour. Approaching the climax Crowley, as Osiris and Hierophant, said to him:

'Child of earth! Wherefore hast thou come to request admission to this Order?'

Victor made the ritual response, 'My soul is wandering in the darkness, seeking for the light of occult knowledge and I believe that in this Order the knowledge of the light may be obtained.'

The voice of his accustomed friend, now awful with the tones of office, asked whether he was prepared, 'In the presence of this assembly to take a great and solemn obligation to keep inviolate the secrets and mysteries of this Order?'

Victor replied, 'I am'.

He was told to kneel and between a triad of Brothers representing Arouest, Horus and Themis, to put his left hand into that of the initiator who had brought him in, and his right upon 'the right triangle,' symbolizing active aspiration towards his Higher Soul.

The Initiation of Victor Neuburg

Crowley gave one knock with his sceptre.

Victor then made the pledge, 'to maintain kindly and benevolent relations with the Fratres and Sorores of the Order, and to prosecute with zeal the occult sciences,' which to fulfil he would not fail 'under the penalty of submitting myself to an awful and avenging punitive current, set in motion by the Chiefs of the Order, by which I should be slain or paralyzed without visible weapon, as if blinded by the lightning flash. So help me the Lord of the Universe and my own Higher Soul.' Crowley then touched him with the sceptre.

After further ceremonies during which he was led about the hall to the west and to the east, Crowley and two others touched sceptres and sword above his head so as to form the Supernal Triad, and Crowley said, 'Frater Omnia Vincam we receive thee into the Order of the Golden Dawn.' After more ceremonies, he was led between the pillars of Isis and Nephthys where the White Triangle was placed upon him.

Omnia Vincam would have been a name chosen by Victor; there would be an opportunity to change it, at each further promotion, though changes was not obligatory.

What strikes me as wrong, and frightful, is not its general form but the words concerning the 'avenging and punitive current, set in motion by the chiefs.' It is occult doctrine that a fault punishes itself in its effect on the character of him who commits it, the hindrance to his progress which it occasions, especially if he be a candidate upon the Path, and possibly other undesired results. But this is through the operation of a mysterious natural law, which seems to have a moral character. If words concerning this are uttered they can never be more than the statement of what is in fact taking place or the agent channelling the consequences of currents already in motion. Whether even this is licit is questionable.

The Christian Church has pronounced its anathemas, or decrees of excommunication; strictly speaking, these were nothing more than the cutting off from its body, but the effect on those who believed their Salvation depended on being in communion with it was as though they had been handed over to the Devil. Madame Blavatsky endorses a Buddhist precept; *not to curse upon any consideration for the curse returns upon the one that utters it*, and quotes the Athenian priestess who refused to pronounce a malediction on Alcibiades, even for desecration of the Mysteries, *for that she was a priestess of prayers and not of curses.*(6)

Victor had to return immediately to Cambridge. He had, from now on, to keep a Magical Record but, his finals being so near, decided not to start anything except the Banishing Ritual for cleansing the atmosphere. To perform this he had to form in his mind's eye a circle of light around himself and within this, to the four points of the compass, four blazing pentagrams.(7) Outside this figure he had to imagine four archangels with wings outstretched, the points touching, making a square above the circle. Then, over his head, he had to conceive a hexagram(8), and through it a column of light descending upon his head. This he did each night before going to bed.

He thought the quality of his sleep improved; against this he remained during the whole of his last term without the astral sight he had had all his life.

He passed his finals obtaining Third Class Honours (9). It was not a brilliant degree, but he had had unusual distractions. Not having twelve guineas to put down, and not thinking it would be useful to him, he did not go up in cap and gown to receive it.

(1) Crowley only puts down the short *Voice of the Silence* under Blavatsky but it is obvious from their writings that both he and Victor were familiar with all her major works.

(2) Crowley has not put down Plato, but I would think only from oversight as he shows acquaintance with the much less occult Aristotle; Victor in any case, was steeped in Plato.

(3) The term is, of course, from Plato's *Symposium*. It is slightly incorrect to suppose that it means paederastic. It means heavenly, or that kind of love which involves the intellectual and higher faculties. It is true that the participants in the dialogue take it for granted that this is impossible to have with their wives; but the implied reason is that these had no intellectual development. They were not educated. The modern usage of the term Uranian was started by Karl Heinrich Ulrichs.

(4) It is a popular fallacy that Krishnamurti has ever denied either the reality of the Masters or his own role as the expected Teacher. On the contrary, he said at the critical moment that now he was sure he had something to teach. But his teaching has been against reliance on external authority and therefore he has turned aside every question touching his authority, pointing out that a thing can be neither more true nor less true according to the authority on which it is said. His whole career has been a crusade against the logical fallacy known as the Argumentum ad hominem: an insistence that the questioner should look within himself and try to answer his own question. The technique is that which Socrates demonstrates so well in the *Meno*,

when, acting as a sort of midwife to the process, he makes the slave-boy discover for himself the answer to a teasing mathematical problem.

(5) My source for this story is a loose, unpaginated sheet amongst Crowley's papers. He had evidently meant to fit it into some literary composition.

(6) *Isis Unveiled,* pp 334 and 608.

(7) The pentagram, or five-pointed star, is the symbol of Man, conceived of as a being endowed with reason and thereby distinguished from the brutes. Sometimes a man is drawn forming the symbol; the feet apart and arms raised at right angles to the body form with the head the five points of the star. Leonardo da Vinci has drawn man so inscribed within a circle. It is a symbol of evolution. It must, however, be drawn the right way up, otherwise it means a man standing on his head, or all proper values inversed; it is then a symbol of involution. The five-pointed star with the apex upwards is a symbol of White Magic; with the apex downwards, of Black Magic.

(8) The hexagram is the six-pointed star composed of two interlaced triangles, signifying spirit reflected in matter 'on earth as it is in Heaven', or the lower self perfectly reflecting the higher or divine spark. It is a symbol of White Magic. The single white triangle upon which Victor placed his hand, and which was later pinned on him during the initiation he had just undergone was the symbol of the aspiration of the lower self towards the higher. The descending triangle, completing the hexagram, would be the answer, inspiration or descent of the holy spirit from above. (The terms above and below are, of course, figurative, no spatial movement being conceived but a spiritual happening.)

(9) The Clerk of Trinity, who obtained this information for me, gave me a reference; p 956 of *The Historical Register of the University of Cambridge to the year 1910.* (CUP, 1917). It was in the Easter Term of 1909 that he sat for and passed the examination.

5
The Magical Retirement of *Omnia Vincam*

On June 16, 1909, Victor left Cambridge for the last time. Crowley had invited him to Boleskine and he travelled to Scotland by the night train in company with another Cambridge man, Kenneth Ward of Emmanuel, who had also been invited. In the afternoon of the 16th they arrived at Foyers, the nearest station, from which it seems they made their own way. Boleskine was an isolated house, almost on Loch Ness, and looking down to it from beneath a high, sheer rampart of rock. Ward had come only to collect a pair of skis Crowley had offered him, and it was when getting these out of the attic that Crowley put his hand on his long lost manuscript of *Liber Legis*, which was underneath them. Victor's experiences at Boleskine were destined to be of a very different order from those remembered so agreeably by Sir Gerald Kelly.

That night Crowley told him he was to go into a Magical Retirement for ten days, during which he would devote himself exclusively to meditation, try to raise Kundalini(1) and reach his Holy Guardian Angel or higher self.

Victor slept late the next morning, being tired from the journey. After a breakfast of tea and toast he had a hot bath, then he was escorted to the chamber prepared for him. This was a room where the floor was covered with a magic circle. There was an altar on which incense was burning, and Victor found a further supply of incense and of charcoal, also a magic sword and an ankh; he had on his magic robe. He was left to his own devices.

It was too cold to be comfortable. Despite the preparations the atmosphere did not seem to him magical and he found it difficult to settle. He walked about the room. Then something came to him. It seemed as though it were memory of an old ritual he had been accustomed to perform, in another land, in a previous life. He started walking round the circle, paced it several times, and recited words in English which seemed to be a translation from some other language unbeknown to him and which he could not identify. It seemed to be about seven gods above and seven gods below and one god. Afterwards he could remember nothing of the words which had come to him, excepting that the whole thing ended with the word or syllable *anch* (if I can read his writing), repeated three times. (Perhaps Egyptian ankh?)

It occurred to him now that he ought to do the Banishing Ritual with which Crowley had taught him every magical enterprise should begin. He thought he had to describe the pentagrams with the sword round the outside of the circle, and was embarrassed because there was so little space left between it and the wall. (Afterwards Crowley told him he had not understood how to do it.)

He then settled himself in a yogic posture and began to meditate, reciting the mantra *Aum tat sat Aum* to raise his level of consciousness. After a time he was repeating only the word *Aum*, allowing his voice to become fainter and fainter as he felt himself become entranced.

His head had fallen outside the circle and he was lying on his back and had visions of sea and sky, then of a beautiful violet light.

He was in this condition when he was fetched to lunch. This consisted of cutlets and potatoes (Crowley had pooh-pooed his vegetarianism), dry toast, rice pudding with stewed rhubarb, and water to drink. He appears to have had his meals alone so that trivial conversation should not break up the atmosphere.

After lunch he wrote up his Magical Diary to date, covering his last days at Cambridge and the morning's session and making some reference to the mystical experiences of his childhood.

At 5.15 he went back to the chamber and resumed the magic posture but although he recited Aum until 7.0 he had no result. As he had become chilled right through, and the effort seemed vain, he went to his bedroom on the ground floor, wrapped himself in his dressing-gown and read Crowley's *Holy Books*.

His record is meticulous(2), having been written up each day, and consists of 127 pages in his hand, his visions becoming progressively more complex. I think I can best give the character of this unique document if I quote the entries for a couple of typical days:

June 21

5.2 am Performed 'Bornless One'(3) Ritual about 10 pm. At midnight, Banishing Ritual.

At about 1.30am my Guru(4) entered and gave me certain advice. At about 2.25am I performed 'Bornless One' and Banishing Rituals, afterwards rising on the planes.

I travelled upwards swiftly and easily again meeting 'Gabriel'.(5) He gave me the same information as before. He was clad in white, with green spots on his wings; upon his head was a Maltese Cross.

After some time I slept by the fire, awaking at about 4.25am. I suffered two emissiones seminis (possibly one only; I am not quite sure) with somatic dreams. This is due probably to one of the following three causes, or of course, any combination of them - (a) my sleeping close to the fire; (b) lack of food; (c) lack of exercise. Personally I back the first cause. (No joke is intended here.)(6)

I again performed the 'Bornless One' Ritual about 4.30am. I left the Chamber just after 5am.

It is now 5.10am. I am tired out, after performing the Banishing Ritual I shall go to bed.

9.25 am Up at 9.2. Washed, brushed teeth.

9.18 [sic] Brekker. Egg, bacon, tea, a little water. I feel pretty fit but a little tired. I shall retire to the chamber almost immediately, when I have exchanged my piggers for my robe. I slept well.

9.30am: I depart for the chamber.

Mid-day. Almost immediately on reaching the Chamber did I perform the Preliminary Invocation. I then meditated upon myself for an hour, sometimes reading Thelema. Just after 11 am I performed the Banishing Ritual, the Preliminary Ritual, burnt incense, recited *Aum Mani padme Hum*, and rose upon the planes. I went very far indeed. Early I met my Angel. I slew him.(7) I then rose through many planes; eventually I was detained by my Mother, a huge brown woman, my Father, a little green man; a voluptuous woman; and an hermaphrodite. They sought one by one to detain me. I passed them all.

At length I reached a coffin, labelled

Resurgam

of the tenth sphere

I was now forcibly drawn into this, but escaped into a whirlpool of light, wherein I was utterly absorbed. Rapidly I sank back, reaching my body at about 11.25.

Then did I meditate and read *Thelema*. (I want some decent blotting-paper. I shall shortly need a new notebook.)

It is now 12.8 I shall return to the Chamber. I have taken a sip of water. I have a

author 1935

Dylan Thomas 1936

Dylan Thomas and Pamela Hansford Johnson under the cliffs at Caswell Bay near the mumbles, Swansea, 1934

Aleister Crowley circa 1910

Victor 1923

anctonbury Ring near Vine Cottage

e Cottage, Sussex

Victor and Kathleen 1923

Victor and his son Victor Edward, 1924

Pragnell shortly before the opening of the Sanctuary

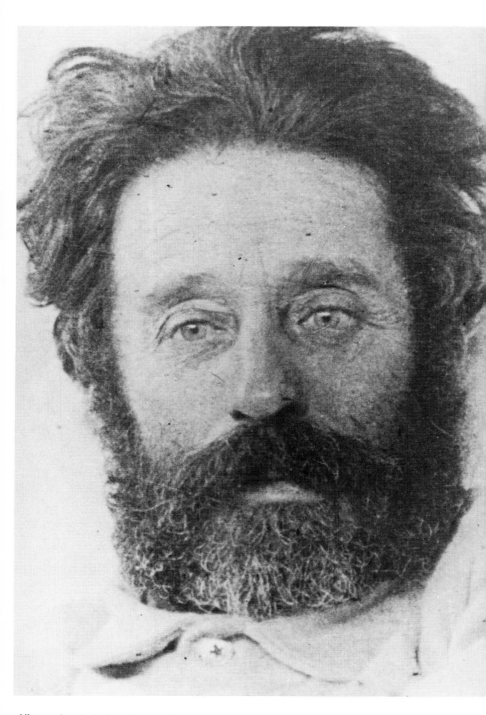

Victor shortly before his death

certain book on Magic with me. This I shall read in the Chamber.

5.57. I studied the Magic Book in the Chamber until 1.20, when I performed the Preliminary Invocation. Afterwards I read and meditated again, being summoned to lunch at 1.50. Egg and spinach, toast, water. I returned to the Chamber at 2.9, where, almost immediately, my guru joined me, and we talked of Magic and other matters. My Guru left in about half an hour. I then spent the time mostly in thought and meditation. I may have slept a little, but scarcely at all, if at all.

At 4.40 I performed the Banishing Ritual and the Preliminary Invocation. Then I burned incense, and said mantra, Aum mani padme hum.

I rose on the planes, reaching rapidly the white light. I struggled through to the top where I was crucified by two angels. I threw the angels off with [ie by means of] the Pentagram, then I floated about in space helplessly, attached to the Cross. This also I got rid of by the Pentagram.

I reached soon after a whirlpool or fountain of red light; struggling through this, I was confronted by a Red Giant against whom I was powerless, though I attacked him furiously by every means in my power. All my weapons and words were useless against him. He cut me to pieces and chased me back to my body, effectually preventing me from rising by falling upon me every time I strove to rise.(8)

I had rather great difficulty in arranging myself in my body after my return, failing once or twice in the effort. At length, however I accomplished the feat successfully.

I was back again a minute or two before five. Took a very hot bath, for I was somewhat wearied. An hour or two after lunch I had a cigarette; I am now smoking another. Smoking staves off hunger excellently.

I find that my Guru - unto whom be peace - has taken the magic book I was studying. I want it back, badly.

It is now 6.14. I shall return to the Chamber. I fear I shall have great difficulty in keeping awake tonight, though I do not feel tired now. I hope to continue this experiment for a week at least and, with luck, more.

My Guru entered about five minutes after I had returned to the Chamber.

7. Dinner. Venison, boiled potatoes, toast, bread-and-butter pudding, Water.

It is now 7.27. I shall return to the Chamber.

I slept until about 10.30, when I was awakened by my Guru, who made the waking process more effectual by 'dowsing' my head in cold water. (He did this also a day or two ago, by the way.) I then received further instruction in the Signs of Horus and Harpocrates, illustrating the signs (apparently) to the satisfaction of the Chief. At 10.45 I began operations, performing first the Preliminary Invocation. I then prepared charcoal, and performed the Banishing Ritual, burned incense, and encanted mantra, Aum tat sat Aum.

I rose at once, slaying the red Giant with the Harpocrates formula; then I slew a Black Giant. I then became a green triangle (apex upwards) in a violet crown or circle; then a blazing comet flaming in the hair of a God; then a flaming star. After this I became absorbed in and identified with white light. This experience was accompanied by extreme ecstasy.

The Magical Dilemma of Victor Neuburg

I found myself at the Court of Horus (he was jet-black), who gave me two tablets inscribed INRI and TARO respectively. I now found that I had no hands they were severed at the wrists. Horus sent me out to gaze at the clear blue heavens, wherein were myriads of stars. He pointed upwards; I could not mount any higher although I tried (or someone tried) to attach the sword and the ankh to my feet.

I had the greatest difficulty in returning, struggling on the floor for some minutes.

At 11.15 I was sufficiently recovered to summon my Guru. I stumbled when going downstairs to fetch this note-book, breathing heavily.

Upon performing the sign of Harpocrates and smoking a cigarette I quite recovered; my Guru is still with me, talking. It is now 11.55. I am quite normal.

My Guru instructs me till 12.30, when he goes to fetch me water. (This last paragraph is intended to cast no reflection upon the eloquence and erudition of my holy Guru).

June 22

1.28am: I have again risen on the plane, the preliminaries being performed by most excellent Guru. I rose to a great height, far beyond the Court of Horus. I began rising at about 12.50. I had many adventures, passing by crowds of beings, most of whom gave me passage upon my presenting my Chief's card, as it were, though many of them ignored me altogether, turning their backs upon me. Three incidents stand out prominently.

I reached a fair garden where there was an enormous, white-clad [illegible] angel, who gave the impression Gabriel. He spoke to me, wishing me to leave my sword and ankh. I refused and he suffered me to depart with them; all I can remember of his speech is, 'Thine is the destiny of the Magi.'

Afterwards I passed through strata, as it were, of the four elements, later reaching a kind of green globe, around which I floated in a little boat with a fair woman; at or about this time I was in a slight state of ecstasy. I would here remark in parenthesis that my physical feet became very painful during this rising, probably because I was in my Japanese yoga posture(9) for an hour or more, I think, inclusive of the time during which my Guru was invoking, etc.

Eventually, after many minor adventures - passing through funnels, voids and so on - I reached a hawk-shaped creature who cut off my hands and feet. I fell back, and had the greatest difficulty in returning. I performed the Harpocrates formula, and lay prostrate on the floor for several minutes, being apparently unable to rise.

Eventually I summoned my Guru, who urged me to perform the Harpocrates formula again. This I did successfully.

I am now quite normal. I returned about 1.10. My Guru gave me instructions and departed. I think I shall sleep in bed comparatively early tonight. I am tired; I must, I think get some air and exercise tomorrow. I forgot to mention that I passed a white cat on a roof during my last journey. I shall now go to bed. It is 1.45. I doubt if I shall be able to wake at six tomorrow as requested.

And so it goes on, restarting at 10 in the morning when, after having woken at 9.40 (not indeed 6.0!) and breakfasted, he was again settled in the chamber to re-begin his meditations. The morning's visions were long and complicated. After lunch and a sulphur bath he began again:

> I started from the place where I was deprived of hands and feet yesterday by the Hawk-headed One. Thereafter I passed a statue of Mercury...I reached a Temple I have known all my life. A maiden met me; she cut me up and sacrificed me upon an altar. After she had said certain formulae over my body, I rose glorified, made the sign and left her. [After many other adventures] I returned through sheer weariness, descending head-first, and finding my body almost without difficulty.

After a second sulphur-bath, between 5.30 and 6, he added, before resuming more, a detail he had forgotten and which is interesting from the homosexual slant:

> I was tempted by a little black boy drawing water from a stream, and a fair woman. I succumbed - O virtuous one! - to the temptations of neither. I am a puritan of the best type.

Having set this down, he did yogic breathing exercises until 7, when he was fetched by Crowley to dinner. At 7.55 he returned to the chamber and resumed meditation, during which he had many visions. Crowley did not approve the quality of these:

> 10.32 My Guru was dissatisfied, upbraiding me bitterly with being among the Qliphoth.(10)

> He is apparently a homosexual sadist(11) for, in giving me thirty-two strokes with a gorse-switch which drew blood, he showed great unction. He performed the ceremony with obvious satisfaction. The ceremony was quite painful, though it aroused no emotion in me save that of laughter. I shall rest for a space.

> My Guru is difficult. Because I laughed, he called me a Masochist! Had I complained he would have called me a coward; had I manifested no emotion, he would have charged me with being callous...

> 1.45 am My worthy Guru advises me to stay up all night. I shall go downstairs and steal a biscuit or two.

> I have been to my Guru; he is very rude, but instructive. Found the biscuits. My fire is out, alas! I shall go to bed. It is 1.53.

The biscuits must have been in Crowley's room, for on a subsequent occasion when he went in for some, hoping Crowley might be awake and speak to him, heavy breathing showed he was asleep and Victor crept out again. Though it is not mentioned in the record, Victor met Rose at Boleskine and was upset; as he later told Hayter Preston, she was drinking heavily and appeared quite sunk.

One evening, Victor went to bed at 9pm. Against this entry in the

Record, Crowley wrote: *At 9pm! Unsavoury slug of sloth!* After this, Victor felt he had to hold out until the small hours, yet one night, too cold to meditate longer, he walked about the house and entered the sitting-room, where he looked into a book about why Queen Elizabeth kept her virginity!

One night Crowley sent him out to cut gorse. He put on both his magic robe and his dressing gown and boots; out on the hillside, in the dark, it took him a long time to find gorse and to cut it and when he had brought it back he fell asleep. Crowley, catching him, upbraided him. On yet another night, Crowley came into his room and beat him on the bare back and buttocks with stinging-nettles.

One morning Victor did yogic breathing exercises until the pain became so excruciating he lay writhing on the floor. That it should have been imagined he had to persist in holding his breath despite the pain, shows appalling ignorance in both pupil and teacher. Crowley made abusive criticism and referred to his Jewishness. In great bitterness, Victor wrote:

My worthy Guru is unnecessarily rude and brutal, I know not why. Probably he does not know himself. He is apparently brutal merely to amuse himself and pass the time away.

Anyhow, I won't stick it any more.

It seems to me that unnecessary and brutal rudeness is the prerogative of a cad of the lowest type. It is the very limit of meanness to grouse at a man because of his race. The 'argument is', I admit, unanswerable by the accused; it is also inexcusable in the accuser. It is ungenerous also to abuse one's position as a Guru; it is like striking an inferior who will be ruined if he retaliates. Were it not for my Vow, I would not stay longer under my Guru's roof. I will not have my family and race perpetually insulted.

Things did not improve. After lunch, he wrote:

My Guru rude; his personalities are becoming monstrous. They are grossly offensive...If I am again insulted I shall depart immediately.

But later, he went out and watched the dawn come up over Loch Ness; soothed and healed by the beauty, he wrote:

It's simply gorgeous. Everything asleep except the birds, who're half awake. The Loch is ripping. I forgive my dear old Guru ten million times. I'd tell him so, only he's asleep. Otherwise I'd take him for a walk, if he'd come.

Crowley asked him to expand the references which he had made to his mystical experience whilst a child and he did so, describing the moments in which he seemed to be right out of the world and yet one with everything:

The Magical Retirement of Omnia Vincam

When in the ecstatic state, I had a consciousness of having always existed: I could not conceive of a time when I was not...While I was an enthusiastic Freethinker and Atheist - which I am still, by the way - the vision occurred, and I cannot remember ever finding anything inconsistent in this...The vision was intense enough to throw into the shade all other events of life. Literally, I lived for it.

He did not think it could be induced by will; neither had it ever come when he was indoors or otherwise than in solitude, though he believed the presence of a sympathetic friend might not be an impediment.

He wrote also of his intimations of past existences, and particularly of one very clear memory - which seemed to him like a re-living - of having been burned at the stake. He had been a priest and it was for heresy, though he had the impression that loyalty to a friend had had something to do with it.

On the eighth day he went through a black patch. He was sure there was no divine mystery to be comprehended. One just went on and on for ever, exactly as one was now. If only it were possible to become extinct! But owing to the nature of the universe that was impossible. As a soul, one was indestructible. He did not believe in the Nirvana of the Buddhists. One had to exist through all eternity.

Crowley, when he read this passage, was most impressed and wrote that it seemed to him a foreshadowing or reflection of the 7=4 (or, in Theosophical parlance, 4th initiation), the ordeal of the abyss. Victor must have been considerably encouraged by this and the record finishes in a much brighter key.

Crowley brought him a beautiful new volume on which he could made a fair copy of the whole. Victor did so, dating it proudly at the end: Boleskine, June 29, 1909.

He obviously thought his ordeal was completed. He was mistaken. Crowley now told him that for the next ten nights he must sleep on the floor, entirely naked, on a litter of gorse. It was the cold more than the prickles which constituted the real torment. The wind whistled under the doors at Boleskine and chilled him, even in retrospect when he remembered it, to the end of his life.

There is no history of tuberculosis in Victor's family. His death from it is likely to have been brought about by this cruel exposure on top of the yogic breathing exercises mis-practised because mis-taught. Madame Blavatsky warned that they could lead to consumption and death. B.S.K.Iyengar (from whom I learned yoga) warns that without the safety restraint, that is without the chin's resting in the notch between the collar bones, alternative nostril breathing and rhythmic retention of the breath is 'lethal'. This is because oxygen is being denied to the brain (instead of its supply to it being increased), and the results are not mystical at all, but can be found in a medical dictionary under 'Asphyxiation'. They should not be attempted until the asanas (gymnastic type exercises) have been mastered, and then only in the presence of a teacher, whose function is to push one's head down if it begins to come up, and stop one at once if one's nostrils begin to flare or even quiver. The slightest movement of the nostrils is a sign the strain is already too much. That Crowley should have watched Victor's writhing on the floor trying to hold his breath, with equanimity, shows his total incapacity as a teacher. All one can say in extenuation is that he was ignorant.

After this Crowley told him he had passed his Probation, and would be made a Neophyte, or 10=1 at the next ceremony. Crowley was to be as stingy in giving grades out as he had been avaricious in obtaining them.

---

(1) In general, I have preferred to avoid the use of Oriental terms, but there is no word in any Western language for Kundalini, because it is a constituent of the body not recognized in Western science; a subtle fire having its seat in the base of the spine, ordinarily dormant but capable of being awakened by spiritual will and aspiration when it will rise up the back (it is felt like a hot fire or rash) and enter the head, where it vivifies the pineal gland, conferring initiation. Though the initial break-through may be made in a matter of minutes, if the time has come, the remaining work is that of a lifetime.

(2) General J F C Fuller, the owner of this document, entitled *The Magical Record of Omnia Vincam*, allowed me to have it in my home and with his permission I had an integral photostat copy made of the whole.

(3) Gerald Yorke explained to me that this crucial term referred to an invocation extracted by somebody in The Golden Dawn (Yeats?) from a book called *Fragments of a Graeco-Egyptian Papyrus on Magic*, translated and commented by Charles Wycliffe Godwin (Cambridge) 1851. I checked this by applying for the book at the British Museum; for those who wish to do likewise, its Catalogue No. is Ac.5624 (Cambridge Antiquarian Society Publications). It is Invocation No 7, on p 12; only it is called in the text, 'The Headless One.' This being a literal translation, showing no mystic's comprehension of the meaning, the Golden Dawn people changed it to 'Bornless One'. I cannot think this is attractive English, but it is nearer to the meaning which is the uncreate or parentless.

To this first entry of the day, Victor himself has put an asterisk against 10pm and written a footnote: This of course refers to the previous night. This remark applies to certain other entries in the record. I would note here that my copy of the Bornless One Ritual, lent me by my Holy Guru, is in manuscript.

(4) Crowley.

(5) Against this, Crowley has put a mark and a footnote: Why not kill the -?

(6) Footnote by Crowley: It is because you are trying to awake the Kundalini and she escapes downwards, owing to the impurity of your soul. Perfect chastity is essential before the first step in yoga is taken. [I do not think Crowley knew sufficient about this to teach.]

(7) Gerald Yorke has explained for me the use of the word 'slew'. It is not meant in the aggressive sense. Victor was trying to attain union with his higher self, and images belonging to the intermediate planes of consciousness which usurped his attention should be, as it were, scrubbed away or deleted.

(8) Crowley puts a footnote: Concerning Red Giant. I will teach thee the sign and god-forms necessary.

(9) This means sitting on his heels.

(10) A Kabbalistic term meaning illusory images of an inferior order.

(11) Crowley has put a footnote: Slandering one's Guru is punished in the thirty-second and lowest Hell.

Beneath this, Victor has put a counter-footnote: A small price to pay for the invention of a new vice.

6
The *Equinox* and Algeria

At the beginning of July they returned to London where Victor helped Crowley bring out *The Equinox*. The office was simply Crowley's flat at 124 Victoria Street, furnished with red curtains and cushions, a stuffed crocodile and several Buddhas. This was almost opposite Aunt Ti's flat, at 125 Victoria Street, so Victor was much backwards and forwards across the road though he had a room of his own at the Adelphi.

Though Victor was virtually sub-editing for Crowley, a good deal of the back-stage work on the *Equinox* was done by General Fuller. Fuller told me Crowley asked him to edit Victor's diary of his *Magical Retirement* at Boleskine so that it could be published in the *Equinox*. It never appeared for Crowley filled the *Equinox* with his own stuff and there was hardly room for anything else. Fuller met Victor a certain amount at Victoria Street. In his first letter to me he wrote, 'He appeared to me to be colourless.' I replied, 'I did not find him colourless.' Later, when he invited me down for the day to his home at Crowborough, General Fuller took occasion, of his own accord, to make amends. 'When I wrote that he seemed to me colourless I did not mean that in a pejorative sense. If one says a person is colourful, that is not always entirely a compliment. Crowley was colourful. His clothes were showy and he took every occasion of dressing up. If he was in a room he was always the centre of attention. Neuburg was inconspicuous. He would be sitting quietly at the side somewhere and probably would not speak unless one said something to him.'

The *Equinox* was a bulky bi-annual, of which the first issue appeared in September 1909. It had as its motto 'The method of science; The aim of religion'. There were articles on the Kabbalah, yoga and other esoteric sciences, poems, stories and book reviews. Relatively outside contributors included Arthur Grimble, George Raffalovich and Frank Harris. Almost every issue contains contributions from Victor.

The *Equinox* and Algeria

Despite the title I discovered not much astrology in it: I had never seen the *Equinox* until I got it out at the British Museum for this research: I examined the few horoscopes Crowley drew and became suspicious when I noticed the moon's place always ended in zero. At home I recalculated them afresh. The basis of the trouble then appeared. The moon moves at a speed varying between 12 and 15 degrees of longitude in 24 hours; only the positions at noon and at midnight each day are given in the ephemerides for astrologers published yearly, the user being expected to work out the longitude for any intermediate time with the aid of the tables of Diurnal Proportional Logarithms appended (unless, indeed, for fine work, he wishes to take account of acceleration or deceleration); and it was this elementary operation at which Crowley boggled.

Crowley wrote an autobiography; the published volumes ended in 1904, before the story really begins. The rest was in typescript, and in the possession of Gerald Yorke who lent it to me with other manuscripts, *The Vision and the Voice* and *The Paris Working*, which I shall refer to later. Remembering the fear I had had in my youth, it seemed to me strange to have Crowley's manuscripts spread out familiarly on my own floor. I was stepping over them for weeks.

The first volume opened with his rediscovery of the manuscript of *Liber Legis* under the skis at Boleskine where he was there with Victor in June 1909, and his return to London, where Victor is rather lost sight of, except for a description of how Crowley went with a mistress and Victor to see a divorced lady at her flat near Hyde Park. He was distressed to see their hostess and Victor 'flirting'. When they rose to leave, it looked as though the lady would be pleased if Victor stayed and Crowley dragged him out almost by 'main force'.

Having got the first number of the *Equinox* out in September, Crowley proposed that Victor should accompany him for a holiday in Algeria. They arrived in Algiers on November 17, bought some provisions, took the tram to Arba and after lunch started walking south. After two nights in the open and one at a primitive hotel they arrived on November 21 at Aumale. Crowley had brought in his rucksack the copy he had made at the British Museum of the *Calls for the Thirty Aethyrs* dictated to John Dee, Queen Elizabeth's astrologer, by Edward Kelly, who claimed inspiration by the angels. They are in a curious language which has to read backwards, and they also have to be called in reverse order, starting with the thirtieth. This and the twenty-ninth Crowley had called some years previously. He now wanted to do the rest.

In Aumale they bought notebooks. These were for Victor, for Crowley was to make the *Calls* and relate what visions appeared to him, while Victor acted as scribe. For Victor, Africa itself was new and even the ordinary sights of the day, Arabs going about in their own dress with donkeys and camels must have been emotional for him. In addition, they were embarking on a psychic adventure of unknown consequence. In the evening of November 23, after their meal, they went to look for a secluded place. Looking at an ephemeris for 1909, I saw that on this date there would have been a three-quarter moon approaching the full, riding high in the sky by 8-9 o'clock, the time when they began the operation. I think one must imagine Victor seating himself in such a position that the moon fell on his exercise book.

Crowley made the *Call* and began to dictate. Gerald Yorke had brought me photostats of the sheets of Victor's writing, which became larger and larger in his efforts to keep up with the speed of Crowley's utterances as he described the appearance of a most frightful monster.

I ask myself what these Angels, which seem so much more like demons, were supposed to be. It is an occultist's axiom that the candidate's effort to acquire any virtue calls up as much of the opposite vice as may be latent in his own nature. There is some indication that the series of *Calls* was regarded as a scheme of initiations although the Aethyrs are referred to as though they had independent existence. I don't believe Crowley had thought this out; in any case, the communications, in which all his special obsessions appear, seem very much a projection of his own personality.

The next day, November 24(1), they went on to Sidi Aissa where they called the twenty-seventh Aethyr. The following day, in the desert between 1 and 2 in the afternoon, they called the twenty-sixth and in the evening after reaching Ain El Hajel they called the twenty-fifth. In the afternoon of the next day they called the twenty-fourth Aethyr, and on November 28, continuing their journey over semi-desert, they reached Bou Saada where in the morning and afternoon they called the twenty-third and twenty-second.

Bou Saada they found delightful. It was a place of white-walled houses, clustered on a hill in the desert to which fertility was brought by a stream below, bordered with palm trees, orchards and gardens with brightly coloured flowers, made private by cactus hedges. The scents on the air were subtle and fascinating, and as every path they took led them to something of interest they stayed for several days.

It was their custom to ignore the local *heure de sieste*. On December 3, immediately after lunch, they set out to climb the nearby Mount Dal'leh Addin where they called the fourteenth Aethyr. This took them from 2.50 until 3.15. They were beginning the descent when suddenly Crowley was seized by a compulsion, or as he puts it, 'heard a command'.

They climbed back to the summit and picked up small boulders or big stones and arranged them so as to form a circle. Within this they traced in the sand magic words. In the centre of the design they built an altar. On the altar they placed themselves and 'in the sight of the sun' performed a homosexual act, Victor taking the active role. They dedicated it to Pan.

This was the first occasion on which they had ritually dedicated a sexual act. Crowley says he had long known it did not detract from the glory of God but that it was only in this moment he realized it could be done to the glory of God and be made a sacrament. He felt that he had overcome a dualism which he now detected in his previous conception of things as being divided into spiritual and physical, and resolved the opposition between the one life and its many manifestations. He believed that he had passed the initiation entitling himself to become a Master of the Temple, or 8=3. He descended the mountain, and awaited nightfall, Victor presumably with him.

I would make an observation here concerning Crowley's presumption in assuming he had attained a super-human grade. He drew a horoscope (moon in wrong place) for the moment, at 11.15, at which he believed that mantle had descended on him. With this claim to have transcended the condition of ordinary man, he had ceased to be completely sane. By December 6, still at Bou Saada, they had worked their way down to the tenth Aethyr, the most critical, representing the Abyss. Kelly described its indwelling demon, Choronzon, as 'that mighty devil'. It was the power of Chaos which had to be conjured, faced and vanquished.

In the early afternoon they walked a long way from the town and came to a valley of fine sand. In this they traced a circle, fortified by the Kabbalistic words, TETRAGRAMMATON, SHADDAI EL CHAI and ARARITA, within the protection of which Victor was to sit. Outside the circle they traced a triangle, wherein Choronzon 'the first and deadliest of all the powers of evil', was to be invoked and confined. They fortified this also with holy words and in the three corners Crowley killed three pigeons he had brought from Bou Saada so that the subtle counterpart of their blood would provide material for Choronzon to make a semi-physical body in which to manifest himself; Crowley was careful that none of the blood fell outside the triangle so that Choronzon could not break out of it.

Victor, ensconced within the circle, with his magical dagger and his exercise book now swore an oath of the most awful solemnity:

'I, Omnia Vincam, a Probationer of the *Argentinum Astrum*, hereby solemnly promise upon my magical honour and swear by Adonai the angel that guardeth me, that I will defend this magic circle of Art with thoughts and words and deeds. I promise to threaten with the dagger and command back into the triangle the spirit incontinent if he should strive to escape from it; and to strike with the dagger at anything that may seek to enter this Circle, were it in appearance the body of the Seer himself. And I will be exceedingly wary, armed against force and cunning; and I will preserve with my life the inviolability of this circle. Amen. And I summon mine Holy Guardian Angel to witness this mine oath, the which if I break, may I perish, forsaken of him. Amen and Amen.'

Victor then performed the Banishing Ritual.

Crowley, who had changed into a black robe, had by now entered the triangle had at 2pm made the *Call*. Nothing became immediately visible but Victor heard a voice from within the triangle cry out, 'Zazas, Zazas, Nasatanda Zazas', followed by many blasphemies. It seemed to him that the voice simulated Crowley's. Now Victor began to see things; within the triangle was the form of a beautiful woman who resembled a courtesan he had known in Paris. She called to him with soft words and made seductive gestures but he recognized that it must be the demon who had assumed this form in order to lure him out of the circle and he resisted the enticement.

She then begged his forgiveness for having tried to tempt him, acknowledged his inviolability and asked to be allowed to come and lay her head beneath his foot in token of service. Victor recognised this as an appeal to his pride and would not allow the demon to leave the triangle.

The demon changed into an old man, then into a snake; then, in a voice simulating Crowley's, he begged for water to quench his thirst. Victor recognized this as an appeal to his pity and gave it no heed. In the name of the Most High, Victor conjured the demon to declaim his nature. The demon mocked him, declared that he feared not the pentagon, that he was Master of the triangle and at his name was 333.

Victor invoked his Holy Guardian Angel and Crowley also. The demon declared that he knew the names of their Holy Guardian Angels and had power over them. Victor replied that he knew more than the demon and feared him not and again ordered him to proclaim his nature. The demon cried out that his name was Dispersion and therefore he could not be mastered in argument. Victor raised the dagger and the demon taunted him for thinking to frighten him. While Victor was trying to write down his words the demon pushed sand over the edge of the circle so that the boundary of the protective figure became impaired.

Then, in the form of a naked man, the demon leaped into the circle and upon Victor, throwing him to the ground. They rolled over in the sand and the demon sought Victor's throat with its teeth, then tried to bite through the bones at the back of his neck. Victor stabbed at him with his dagger and was able eventually to drive him back into the triangle. He retraced the arc of the circle where the sand had been pushed over it.

The demon within the triangle wailed, 'The tenth Aethyr is the world of adjectives and there is no substance therein.' Simulating Crowley's voice it begged permission to leave the triangle in order 'to get my clothes'. Victor perceived that this was another ruse and would not allow it to escape from the triangle and menaced it with his dagger.

The demon raged increasingly and Victor said, 'Thou canst not harm a hair of my head.' The demon laughed and mocked but Victor, now completely master of the situation, said, 'Thou has not power!' The demon threatened him with the tortures it could inflict but Victor replied, 'Thou liest.' The demon cried, 'Ask of thy brother *Perdurabo*(2) if I lie!' Victor said this did not concern him.

At last the demon subsided and became invisible. Victor now saw Crowley in his black robe take his Holy Ring and write in the sand the word BABALON(3). Together they made a fire to purify the place and then destroyed both the circle and the triangle. The whole operation had lasted two hours and they were so exhausted they hardly knew how to pack up their things and make their way back.

What had really happened? The commonsense explanation would be that it was Crowley who had said all the things and, shedding his robe, leapt upon Victor. But for what reason? For Victor, what had happened was proof that Crowley's magic worked, not in the sense intended but all too really. To the end he remained convinced that he had wrestled with a demon that day in the desert. Perhaps he was right, in that he wrestled with a man possessed.

During the morning and afternoon of the following day they rested, but in the evening they went out again, and called the ninth Aethyr. The next day, December 8, they continued their journey to the south-east, their goal being Biskra, over a hundred miles way. French officials were polite but expressed concern regarding their intention to cross this wild country on foot, sleeping in the open, and warned them they might be attacked by brigands. The Arabs added to this and said there were evil spirits in the desert! Also that they should be careful not to be drowned. This seemed to Victor and Crowley a strange warning to receive on the fringes of the Sahara, where water was the rarest element, but it appeared that what the Arabs feared for them was a cloudburst which could fill any narrow ravine or hollow with such rapidity they might be unable to scramble out before being overwhelmed. (Elizabeth Eberhard is believed to have been washed to her death in such a manner in this area.)

A few miles beyond Bou Saada the road finished and they felt their last link with civilization had been broken. They walked all day, climbing all the time, until sundown. They made themselves an evening meal and when they had eaten, they called the eighth Aethyr, which took from 7.10 until 8.10. After this they lay down on a patch of grass on a sandy slope and slept under the stars.

In the morning they went on and presently caught up with a road again. By evening they reached an inn, but it was closed and they were told it would open only when the coach arrived. To pass the time they strolled across the sand, meaning to climb a small hill from which they could get a moonlight view. They felt their feet becoming chilly and could not understand why. Crowley put his hand to the sand and snatched it back a though he had touched a red hot plate, for the sand was freezing cold. They realized it was because in the dry air radiation was rapid and this caused the temperature to fall so low. When they heard the coach they ran down to be at the door of the inn as it opened and spent the next quarter of an hour inside trying to rub their numbed toes back to life.

By December 10, late in the evening, they reached Benisruhr where they called the sixth Aethyr. The fifth they called in the desert between Benisruhr and Tolga after which they again spent the night in the open. On December 15 they descended into Tolga, then walked for three days across the now flatter land, arriving in Biskra on December 16 where they called the fourth Aethyr in the evening. The third and second they called on the mornings of the two following days.

A town of palm trees and camels, Biskra boasted a grandly named Royal Hotel and it was from here that Victor wrote at Crowley's dictation a thirteen-page letter which General Fuller, having preserved it fifty and more years, allowed me to see and borrow in order to make a photostat copy.

18 Dec, 1909

Dear Fuller,

...Tonight I am almost too exhausted to talk, and I couldn't possibly write, so got the regular Scribe to do me this great favour, for which I am extremely grateful.

I cannot possibly express in words my sense of how kind and good he has been throughout. It has been an awful job for him, writing down my ravings at all hours of the day and night, and in the forty-nine Classical positions. God help him for a silly b—. If only he had brains, he'd make an awful good chap. But enough of this distasteful subject.

The next paragraphs move on to refer to practical matters connected with the preparation of the next volume of the *Equinox*. Then, on page 4, there comes this:

I hope to find you a mass of learning on the subject of Kelly (not Gerald. And why they describe him as an artist, God only knows.)

I have gone carefully through the proofs the *Temple* and dear, kind Victor has been good enough to glance at them, but is trying to soak up the credit. I have had an awful job keeping him off these Arab boys. He has a frightful lust for brown bottoms, because when he was at school he was kicked by a man with brown boots; and being a masochist as well as a paederast, that accounts for it.

Coming on this passage so unexpectedly gave me the biggest single jolt I sustained while doing this research. In one sense I was grateful to Vicky for having left a statement in his own hand concerning his homosexuality, which I could produce should anybody tax me with having invented it. It startled me because I had always thought of his relationship with Crowley as a unique thing. Indeed even after this long research I still have not met a single person who believes Victor had relations with any male excepting Crowley.

The letter contains passages of unprintable obscenity. I do not refer merely to the lavish sprinkling of four-letter words but to the utter offensiveness of some of the ideas introduced. I feel that Victor should have refused to write these down.

I think General Fuller had not realized what he had passed me. He had picked it out from a huge mound of unsorted papers he had tipped from a drawer onto a table, and given it to me because it was in Victor Neuburg's handwriting. I was well into it when some memory of its content must have stirred him to anxiety, and he exclaimed in sudden alarm, 'What is it I've given you? I didn't read it myself, first!' I said, divining the cause of his anxiety, 'It's all right. I'm reading purely in the spirit of a researcher.' He said, 'I passed a Crowley letter to a man once without taking the precaution of reading through it first and he was frightfully cross with me for passing him obscene matter, unwarned.'

On the last day of 1909, they set sail from Algiers for Southampton.

---

(1) This, November 24, 1909, was the day on which Crowley's wife, Rose, obtained her divorce from him; the action was raised at her instance and the ground was adultery. This information was communicated to me by the Principal Clerk of the Court of Session, Edinburgh. I made inquiry because I had always been puzzled by the loosely given information that she obtained a divorce on this ground at a time when this was not sufficient reason in English law for a woman to obtain a divorce against a man. I went to Somerset House, found that their books had no record of this case and obtained from a helpful clerk the address of the equivalent department in Scotland in case it should have taken place there, which in fact it had.

(2) Crowley.

(3) A name of Venus as bride of Chaos.

7
The Rites of Eleusis

May 9, 1910, found Victor, in company with Crowley and the violinist, Leila Waddell (1) and some others at the house of a Commander Marston in Dorset, where it was decided to invoke Mars. Victor was put into the triangle so that he should become possessed by the god and deliver his message; then questions were put to him. Commander Marston asked whether there was going to be a war. Victor's lips framed the oracle that there would be two wars within the next five years, that the storm centre of the first would be Turkey (2) and the second Germany, and that the result would be the destruction of both nations. Victor must have danced in connection with their invocation, for Commander Marston now suggested the performance should be staged in a place where more people and the press could be invited.

A project was elaborated. While Victor danced the god down, Leila Waddell would play the violin and Crowley recite verses explaining what was happening. He composed these in collaboration with Raffalovich. They spent the early summer in preparation of the texts and costumes.

It was during the early summer that Ethel Archer came into the picture. In her early twenties, with brown, fine hair and a little learning in Greek, she was married to the artist, Eugene Wieland, but used her maiden name on the poems she submitted to the *Equinox*. They were love poems addressed to girls and when she turned up in person Victor, in his direct, naive way, made some remark about this and called her Sappho. A clergyman's daughter, she protested hotly that he had misunderstood and that they were to *herself* as she imagined a man might see her. She accepted the name of Sappho, however, for its lustre.

When I saw her at her flat in Fulham in 1961, she was grey-haired and failing. I only saw her once. Indeed, I was only just in time, for she had a stroke soon after and died. It was from Ethel Archer that I got a description of the first performance of The Rites of Eleusis at which she was present with her husband.

It was in Crowley's flat in Victoria Street. Arriving early they were met by Victor who took them into the sitting-room. This was in semi-darkness; the curtains having been drawn to shut out the light sky of a summer evening; the only illumination came from a swinging silver censer, and the atmosphere was thick with incense. The usual furniture had been moved out of the way and cushions were ranged round the sides of walls where the guests were to sit. Victor found a place for them to settle themselves and then brought a huge beaker, containing a brownish liquid, which he explained had been mixed by Crowley who was in an adjacent room. He had instructions this should be passed round as a loving-cup but warned them that in his opinion they would be wise if they did not drink much of it. 'It's got alkaloids of opium in it.' It tasted like rotten apples. A Dr Jensen was helping to officiate and they lost sight of Victor and when they saw him next he was in a white robe moving mysteriously to the strains of a violin. All eyes were on the dancing figure.

'Where had he learned to dance?' I asked.

'I don't know. It was just something he made up.'

'What sort of dancing was it?'

She raised her arms above her head, as though trying to recapture a gesture he had made and said, 'He kept turning round and round.'

'Like a dervish!' I exclaimed. She agreed; and I supposed that while in Algeria he must have seen dervishes dancing which had given him the inspiration. I remembered a conversation I had had many years ago with Vilayat. I had asked him the purpose of the dancing dervishes and he had replied, 'It's a way of getting into the astral. They turn and turn and turn and turn, until they are so giddy and so tired their bodies drop off them.'

'He fell!', Ethel Archer said. 'He lay unconscious for some minutes.'

She thought it must have been the effect of the drug although on herself and her husband it was quite otherwise; they felt extraordinarily pepped up and lively. It took about a week to wear off. Ethel Archer also mentioned to me that Crowley had told her a yogic breathing exercise, which on her return home she practised. At first she felt no result at all, so , although he had advised her not to do if for very long, she persisted. All at once her nose and mouth were full of blood and she lost consciousness. She never told him, and did not wish him to be blamed for this.

One of the items which came to me in Anthony d'Offay's collection was a letter in Victor's handwriting, on the headed paper of the *Equinox* to Ethel Archer's husband:

The Equinox

June 15th, 1910

Dear Mr Wieland,

Crowley has departed for some little time: I am glad the effects of the drug have passed off from Mrs Wieland and yourself.

You at least had an exciting time, if not a very pleasant one!

As for the people who were kind in their attentions, I simply don't believe they exist!

Greetings to Mrs Wieland and yourself.

Sincerely

Victor B Neuburg.

PS The poems are quite good.

This is obviously the original of which a hotted up version, represented as having been addressed to Ethel Archer herself, which appears in her book *The Hieroglyph*.(3)

General Fuller told me that with regard to these performances in Victoria Street there was no impropriety at all. He attended the whole lot, taking his wife with him each time and on one occasion his mother as well.

The *Sketch* of August 28 carried an appreciative review. 'After further ceremonies, Frater Omnia Vincam was commanded to dance 'the dance of sphinx and Pan in honour of our lady Artemis.' A young poet, whose verse is often read, astonished by a graceful and beautiful dance, which he continued until he fell exhausted in the middle of the room where, by the way, he lay until the end...A dead silence ensued. After a long pause the figure enthroned [Leila Waddell] took a violin and played...'

Victor's fall, however, was not in the ordinary sense an accident. In Crowley's typescript autobiography I came upon this passage:

The dialogue and action were little more than a setting for the soloists. These were principally three; myself..., Leila Waddell, the violinist, and Neuburg, dancer. I sometimes suspect he was the best of the three. He possessed extraordinary powers. He gave the impression that he did not touch the ground at all, and he would go round and round the circle at a pace so great that one constantly expected him to be shot off tangentially. In the absence of accurate measurements one does not like to suggest there was some unknown force at work, and yet I have seen so many undeniable phenomena take place in his presence that I feel quite sure in my own mind that he was generating energies of a very peculiar kind. The idea of his dance was, as a rule, to exhaust himself completely. Sometimes he failed to lose himself in which case, of course, nothing happened; but when he succeeded the effect was superb. It was astonishing to see his body suddenly collapse and shoot across the polished floor like a curling stone.

It was during these performances that Cremers, having recently arrived from the United States, made her first appearance in the Crowley circle. She came as a spectator; and always maintained that although much in the general ambience seemed to her sham something really did happen when Victor danced. She felt that at a certain moment, while he danced 'down' the god, a possession by the god did take place.

Cremers, since my extraordinary meeting with her at Vicky's, had always been a mystery character to me: during this research, I received information concerning her from an unexpected quarter. My letter in the *Daily Telegraph* was answered by a Mrs Joyce Saunders whose mother, Olivia Haddon, had at one time been interested in Crowley's ideas and joined his 'mixed masonry', as Mrs Saunders called it. She had little to tell me about Victor but she mentioned having known Vittoria Cremers, and I was so electrified that I went down to Bognor Regis to see her at her home.

Mrs Saunders emphasized the reserve which Cremers had always maintained concerning the facts of her life, and seemed herself affected by it. Her brother had been Cremers's executor but she had destroyed all papers before her death, intending completely to obliterate her tracks. Though she had been a close friend of the family for many years she had always maintained secrecy concerning her origin. Her mother was French. Cremers was illegitimate. It was understood that her father was a member of an enormously wealthy family of Jewish financiers; they believed it was one of the Rothschilds. While he made her an allowance she was almost obsessively concerned with not causing him embarrassment by allowing the connection to be known. She had married a Russian, Baron Louis Cremers, from whom she had her name. She was really a Baroness but would not use her title and was always called Cremers, as though she were a man. She wore her hair cut in a short bob before women did cut their hair. She had lived for many years in the United States where, acting as an under-cover agent, she had helped the New York police clean up a drug peddling and prostitution racket.

This sounded a strange career for a woman who had first been described to me as 'a Buddhist initiate'. but I remembered the sinister sounding references to Jack the Ripper which I had heard the day she came to Vicky's. 'Did you ever hear of Jack the Ripper in connection with her?' I asked.

'She knew Jack the Ripper,' said Mrs Saunders shortly. But she stopped and would not say any more. It was plain she admired Cremers for she spoke of her wonderful personality and luminous eyes.

When, in Crowley's then unpublished autobiography, I came to Cremers' entry to the Rites of Eleusis I was excited. There was, however, almost nothing concerning their relations save for a generalized statement that she set herself to work against him and take away his pupils. But there was the Jack the Ripper story! And despite the enmity between them he tells it in a way which is to her credit. (On the other hand he maintained she ran a drug peddling and prostitution racket in New York and, also that she was a Lesbian. Heim had told me this but I would not consider either Heim or Crowley trustworthy on such a matter.) But to the Ripper story which antedated the New York period, for the year of the Ripper murders in London was 1888.

According to Crowley, it was the novelist Mabel Collins who confided to Cremers her lover was behaving so strangely that she was afraid he was Jack the Ripper. The lover was Dr Roslyn d'O Stephenson - alias Dr Roslyn d'Onston, rightly Robert d'Onston Stephenson, not a doctor. The story told by Crowley sounded so melodramatic and impossible that I thought he had made it up.

Nevertheless, I wrote to Mrs Saunders telling her the story I had found amongst Crowley's papers and asked her to comment. Her reply contained no details but confirmed the story in the particular which surprised me most:

I always remember Cremers saying she knew Jack the Ripper quite well through her dear friend Mabel Collins.

Since then, more has come out about this, in two books, *Jack the Ripper, Summing Up and Verdict*, by Colin Wilson (Bantam, 1987) and *Jack the Ripper, The Bloody Truth*, Melvin Harris (Columbus, 1987). Both take as their source the notes left by a journalist, Bernard O'Donnell, who obtained an interview with Cremers but never published because he felt, had not got the whole of the story. Colin Wilson says it was Hayter Preston who told O'Donnell that Cremers could tell a story about Jack the Ripper, and that makes me think O'Donnell must have been that young newspaperman who kept trying to talk to her that afternoon at Vicky's. I thought I heard Runia refer to him as Donald, but I could have misheard O'Donnell as Donald. If it was he, he did not make on me the impression of a profound person. But, according to him, what finally convinced Cremers d'Onston was the author of the crimes was that he assured her there would be no more of them.

In fact, I think she was mistaken. In excusal of her and Mabel Collins's suspicions, he called on the police, talking so strangely about the crimes he almost had them suspecting him, though they seem to have decided he was merely mad.

I happen to have primary material, which points in a different direction, which I shall disclose in a forthcoming book *Sickert and The Ripper Crimes.*

Some of the dances Victor performed were invocations to the Moon and years afterwards he was to tell Commander King Bull that on one occasion Crowley omitted to speak the ritual words which would have relieved him from the possession before the end of the ceremony. This was a serious piece of negligence, if negligence it was, because it left Victor possessed. He had dismissed the deity himself as best he could but, looking back, it seemed that for a considerable period of years he had suffered from a greater than usual possession by the moon.

The evenings at Victoria Street were such a success that Crowley booked the Caxton Hall, Westminster, for seven successive Wednesdays in October and November, at 9pm. An entrance fee of £5 5s. was charged for the series. Victor danced an allegory in which, as Mars, he sought to understand the riddle of the universe, and appealed on successive evenings to Saturn, Jupiter, the Sun, Venus, Mercury and the Moon; all confessing their inability to provide the solution they all turned in the end to Pan, who did so. To represent these other celestial bodies, additional persons were brought in.

Amongst these was a young girl of unearthly pallor; a fillet of silver leaves crowned her dark hair which fell loose about her form, robed in shining white. She was the moon.

Concerning this girl, who was to become tragically involved, Dame Rebecca West has written to me:

I was a fellow student of Joan Hayes at the Royal Academy of Dramatic Art in the year 1910. She had a beautiful face of the Russian ballet type, oval with beautifully defined eyebrows; her hair was very black and her skin white. Most girls at that time did not use powder but a curious thing called papier poudre, and we thought it rather dashing of her to use powder - and terribly dashing when she took to using a pale blue or pale green powder to intensify the whiteness of her skin. This she had been taught to do by a famous beauty of the time ... a poor girl who was just too marvellous to look upon, and could not act at all, and had come before the days of the photographic model. She had the body of a child of twelve. She was a freak of nature, though a very lovely one. She was both short and slight. It was as if her growth had been checked. She had absolutely no talent of any sort, as actress or dancer. Her delivery was wooden and her movement stiff. She was also quite stupid on general matters. But her beauty was extraordinary, and she was sweet natured. Joan Hayes was a delightful, kind sympathetic friend.

She had two sisters. One was a famous show-girl called Kathleen Hayes, the other was also on the stage. Their father was, I thought, a Frenchman; and he had come over to England because in some curious way he had been ruined by the Dreyfus case. I think they were possibly Jewish. She was not in the least what one would have expected from the daughter of a man who kept a lodging house in the Brixton Road. She was by the way frank and humorous about her home. She spoke beautiful English and odd French, she had good manners, and a certain air of refinement was evident in everything she did and said, but there was something odd and isolated about her, plus an air of second rate theatre. Joan's fees were paid by somebody very odd - I can't remember if it was the local doctor or the grocer. Anyway he came with his wife to see her act and I met them. Or was it a bookmaker? I remember a cheerful and vulgar pair.

Joan took a job appearing as a figurante in some ceremonial shows which were given by Crowley. She either applied for the job as a result of seeing it advertised or was sent there by an agent. I don't think Joan had any ideas which would have led her to Crowley. She was a very simple-minded girl, who read in order to develop herself but wouldn't have known the difference between Marie Corelli and Thomas Hardy.

Meanwhile, Ethel Archer wrote Victor a poem, which was later printed in her first volume, *The Whirlpool*:

To VBN
What shadow stirs the sentient air?
Like some dim whirling flame-flower from the loom
Of darkness; swifter circling mid the gloom
Of incense laden shadow to the air
Of softly chanted mantras; till the prayer
So oft repeated fills the sombre room

The Magical Dilemma of Victor Neuburg

With magic mighty as the dusky plume
Of the concealed one by whom we swear!

Victor! Twice Victor! By these golden lays
Of many-moulded music, hear our praise!
Accept our homage, whilst other spirit whirls
With thine; in fiercest ecstasy unfurls
Itself of its own beauty, passion's pearls.

To this Victor replied with a poem, unfortunately not one of his best, which makes me think it was written out of polite gallantry. He salutes her as a tormented soul from Lesbos but includes a mysterious couple of lines;

Thou lyric laughter of the enfranchised Male,
Thou fury of the eternal Woman's dirge!

I think the first of these is superb. But is it her he is saluting, or, as I think, his own freedom?

Ethel Archer from now on was increasingly in the office of the *Equinox*, fascinated by Crowley and Victor. Victor was always reading proofs and when coal had to be put on the fire he would pick it up with his fingers. In consequence his hands were usually black from printers' ink and coal dust. Crowley would say, 'Show me your hands, Victor!' And Victor would put them behind his back had say, 'Shan't!' like a child.

'He was absolutely fay!' said Ethel Archer. I wondered if she was aware that word had acquired, modernly, the meaning of homosexual; from a remark she had made earlier I realized she knew he was so but from the way in which she spoke the word, with an eerie look, it was evident she was giving it its literal meaning. The next moment she said, 'He was a leprechaun! No, not a leprechaun; they're Irish. What's like a leprechaun, but not Irish?'

'A sprite?' I suggested.

'Puck!' she said. It was in his laughter that she felt something aeriel, belonging to the woodlands rather than to the realms of men. 'It was quite unearthly'. Sitting suddenly bolt forward, her eyes straining as though into another region, she said, 'He wasn't human!'

The Rites of Eleusis

(1) Amongst the books I acquired from Anthony d'Offay was one about New Zealand, inscribed inside: 'To my Good Samaritan Victor Neuburg, from the pilgrim *Cestrius* for Maoriland, Kia Ora (good fortune) En passant June 24, '10, Leila Waddell.'

(2) There was the Balkan war in 1912, and of course the Great War in 1914.

(3) The 'hotted up' version in *The Hieroglyph* runs:

Dear Miss Strickland,

Salutation, and thanks much for the screed. We are glad you survived the fearsome ordeal; and trust that all is well with thee and thine. As to the persons who were kind in their attentions, believe me they simply don't exist! - Thine in the Mysteries,

Benjamin N

PS When will you come again?

It will be noticed that the significant alterations are (a) that the letter is made to be addressed to herself instead of to her husband; (b) that the signature is altered to 'Thine in the Mysteries' from 'Sincerely,' and (c) that the PS is altered into an invitation to come again.

Curiously, I found the original of this invitation imputed to Vicky when, Ethel Archer having died, Anthony d'Offay acquired a great mass of her papers and allowed me to see them. There were many manuscripts of her own poems and on the back of one I discerned a scribble in faint pencil in a hand which had become familiar:

124, Victoria Street, SW

July, 1910

Dear Mrs Wieland,

I offered this after you had gone the other day. It is quite good; you should finish it off. When will you come again?

Yours,

Aleister Crowley.

With regard to the slight alteration of names in *The Hieroglyph*, Ethel Archer said when I spoke with her that she had used Crowley, Victor, herself and her husband as models for the characters of Swaroff, Newton, Iris Strickland Blitzen, but she avowed that she had freely fictionalized the events in which she had involved them. She had not given Victor an opportunity of seeing the manuscript and was horrified when I told her I had found the book in Victor's library.

8
The Triumph of Pan

The Triumph of Pan(1), Victor's second book, was published from the Equinox in 1910. As a reward for turning the pages of the Bookseller for the whole of that year at the British Museum, I found it listed for the week beginning December 16.

There are 182 pages in the book, the title poem occupying fifteen pages. At the commencement are the words *Lampada Tradam*, meaning 'I carry the light.' They constituted his new motto as a Zelator and show he had now obtained this grade and was a 2=9.

The title poem, which consist of fifty-four eight-line stanzas, begins:
> *There are three gods who in their talons hold me;*

The first of these is a woman, who seeks him for her lover. Her longings are 'soft and pure',
> *But while I love her, she consumeth me;*
> *She withereth my soul, that erst was free.*

Is this Joan Hayes, already?

The second predator I am unable to place, unless it be Pan himself.

The third is obviously Crowley:
> *Lastly, there is one Great One, cold and burning,*
> *Crafty and hot in lust,*
> *Who would make me a Sapphist and an Urning,*
> *A Lesbian of the dust.*
> ...
> *The dung of all dead ages clings to him,*
> *And a fierce light shines through;*
> *They are the dead who once, long, long since, knew him;*
> *The Pagan and the Jew*
> *Have lent him, one by one,*
> *Seed with their orison,*
> *But he hath spurned their offerings, seeking me,*
> *A God, a victim slain in majesty.*
> ...

The Triumph of Pan

Here in the dust I lie, a broken shadow.

...

I am corrupted utterly; and whole.

...

But we, my God have been
Sublimely wise; obscene
In passion;...

It is, of course, homosexual poetry; in its category grander than anything I know, not excluding Verlaine. The sand blows through many of the lines and images.

> *....the sun is glowing*
> *Over the eternal sand,*
> *The endless road grows steeper; we are going*
> *Into a nameless land.*
>
> *...*

It is Dal'leh Addin which they are ascending, but also a spiritual territory:

> *No way may lead us back; our track is hidden*
> *In dust and sand and grass,*
> *For lo! we journey on a road forbidden,*
> *Where no man sees us pass.*
>
> *....*
>
> *....no stay*
> *We make, for who looks back shall lose the way.*

Amidst the concatenation of mixed images which follows, rises one superb line:

> *And we have passed the bounds of men's derision;*
> *Men shall stand naked, unashamed and free,*
> *To flaunt abroad their new-born ecstasy!*
>
> *...*

The end of what must surely be the most outspoken poem of its kind ever to have seen publication, read:

> *...the lure is mine, and I am fearless,*
> *Naked, and free, and young;*
> *The torch is out; no longer night is cheerless*
> *The hot young day is sprung*
> *From out the loins of God!*
> *Rise from the barren sod,*
> *Raise high the Paean of the God in Man!*

Io Triumph! Hail to the new-born Pan!

It represents the time when he was at his greatest emotional height in the pride of his powers, ecstatic. He was still unbroken, a wave which has not yet struck rocks big enough to curb its impetus.

The title-poem is followed by a number of shorter lyrics. Of these, 'The Lost Shepherd' is also a homosexual poem, though there is a blind in as much as the first six stanzas, beginning;

> *She walks among the starry ways,*
> *A crimson full-blown rose;*
>
> ...

and last (XVI), ending

> ...
>
> *She is born at midnight on the stream,*
> *A starry full blown rose.*

constitute a kind of cup which, though beautiful, has no connection with and forms a separate entity from the core of the poem, beginning in verse VII with:

> *I was a shepherd in other days,*
>
> ...
>
> *I found the groves of Pan: I came*
> *At length to a daisied field,*
>
> ...

What follows is a rape of the shepherd. Afterwards,

> *...in the morning Pan rose and fled*
> *And left me alone to sleep;*
> *And long I lay in slumber dead.*
> *Then on hands and knees did I creep*
> *Back to the shade of the sheltering trees;*
> *And I found my sheep on the shady leas;*
> *And my body was flushed, and my cheeks were red,*
> *And my eyes too bright to weep.*

Curiously, this poem is dedicated to Ethel Archer. I asked her about this. She said Vicky let her see the whole book when it was in proof and, explaining that he would like to dedicate a poem to each of his friends, invited her to choose one or two with which she would like her name associated. She chose 'The Cauldron' and 'The Lost Shepherd'.

The Triumph of Pan

Not all the dedicates were consulted. General Fuller received a piece about somebody being ritually stoned to death. I wrote to him about this and he replied:

I have no idea why VN dedicated it to me, and on re-reading it can see no reason why he should have. This applies to most of the dedicatees, many of whom I knew. It would seem that he dished out the dedications in a haphazard way, including as many of his friends as there were poems.

Some of the poems were written for girls with whom Victor had fleeting contact. Cammell showed me his copy of *The Triumph of Pan*, in which he had made notes concerning some of the dedicatees whose names had been supplied by Dr E.T.Jensen, formerly of Crowley's circle. Beneath the poem 'Dolly', I read 'Dolly was a fille de joie, formerly a chorus girl.' 'A Meeting' is dedicated to Nora: 'Nora was a lady of pleasure VBN met in Bournemouth in 1910.' 'Night Piece' is dedicated to Bruna: 'Bruna was a fille de joie and friend of VBN.'

John Symonds put me in touch with the widow of one of Crowley's disciples, Noel Fitzgerald. She also had notes on the dedicatees, unfortunately from the same source though in cruder language and slightly amplified, eg 'Nora was a tart VBN met the night in Bournemouth.' She may have been a tart but she got a lovely poem, beginning:

> Violet skies all rimmed in tune,
>> Soft blue light of the plenilune:
> Oh, the sway of the idle moon!

These tributes to the lightly loving ladies contrast with lines written in 'A Nocturne' (not included in *The Triumph of Pan* but published in the *Equinox*, no 5) to a feminine figure who appeared before his inner eye, as though in a dream, and who seemed to be his true love:

> ...tiny rosebuds
> Girt thy green mantle, and thy yellow hair
> Glittered with the dust of the stars.

Most of the lines from 'A Nocturne' were later incorporated in a much longer poem, 'Rosa Ignota', which appeared in the *Equinox*, No 10. I spent a long time trying to identify this girl. She was not Joan Hayes, for the colour of the hair was wrong, as were other details. None of Victor's friends could think of any girl he had known who fitted the description I came to the conclusion that she must be a figure whom he had known only in dreams, like 'Strong-heart' and the 'Grey Friend'. I was not far off the truth; yet I did not obtain the solution of the mystery until I was near the very end of my researches.

Other dedicatees include Crowley, Norman Mudd, Kenneth Ward, George Raffalovitch, Arthur Grimble, Commander Marston, Leila Waddell, Oscar Levy (translator of Nietzsche), Edward Storer, R.Noel Warren, R.B.Hazelden, Rae Fraser, Dorothy Taylor, Ragna Temp (dedicatee of 'Sleep on the Hills'), E.J.Wieland, Wilfred Merton, Vicky's mother, Aunt Ti, his cousin C.H.Davis and Rudolph C.Skinner. The book as a whole was dedicated to Gerald Pinsent.

But in the light of future events the most significant dedicatee is Joan Hayes. It is disappointing that the series of poems dedicated to her, 'The Songs of Sigurd', seem to have no possible bearing on a personal relationship. It is about a Norseman in the land of the Saxons; Vicky had an unexpected vein of interest in Vikings, their myths and their long ships.

The latter part of the book consists of the earlier composed *Olivia Vane* series, from which I have quoted when dealing with the period during which they were written.

At the end of the book appear lines which seem very special because they are printed in red and occupy a page to themselves. Indeed their meaning is very special and seems to prove my thesis, which I elaborated earlier, as to what Victor and Crowley really purposed in their relations

I cannot avail myself of red print so I will use italic:
> *There is a maiden harp-player, and a silver lute is held*
> *In the hands of an hermaphrodite; this thing shall be fulfilled.*

This volume of Victor's poems, *The Triumph of Pan*, was the subject of the first letter from John Middleton Murry to Katherine Mansfield. She was a contributor to A.R.Orage's periodical *New Age* - as indeed was Victor. I am indebted to Mr Charles Stephens of Liverpool, the grandson of another contributor, for sending me photostats of some pages of the issue of 28 December 1911, which carried not only an article by H F Stephens but a translation by Victor B Neuburg of 'The Englishman Abroad', from the German of Karl Hillebrand. It was in that same month that Katherine Mansfield and Murry met at a dinner party. Interested, he gave her a book, apparently by hand, and asked her to review it for the new periodical which he had just started, *Rhythm*. She asked him to tell her something about the author. This gave Murry the occasion to write her his first letter:'(2)

The Triumph of Pan

Jan 27, 1912

Dear Miss Katherine Mansfield,

I don't know very much about the man Neuberg [sic] - but what I do know I'll try to tell you. He is or rather was one of Aleister Crowley's push in the advanced spiritualist - obscene yet divine - stunt, εραστησ Crowley's part being always pathic...

This is true, but it was a pity for Victor that he should become known in this way. The reputation then acquired would damage him in later life. Nevertheless, Katherine Mansfield wrote a nice review, occupying nearly a page of *Rhythm* and carrying seventeen lines of quotation from Victor's verse. The poem she appeared to like the most was 'Sleep on the Hills':

> *There is peace on the hills to gather,*
> *There a sad, proud soul may sleep*
> *Gold gorse and green purple heather,*
> *Hold the tears that the salt winds weep,*
> *And we will lie down together.*

So Victor was on the fringe of that circle. Did he actually meet those by whom he and his work and life were discussed? I am trying to remember. I know that the name of Orage passed his lips, as being that of a great literary editor of the days before we were born, and remember his paying a special tribute to Beatrice Hastings who lived with Orage, contributed to *New Age* and helped behind the scenes. In Vicky's view, her importance had not been sufficiently estimated (Theosophists are grateful to her for her defence of Madame Blavatsky). Vicky only once mentioned John Middleton Murry in my hearing; I cannot remember the exact words, but the impression they left on me was that he thought of Murry as a person who tried to understand without understanding.

(1) Several of the poems in *The Triumph of Pan* are reproduced in *The Cambridge Poets, 1900-13*, in which Victor Neuburg is accorded the same number of pages as Rupert Brooke.

(2) *The letters of John Middleton Murry to Katherine Mansfield*, ed C.A.Hoskins (Constable, 1983), p 16.

9
The Desert

The Triumph of Pan received a great many reviews but Victor did not see them as they appeared, for Crowley was impatient to get back to Africa. Crowley installed Ethel Archer and her husband in his flat at Victoria Street, with instructions to hold the fort, and departed with Victor. At Marseilles they were held up for a couple of days waiting for a boat to Algiers. Victor sent a postcard to Ethel Archer from the Hotel de la Regence, dated and postmarked December 9, 1910.

If there's time, send me a set of proofs to Biskra; both AC and I would like a chance of seeing your book before it goes to press. If there's no time, never mind. We go today.

Thine,

Victor

The book referred to is her book of poems *The Whirlpool*, which was being published by Equinox, and on the verso Victor has written, across the picture:

Ask Bunko to send me an ordinary *Pan* to Biskra beside the others and send news of *The Whirlpool*

With best wishes form

Victor B Neuburg ∴ /.

This is the first thing I have of his, where he uses the two dots, one each side of a slanting line. They do not appear in his letter to Wieland of the previous June but from this time on were always to appear after his signature. They have puzzled many people and I have been asked if they are an astrological symbol. They are not, but they might be Rosicrucian. Most Rosicrucian Orders use dots, usually arranged in pyramids, but in a manner differing slightly from one Order to another and according to the grade. I presume that this particular formation was the one Victor was entitled to as a Zelator, or 2=9.

From Algiers they took the train to Bou Saada, where they must have spent six nights. From Bou Saada Victor sent a second postcard to Ethel Archer:

The Desert

Dec 14, 1910

Greetings to you and Bunko. We start walking tomorrow. Ask Bunko to send a free, ordinary *Pan* to W K Sanderson, Vote Office, House of Commons.

Best wishes from

Victor B N './.

This time he and Crowley intended to strike deeper into the Saharan Atlas Mountains so they obtained camels with a man to drive them and a boy to look after them. They made their first evening halt with a sheikh who held a kind of mystical school and talked with him far into the night, which they spent as his guests.

In the morning they struck upwards towards a mountain pass. To follow their day-to-day progress from Crowley's typescript would occupy too much space. Briefly, they ran into rain. Neither Victor nor Crowley had even conceived of rain of such an order. In fact they were caught in a storm which entered into history. They had difficulties in putting up a tent, reminiscent of *Three Men In A Boat*. It was an Arab lean-to made of a blanket and sticks, some of which plainly served the structure while others had no function they were able to discover save to stick into them.

The camels were wretched. The camel-driver and boy complained ceaselessly; they said the beasts were too cold and hungry to go on. As they had brought no food for them, and there was no way to give them shelter, it did not seem to Crowley or Victor that simply to stop moving would be any solution. Eventually the man and boy staged a sit-down strike. They sat in an empty tomb and said they would go no further. Crowley and Victor called their bluff and went on by themselves on the camels, for by now they had learned to make them go in the direction they wanted. When at last the downpour ceased, on the third night out, they contrived to make a fire and spent the hours until dawn removing their clothes and drying them.

The driver and boy, not wishing to lose the camels, caught up eventually but Crowley and Victor decided to do without them and to continue on foot. They had intended to do a pendant to the Aethyrs but neither of them felt in the mood for magic.

Most of the time they spent in the open. On one occasion, according to Crowley, they covered 100 miles in a day and a half though I suspect exaggeration.

On the flat, featureless desert, where no moving thing was seen from horizon to horizon, the sense of isolation from the ordinary events of life was complete. The smallest physical detail had absolute value. It was possible, as 'not on even the holiest honeymoon'

to love as it is impossible to do in any other conditions. Every moment of one's life becomes charged with unimaginable intensity, since there is nothing to interfere with one's absorption.

After this, it is surprising to read:

I left Neuburg in Biskra to recuperate.

That is how Crowley puts it. The Raeburns, years afterwards when Victor told them about it, understood something very different: 'Crowley abandoned him in the desert.'

Victor felt this was a most unfriendly and unkind desertion. If, as is probable, Crowley had taken the map and compass he may have feared being lost. It is plain that he was in utter desolation; and I suppose it was in this moment that he turned to beseech help of the Great White Brotherhood.

> The Master heard; with his remembering hand
> He scrawled a message in the wrinkled sand.

Victor regained the coast at Bône and left from the port of Tunis.

10
Triangles

ictor's story now enters what, to me, is the most confused period.
/hat I see is a series of triangles in which he was involved; but they
re triangles which, because of the homosexual undertow, could be
nterpreted in different senses. It is difficult to be sure and because
ne is dealing with real people, who had real feeling, one does not like
o juggle with them like puppets. The position is not made easier by
ne fact that the whole thing has become overgrown by a jungle of
·gend, most of which is based on misunderstanding and misinfor-
nation. Slashing this aside I shall present only the barest bones of the
ituation which has emerged from my researches.

irst there was a triangle of Crowley, Victor and Joan Hayes; then a
ubsidiary one composed of Victor, Joan Hayes and Ethel Archer. I
vill treat the latter first because it bears on Ethel Archer's capacity as
 witness. I found her almost hysterical on the subject of Joan Hayes;
he spoke of her with extreme antipathy and I marvelled that any-
ody could speak in tones so charged with hatred of a girl whose
uneral she had attended half a century ago. 'She made him [Victor]
·romise not to see me. I didn't see him for ages and when I did I
sked him where he'd got to and he said "She asked me to promise
ιot to see you again."'

Victor and I were not having an affair!' she added, suddenly fearing
his might give me a false impression.

 am sure they were not. In Anthony d'Offay's collection I got a
ιumber of letters written by Victor to Ethel Archer at different peri-
·ds. All are to do with printers' proofs and the like; and the tone,
hough friendly, is incompatible with anything more than comrade-
iness.

Nevertheless jealousy can exist without 'an affair' being involved.
Ethel Archer's attitude to Victor was obviously complicated and
ımbivalent. When she forgot Joan she read to me from *The Triumph of
?an*, in a voice that quivered and said, 'it's simply too beautiful'. She
ieemed to have been carried back to another world. But any question

concerning Joan and she was immediately beside herself, Victor became engulfed in the wave of vitriolic emotion and nothing was too bad to say of either of them.

Dame Rebecca West declared that Joan was quite undeserving of the comments Ethel Archer made on her moral character.

Dame Rebecca wrote:

I know her family background was probably sordid, but...that she was an innocent girl I am certain. I met her every day in term-time for a year, and I took her home several times and exposed her to the really very shrewd gaze of my mother, who thought she was a nice, stupid, very affected, good natured girl, with a tragedy ahead of her because of her ambition and her quite evident lack of gifts.

What is interesting about the whole story is that Joan Hayes had almost no personality, except this sweetness of which I have spoken, and a sparrow-like chirping activity.

She recollected that somebody at RADA had told them a risqué story which neither *she nor Joan* understood.

While completely accepting this picture of Joan at the time when Dame Rebecca knew her, it seems possible she altered considerably after she left R.A.D.A. and became part of Crowley's circle. Dame Rebecca herself wrote:

I lost touch with Joan Hayes, but went to some cellar theatre and saw her acting...in some avant garde play. She acted so badly that I was embarrassed and did not go round to see her. I was also conscious of a disagreeable change in her, something affected and queer.

From all Ethel Archer said I retain one cameo: she described Joan standing behind Crowley's chair as he sat at a table, running her hands through his hair and calling him 'Aleister'.

'Not even Victor called him Aleister!' she said to make me realise the enormity of the familiarity.

'What did Victor call him?' I asked with sudden curiosity.

'A C usually. Or Holy Guru. Or by his surname.'

She represented Crowley as detesting Joan, and quoted him as having spoken about her, and to her, in terms which, if he did employ them, were offensive to a degree.

Yet Hayter Preston believed strongly that Crowley had intercourse with Joan before Victor did. I had always known that Hayter Preston was one of the most important people to see with regard to Victor's story, yet I had had no idea that his friendship went back to those

Triangles

days.

I wrote to him c/o The P.E.N. and a few days later he was having tea with me. To me he had been simply a name, the Literary Editor of the *Sunday Referee*; he was a big, friendly man with blue eyes; his friendship with Victor, to my surprise, went back to 1911.

Curiously enough, he had met Ione de Forest, even before he met Victor. It was in a bar, perhaps at the Cosmo Club and she was with a theatrical agent called Alec Bland. His impression was that she was neurotic. Ione de Forest was the stage name of Joan Hayes.

Preston at this time was a young freelance journalist, a poet and Freethinker. One day when he went to the office of the Secular Society off the Farringdon Road, he happened to have under his arm a volume of poems by Ezra Pound whom he much admired. G.W. Foote was there, talking with some others; they noticed the book he had and told him that if he was interested in modern poetry he ought to meet Victor Neuburg, one of their members. They gave him Victor's address, at York Buildings, the Adelphi.

Preston went there. It was a couple of houses down as one descended from John Street to the river. There was an Adam doorway and a rather dark staircase. Victor's room was on the second floor. It, too, was rather dark. There were piles of books on the floor and in corners. Victor let him in, 'small and birdlike,' a shock of hair and a head too big for his body.

I had often wondered whether had I known Victor in the days of his strange relationship with Crowley I would have felt his personality to be in any way different. I asked Preston. 'No' he said, He was younger of course, 'As he grew older the face grew more lined and greyer. He used to have a fine skin. But he changed remarkably little over the years.'

Sketching the pattern of Victor's daily life, he said. 'There was no kitchen attached to his room. He did not cook. He ate out. At Lyons usually. Or he would go for a meal to his Aunt's in Victoria Street. Once I went with him into Coutts' Bank in the Strand where he cashed a cheque from his Aunt and we had lunch at Simpson's'.

He met Crowley through Victor; and disliked him. He lunched again at Simpson's with Victor, Crowley and Crowley's mother. Crowley took the menu and said, 'You can have boiled toads, Mother, or fried

Jesu.' His mother was obviously upset, and Preston could not understand Victor's association with a man whose sense of humour was so puerile. Preston found Crowley vulgar, coarse, overwhelmingly conceited and fake.

I had always thought of Preston as having had from the beginning the completely Secularist and Rationalist attitude for which he was known but he surprised me by saying: 'I had read the books of Eliphas Levi before I met Victor!' he had had a brief experience with an esoteric group in Paris and considered Crowley's attitude to magic much less refined than that which he had encountered there. 'Everything he touched would become fake!' He paid the chef of a London hotel to name a dish after him, *Sole à lá Crowley*. He commissioned Augustus John to do a portrait of him. He had his own books bound in vellum. He got through an inherited fortune of between thirty and forty thousand pounds and was battening on Victor. 'Victor could only get the money through his family and through him Crowley was bleeding them.'

I have confirmation of this from a Mrs Baker, who did not know the family until much later but understood from his Aunt Fanny that while they were in Algeria, Victor's mother received a telegram from Crowley reading: *Send £500 or you will never see your son again.* There was a family conference at which his Uncle Edward declared that this was just another ruse to get money out of them. His mother, frightened that Victor was really being held to ransom, dissolved in tears. Mrs Baker did not know whether the money was sent or not.

One evening Victor took Preston to Crowley's flat in Victoria Street. In a half-open drawer Preston glimpsed a pile of visiting cards printed for *Lord Boleskine*. When Crowley left the room for a moment, Preston took them out and put them on the table in front of Victor and said, 'Why does he call himself LordBoleskine?'

Victor had nothing to answer. But when Crowley returned Victor said, 'Teddie asked why you call yourself Boleskine.'

Crowley said bluffingly, 'I'm the laird up there. Laird means Lord.'

With regard to Joan - or de Forest, as Preston always heard her called - he did not know the exact story. He did not think she was 'a promiscuous girl by nature', or even particularly sensual, but he thought she had been disorientated by Crowley.

Triangles

He thought it possible that Victor's affair with de Forest was an attempt to get away from Crowley, or to gain some emotional independence of him.

No enlightenment is to be had from Crowley's autobiography, which does not mention Joan or Ethel Archer, the pages for this period being consumed with another matter about which I first heard from General Fuller.

'I broke with him because he let a friend of mine down,' General Fuller said. 'George Cecil Jones had a peculiarity, which was that he told the truth!'

The day after my visit to General Fuller I went to Colindale to get out the *Sunday Times* for April 1911, and to find out what the case of which he had told me was about. The report was in the issue for April 26 and referred to the following paragraph, which had appeared in the *Looking Glass* in November 1910.

Two of Crowley's friends and associates are still associated with him; one the rascally Buddhist monk Allan Bennett; the other a person of the name of George Cecil Jones, who was for some time employed at Basingstoke in metallurgy...Crowley and Bennett lived together, and there were rumours of unmentionable immoralities which were carried out under their roof.

Jones' case was that anybody reading his name sandwiched between the names of Crowley and Bennett would connect him with the unsavoury reference and his suit was for libel. Crowley turned up at the hearing in the role of a spectator. Mr Justice Scrutton, at one moment, expressed doubt whether it was in order to hear evidence concerning Crowley's character, Crowley not being a party in the case; eventually he allowed that it was and commented, 'This trial is becoming very much like the trial in *Alice in Wonderland*'.

General Fuller went into the box for Jones and was asked whether he could see Crowley sitting in court. He said he could. Crowley beamed and remained where he was.

A Dr Berridge was called and this dialogue took place:

Dr Berridge : On one occasion when Crowley was over here as an envoy on official matters concerning the Order, I had an opportunity of speaking alone with him and I said to him, 'Do you know what they accuse you of?' - meaning the members of the Order. I will not express it too plainly as I see there are ladies in the court.

Mr Justice Scrutton: Any ladies who may be in this court probably are beyond any scruples of that sort.

The Magical Dilemma of Victor Neuburg

Dr Berridge: Well, I said: 'They accuse you of unnatural vice': and he made a very peculiar answer: he neither admitted nor denied it.

Jones lost his case. Victor was not in court, yet the affair affected him as it affected everybody in Crowley's entourage.

On this same afternoon General Fuller gave me a different reason for his having broken with Crowley, 'I opened a letter from him at breakfast. It was in a large envelope and a whole lot of obscene postcards fell out, that he had bought in Port Said. At night, when drunk, it may seem funny to put obscene postcards in an envelope, but when one opens it, in the morning, and has them fall out on the breakfast table, it is merely disgusting. It could have been opened in transit and it could have been wondered why I should be the recipient of such stuff. I decided I could no longer be associated with him.'

Crowley was not prepared for the thinning of support (Raffalovich was one of those who left in the wake of Fuller) which the comedy cost him. No prosecutions followed from the failure of Jones' action for libel but because of the general alarm Crowley's name had to disappear as Editor of the *Equinox*. Victor's name now appeared as Sub-Editor; the Editor being given as Mary D'Este Sturges; she was Crowley's newest friend.

In the midst of this reorganization, Joan Hayes married. The certificate I drew from Somerset House showed me, *inter alia*, the true spelling of her name:

At St Georges, Hanover Square, W1, 22nd December 1911. Wilfred Merton, 23 years, Bachelor, Engraver. 31 Green Street, Mayfair and Jeanne Heyse, otherwise Ione de Forest, 19 years, Spinster. Artist (Painter). 167, Brixton Road. Father : Francis Heyse, of Independent Means. Witnesses: Zachary Merton, Kathleen Heyse.

A new triangle had emerged Merton, Victor and Joan. Before I could treat this, I felt I must discover whether Merton was alive and inserted an advertisement in *The Times*. I had a reply from a man who told me Merton was dead but that he had been his friend for many years in later life. 'Wilfred Merton was the nicest person you could meet.' he said. 'By blood he was entirely German. He had taken the name of the man his mother married, Zachary Merton. Zachary Merton was immensely rich. He had an income of between £50,000 and £60,000 a year. He was head of a big copper combine. Before Wilfred came of age he had been known as Schmiechen.' (I realised this must be the 'wealthy undergraduate named Schmiechen' who had helped Victor finance publication of his first book, *The Green*

Triangles

Garland, while at Cambridge. Far from being a newcomer in the story, he had been in it from an early date.) Wilfred, my informant said, had as a child 'been dandled on the knee of Madame Blavatsky.(1)' His parents were Theosophists but they separated without having married.

After the ceremony at St George's, Joan, Merton and Victor travelled to Paris together, the best of friends. Even Ethel Archer, who loathed Joan, conceded that Merton knew the situation which had existed previously with Victor. She expressed doubt, however, whether as Joan said, he had given permission for its continuance.

On their return Joan and Merton went to live in Cardinal Mansions, Westminster, and Joan became an arts student and took a room in Rossetti Studios, Flood Street. It was now that she met Nina Hamnett. About the beginning of June, five or six months after marriage, she left Merton and installed herself in the studio. Preston said Victor took a cottage for her in Essex where they went at week-ends. Merton filed a suit for divorce and it is generally assumed that this was for adultery and the co-respondent was Victor, though I have been unable to obtain proof.

Dame Rebecca West who had left the stage for journalism had one final, unexpected glimpse of Joan, peculiar and disturbing:

I then worked on the *Freewoman*, and at a meeting addressed by the Editor, Dora Marsden, Joan appeared, accompanied by a man who was, I suppose, Victor Neuburg. She came at the end of the meeting to ask a question of Dora Marsden, but Dora had already gone; she had left with a party of friends while Joan waited in the wrong passage. I said to her, 'Is there anything I can do for you about this?' or words to that effect, meaning, 'Shall I arrange a meeting when I see Dora tomorrow or the next day?' Joan looked at me with positive hatred and said, with a malicious laugh, 'What could you do for me?' I had been so glad to see her and felt such gratitude for her kindness, that I had nothing but friendship for her when I spoke - and as she knew that I was writing for the *Freewoman* it seemed odd that she should not take what I had said as quite reasonable and polite. I was with a young man who was so startled by the force of Joan's remark that he took two steps backward.

There is one other thing which I mention with hesitation. Runia, when I saw her in the summer of 1940, after Vicky's death, told me he had told her the problem of Joan Hayes was that she was very small. Not only was she slight of stature and weight, and small breasted, her internal passages were small, too small to allow of penetration. When I saw Runia again, in 1961, and sought to check this story with her, as I wanted to write Vicky's biography, she repudiated it and said she had never heard of a girl like that. I therefore did not mention it in the first edition. Yet if it were true, it would explain the strange exclamation she made to Rebecca West, 'What could you do for me?'

(1) It seems the father must have been the German Theosophist, Hermann Schmiechen, a friend of Mme Blavatsky, who drew the picture of the Masters now treasured at Adyar; an unexpected, yet oddly significant link-up.

11
The Moon Above the Tower

What was Victor's position and feeling in all this? Regarding his relationship with Crowley, I have no difficulty. He talked to me about it. I have its wave-length. I never heard of Joan from him.

Insight came from one of the items in d'Offay's collection: a long, unpublished poem by Victor, entitled 'The New Diana'. The whole is in his hand, and is dated - *Finished 28.9.12*. It consists of eighty-two foolscap pages, comprising prelims, argument, prologue, seventy stanzas and an epilogue. In the Kabbalah, 70 is the numerator of LIL (night) and in the argument Victor warns the Disciple not to set his foot upon the Path unless he can keep to it, for:

There is one who all but fell into the abyss, through the Wiles of a Syren; for she by her seductions closed against him the Way of Initiation...Even to the brink of Hell was lured that Disciple; the White Breasts and dark eyes of Lilith stood even between him and the Great Gods, wherefore the gods smote him heavily for his Perfidy to Them and his Master. And this Syren was the Projection of the Disciple himself upon the Screen of the visible Universe, even as Lilith was a projection of the God Adonai.

Lilith is the dark side of the moon, or in human terms a person of opposite sex to the Disciple whose influence is detrimental to progress on the path. There is a tradition that no sooner has he set his foot seriously upon it than such a temptation appears.(1)

The poems opens:
> There is a tower whereby the white moon sails,
> A tower within a city of the west;
>
> ....
> ...the starlit summer glows and pales
> In calm, unending sleep.

I thought for a long time about the setting of this poem until it flashed on me suddenly that the tower, to which reference is made several times, could only be the old Shot Tower on the South Bank, opposite York Buildings, the Victoria Embankment Gardens, and Cleopatra's

Needle. So *that* was the view which Victor saw when, unable to sleep, he looked up at the great silver disk and wrote:

> II
>
> ....
>
> *She lies above the Tower,*
> *And dreams.*
>
> V
>
> *My little wilderness of tangled dreams,*
> *Under the moon-enchanted lonely tower,*
> *My little land...*
> *Where in I pass the morn's first shaded hour -*
> *My solitude....*

He becomes more and more enchanted:

> VI
>
> *I still worship Thee*
>
> ...
>
> *I see Thee pass*
> *Along the summer Grass,*
> *And as Thou passest grows day's light more strong*
>
> VII
>
> *The striving starlight through the pale blue skies*
> *Breaks in a cluster-cloud...*
>
> ...
>
> *Under the lids of Artemis' shut eyes*
> *Let me awake again*

The memory of earlier incarnations comes in a series of fragmentary glimpses:

> VII
>
> *I bore...*
> *A little vine, a golden lily, a cross,*
> *A little box of nard, a swan with wings*
> *Of gleaming silver, a shield with golden boss*
>
> ....
>
> IX
>
> *I bore a panther-skin in Argive woods,*
>
> ...
>
> X
>
> *I have known love, nor count my knowledge loss,*
> *Because at full-moon time I lie in pain*
> *Watching the skies...*

The Moon above the Tower

XI
I have passed through a wilderness of Pan
....
I left the fires
Unto the guardian sires
Who watched so long for a little sign that ran
At length along the grass;
They heard it pass:
One side the path the quick lay, and one side the dead.
XVIII
In a deserted field a statue raises
Bare silver arms into a light, pale sky;
With words in unknown tongues...
It seems to speak forgotten lore; and I
Lie on the sward,
And hail Adonis lord

In agony, he cried:
XXVII
Diana! I have left the mystic Way.

He was born into an alien time, wherein Her worship was forgotten.

The Goddess asks him sternly why he has taken an earthly love, which exiles him from light and sun, and from Her service. The *Epilogue* concludes in bleakest strains;

...
the hour is fled, and the glory
Is fled from the world I knew:
And here I have told my story -
I that was counted true,
Fell. Now, what may I do?
My life is dead! Save dying,
There is nothing more to be feared
For no man lives by lying,
When the scroll of his fame is smeared.
When his soul is foully seared.
And a man must dree his weird.(2)

What is the meaning of the appalling despair in which Victor Neuburg languished under the full moon of the summer solstice of 1912? I verified that it does at this time lie above the tower. The old Shot Tower is no more but I remember where it used to be and on the night of the summer solstice of 1963, I went and stood on the Embankment below York Buildings and waited for the moon to rise until at last it was over the place where Victor had seen it half a century ago.

When Joan first appeared in Crowley's circle it was to represent the moon and as Victor saw her, white and silver in a mysterious light, she must have seemed to him the personification of his true Goddess, the unearthly Diana. It was on finding himself trapped in a narrow domestic alley, in a tête à tête with someone who would come between him and the Argentinum Astrum that as he gazed at the great white moon above the tower, and felt all he would lose, he wrote in such suicidal anguish.

But it was Joan who took her life.

It was Nina Hamnett who found the body. As she told the Coroner on Saturday, August 3, 1912, she had seen Joan on Thursday August 1, having come in response to a wire. She arrived between ten and eleven in the evening; she found Joan packing. Joan was very cheerful and said she was going away, and said she would give Nina some dresses if she would come back at eleven in the morning to collect them. As Nina was going Joan put an envelope into her hand and said in a most natural way 'Would you mind?'

On the envelope was writen: *To be opened if I cannot see you at 11 o'clock on Friday morning.* When she arrived on Friday at 11 Nina found another envelope addressed to herself, pinned to the outside of the door. It contained the key of the studio. Nina let herself in and saw Joan's body on the divan. A revolver lay on the floor by her slippers. Seeing that she was dead Nina withdrew and called the caretaker, who fetched in a policeman.

Nina told the Coroner that she had known Joan under the name of Ione de Forest. Joan had told her nothing of her private life. It was only in the last two months she had known Joan was married. She had not opened the note which Joan had put into her hand on the Thursday evening. The Coroner opened it. It contained two items, the certificate of marriage between Joan and Wilfred Merton and a gun licence issued to Joan, in the name of de Forest, on July 18, at Sloane Square.

Wifred Merton, with Derek Curtis Bennett to represent him, said that

On Friday, August 2, at lunchtime, he had received by post a letter from Joan. Opening it, he found a sheet on which she had written four words. These were: 'You have killed me'. Answering a question from the Coroner, he said he did not know why she should have written these words to him.

Answering further he said, 'She was neurotic; her nerves were highly strung, and she was subject to fits of hysterics...She suggested suicide once or twice...She suggested chloroform.' Asked if she took drugs he replied that he did not know but added, 'She was not quite normal. I could never get her to see a doctor.' Merton said he was the petitioner in divorce proceedings and had not seen or had communication with her, save through their solicitors, since she left him two months previously; nevertheless, he was making her an allowance.

Mr E.S.P.Haynes, solicitor for the deceased, said he had been instructed not to defend the divorce proceedings. The deceased had told him that when they were over she would take her life but he had not thought there was any immediate danger, or he would have done something. He had now received a letter from her in which she thanked him for his kindness and said she could not bear the position any longer. Replying to Curtis Bennett he said he had thought the husband's offer of £300 a year alimony extremely handsome. There was even talk of a further voluntary settlement by the husband after the divorce proceedings had been settled.

The deceased had addressed a letter to the Coroner which was read:

No 5, Cardinal Mansions,

Westminster

The last statement of Jeanne Merton, wife of Wilfred Merton, of the above address, written at her present residence at Rossetti Studios, where she has been living under her professional name of Ione de Forest, being an art student. I hereby state that although of sound mind I intend committing suicide tonight because of the intolerable position my extremely rash and unfortunate marriage has placed me in. It is my wish my body should be cremated.

The verdict was returned and recorded on the death certificate I drew from Somerset House:

2nd August, 1912. In flat, Rossetti Studios, Flood Street, Chelsea. Jeanne Merton, Female. 21 years. Found dead. Syncope from a revolver wound of the heart, self inflicted, and deceased did kill herself while temporarily insane.

Victor was not in court because at the time of the inquest he did not know Joan was dead. He had gone down to the cottage in Essex, says

The Magical Dilemma of Victor Neuburg

Preston, expecting either to find her there or that she would join him later. She did not come and he supposed she had been delayed he returned to London on the Sunday night or Monday morning. The inquest had been on the Saturday.

'When I got back, she was dead!' he told Preston, dazedly.(3)

Runia, when she told me the story in 1940, averred, on the basis of what Vicky had told her, that it was because, anatomically, Joan Hayes was unable to be, in the complete sense, anybody's wife, a condition with which, she told Vicky, Merton was less patient than he, that she ended her life.

(1) 'When you knock on the door of the heavens, it is the Gates of Hell which first open: *always*, by ineluctable law.' This was written to me in 1945 by the Frenchman Vivian. Suppressing the source, I repeated this dictum to Gerald Yorke when he brought me the Crowley papers. His rejoinder was, 'But when you see them, you don't think they're the Gates of Hell, or you wouldn't go through them! You think they're the Doors of Heaven. You think the marsh-light is the real light. The Devil appears in the guise of an Angel.'

These two dicta are complementary. Vivian's point (which has been made also by Blavatsky), is that it is the aspiration itself which calls into resistance all that is opposed to it and so manifests the extent of the candidate's liability. 'Movements which have in their title the word *Universal* are specially liable to schism. Those which take as their watchword Liberty fall quickest prey to a tyrant. While if you even come on a Lodge with the name of *Fraternity*, you can be sure the members are at odds to the extent they hardly know how to endure each other at all!' The candidate who chose as his aim a specified virtue chose the field in which he would be tried.

It was also said, *chez* Vivian, 'Every initiation is a test in discernment.'

(2) See *The City of Dreadful Night* (V 25), by James Thomson the younger, one of the poets who had most influence on Victor.

(3) I am aware that Calder-Marshall, in his book *The Magic Of My Youth*, gives a different version, according to which Victor was with Ione de Forest on the night that she took her life, Thursday, August 1, and walked out after a violent scene; I think, however, that Calder-Marshall's source is false. I had some correspondence with him about this: though he knew Victor, at a later date, in Steyning, it was not from Victor that he heard the story.

12
Templars and the Tradition of Sheikh El Djebel

In order to understand the next chapter in the history of Vicky and Crowley, it is necessary to have some knowledge of the affairs of the Knights Templar. This was an order founded in 1119, ostensibly for the purpose of protecting pilgrims to the Holy Land from attacks by Muslims. Within two hundred years it had grown to a military power and an affluence such as made it one of the most important forces in Europe. By this time, however, exceedingly strange rumours were current. Pope Clement V, even before he became Pope, heard of these from Philippe IV of France. Perhaps because he found the rumours impossible to believe, Clement V did little about it, although shortly after his coronation he wrote to the Grand Master of the Order of the Knights Templar, Jacques de Molay (born 1244) and suggested that the Knights Templar amalgamate with the Knights Hospitaler.

Jacques de Molay replied with a letter giving sixteen reasons why he did not think this would be a good idea. Some of these reasons are so small, so hair-splitting and so repetitious, so subdivided to make their number the greater, that I felt he had some other over-riding reason which he found impossible to give.

The Pope did nothing further in the matter.

Philippe of France made the next move and it was a dramatic one. He ordered the arrest of all the Templars in France. It was done suddenly, so that they were unprepared and seems to have been an overnight coup.

The king was the real prosecutor and the gravamen of the accusation is contained in a letter to his officers of September 14, 1307, in which he commands them to make the arrests. It is too long to quote in full, but I have translated the key passages from the Latin.

Philippe, by grace of god king of France, to his dear and faithful seigneur Onival, the knight Jean de Tourville and the bailiff of Rouen, greetings.

A bitter thing, a thing to weep on, a thing horrible to think of, terrible to hear, a detestable crime, an execrable wickedness, an abominable act, a frightful infamy, a thing strange to all humanity has, thanks to the report of several persons worthy of faith, come to our ears, not without striking us with heavy stupor and causing us to shudder with violent horror...

...it has come to us that the brothers of the Order to the Knights Templar...at the moment of their entry into the Order, when they take their vow, have presented to them His image [the image of Chris on the Cross] which with miserable blindness they thrice deny and with horrible crudity thrice spit upon. After this they take off all their clothes, which they have worn in civil life; naked they are kissed by him who receives them, or by his representative , upon the base of the spine first, then upon the navel and then upon the mouth. After...they give themselves to one another in a horrible and fearful concubinage.

To this letter Philippe adds in the French of his time, the better to be understood, detailed instructions as to how the arrests should be carried out, and the questions which should be put to the persons arrested:

They must be asked, carefully and seriously, to say under oath in what manner they were received [in to the Order] and what oaths or promises they made...

To prepare the interrogators for what they should expect to hear, he told them what he knew already.

Then he [the commander or Master], makes him take his clothes off, kisses him at the base of the spine. under the belt, on the navel and on the mouth, and tells him that if one of the brothers of the Order should wish to lie with him carnally he must suffer it, because he must and is bound to suffer, according to the statue of the Order, and several of them, after the manner of Sodom, join with each other....

Further on Philippe writes of:

An idol which is in the form of a man's head with a great beard, which head they kiss and worship in their provincial chapters; but his is not known by all the brothers but only by the Grand Master and the senior brethren.

This is the earliest reference to Baphomet.

The trial lasted nearly seven years. There is an excellent resumé in the Introduction to a recently printed edition of the principle documents, *Le Dossier de L'Affaire des Templiers, édité et traduit par Georges Lizerand* (Les Belles Lettres) Paris, 1964, in which the Latin or Old French (as the case may be) is given with a translation into modern French. I lifted these extracts from this edition though I have made my own translation from the old texts so as not to be a remove from them. The case was eventually taken out of the jurisdiction of the secular into an ecclesiastical court, where the prisoners were treated with greater courtesy and, surprisingly, remarkable consideration. Having signed a partial avowal, under torture, de Molay now reserved his defence. He said he would be prepared to give a full explanation to the Pope; but to him only. It does not seem that an audience was granted but the Pope appointed a special commission of Cardinals to see de Molay privately, and to reconcile him to the Church, with those of the Knights closest to him in the affair. This, however, was at the cost of a penitential confession and when a sentence of imprisonment for life was read out to him on March 19, 1314, de Molay declared that the prepared statement by which he had purchased his life was nonsense; one of those with him, Geoffrey de Charnay, did likewise. The King, hearing of this, snatched them both back and had them burned outside the Palace courtyard. Precautions were such that nobody representing the Church learned of it until it was done.

What was the truth of it? I think one can put aside all the learned commentaries which have been written, and begin with King Philippe's text. Despite the indignation and incomprehension that informs it, it seems to me that there transpires the structure of a genuine rite. The places touched with a kiss are the sites of psychic centres, called in Hindu science chakras; the phrase 'at the base of the spine' is to be taken literally; it is not a euphemism, and the touching is for the purpose of awakening kundalini. On the evidence of this document I would say that the rite was devised by someone familiar with Hindu scriptures (not necessarily at first hand), who incorporated the knowledge into the framework of a Western proto-Rosicrucian ritual. Even today there exist lines of initiation in which the candidate is touched on the higher chakras of breast and head, those situated lower being omitted. It is usually done with an instrument; yet the chaste Albigenses initiated with a kiss on the mouth. The rite of disrobing is also very eloquent.

How did the Templars come to their knowledge of Oriental science? It was an item in the indictment that they were in secret converse with the Assassins, an extreme Ismaili sect founded by Hassan-ben-Sabbah. This man, born in 1054, was one of the most extraordinary who ever lived and his influence upon history has never perhaps been sufficiently appreciated. A Persian, he and the poet Omar Khayyam as youths shared a tutor at the University of Naishapur. Hassan travelled widely, taking the highest initiation of the Ismaili and studying the secret doctrine in Egypt. He returned to Persia and with a small band of his faithful, Fidawi, garbed in white tunics with red girdles, took possession of a number of old forts in the mountains south of the Caspian. He took no title but was called by his people Sheikh el Djebel, Lord of the Mountains, popularly mistranslated Old Man of the Mountain.

He gave a teaching in seven initiations. In the lowest grade, his men, who were Muslims by birth, were not disturbed as to the fundamentals of their belief but merely given character training. They were not allowed to bring women within the precincts of the fort and had to live under a regime of the most austere asceticism.

Several attempts were made to dislodge the sect yet, though few in numbers, they were able to keep at bay the whole forces of the country by the assassination of key individuals who marshalled forces against them. The assassin was always chosen personally by Shekh el Djebel, and on his last day sat beside him to be briefed. His drink was drugged and presently he slept and was carried out to a walled secret garden, with lawns, fruit trees and fountains arranged to imitate the description in the Koran of Paradise. When he woke he found himself surrounded by ten beautiful women and ten beautiful youths who played upon musical instruments and offered him sweetmeats and told him that in Paradise all was permitted. He was given a complete day of bliss. In the evening he was again drugged and when he awoke was back on the sofa with Sheikh el Djebel who told him he was sending him to his death but that afterwards he would be in Paradise.

The artificial paradise was a charade for the benefit of simple souls; but the Sheikh's higher initiates were taught to look behind the literal text of the Koran for more mystical meaning; and then to transcend the Koran, to think of the Deity not as male but as androgynous creative essence; to know the sacred science of the Hindus on one hand, and the gnostics on the other; to study Greek philosophy and to pursue truth by the method of Socratic inquiry. They were taught to see morality as belonging to time and place and to regard all laws as relative. In the beginning they had had to pledge absolute obedience to Sheikh el Djebel but at the end he set them free, telling them they must acknowledge no authority in the universe save that of their own judgment.

Sheikh el Djebel was a supreme antinomian; his aim was the evolution of a society of enlightened, autonomous individuals. A vivid account of his life is given in *Le Grande Maître des Assassins* by B Bouthoul (Collin: Paris 1936) British Museum Catalogue No 20010 b 58. It has been said, and I think with reason, that the Templars were the heirs of the Assassins; the white tunic with the red cross, which they wore over their armour, recalls that of the Fidawi. The Templars, however, got the teaching not from Sheikh el Djebel but from his successors in the Lebanon; not from the primal spring but from a source already affected by contact with other cults. In parenthesis the Pope who sanctioned them was Honorius II, to whom is attributed authorship of a magical grimoire which has had an under-cover circulation down the ages.

What I doubt is whether the authorship of an injunction to practise sodomy proceeded from Sheikh el Djebel. He taught certainly, a subtle philosophy which could have been misunderstood. If he did require sodomy it would have been as the ordeal of the one of the initiations and for the purpose of taboo breaking. Loiseleur (*La Doctrine Secrète des Templiers*, Paris 1872) British Museum Catalogue No 4784. ee. 20) puts the view that it was in this sense that it was made the ordeal of entry to the Order of the Knights Templar, and that having once submitted himself the Knight was not obliged to repeat the performance.

The spitting on the cross, which shocks so much, would have been for the purpose of taboo-breaking. The Templars did not regard Jesus as the Son of God in the sense understood by Christians, but they respected him, as do the Muslims, as a prophet. They made a special cult of the two St Johns: the Baptist and the Evangelist. The Baptist, I believe they took for a hermaphrodite figure, and - I am sticking my neck out here - I would say that Leonardo da Vinci knew this tradition and that is why he painted him looking like one. (When I first saw his St Jean in the Louvre I thought it was a Bacchante.)

It is, however, probably significant that the written part of the Templar ritual of initiation contains no mention of Jesus but several of the Virgin Mary. The intuition of the reader must work upon this key. I can give only one pointer, but it is important. The intention of all cults which seem to favour male homosexuality is to exalt the female principle. It does not spring from an anti-feminine bias. Quite the contrary.

One line of occult Lodges took upon itself to bring down the successors of King Philippe. That is why Eliphas Levi sees the French Revolution as 'the vengeance of the Templars.' He asserts (*History of Magic*, p 310) that the term Jacobin was in use before the conspirators met in the Jacobin church, and referred to Jacques de Molay; I do not know how strong is his evidence for this but I think it could have had this meaning within certain circles of *illuminés* and it is certainly interesting, as he points out, that the unhappy Louis XVI was incarcerated in the old fortress of the Templars in Paris while waiting his execution.

I have said nothing of Baphomet. In King Philippe's text it is simply the head of a man with a great beard. Legends have made it the head of a goat or a bovine. A sculptured coffer, found near a Templar Commanderie in Burgundy, shows a horned, nude, bearded figure with long and pendulous womens' breasts and ample male organs. Before it, a naked man kneels in reverence while somebody else cuts the throat of a bull. There is reproduction in Loiseleur *op cit*, looking at which I suddenly wondered whether it was necessary to suppose that Baphomet and the androgyne were one. The bull may be Baphomet; its presence seems Mithraic and suggests a mixed cult. However, Elphas Levi, on whose work Victor and Crowley based themselves, took Baphomet to be Pan, and for the frontispiece of his *Rituel*, Levi drew his own idea of the symbol; a bearded he-goat with woman's breasts, seated cross-legged yogic posture, a five-pointed star upon the forehead, the apex up, to show that it is holy, a blazing torch between the horns, and eagle's wings; the lower limbs are swathed for modesty, while from the private regions rises a caduceus, symbolizing sublimation. In his text, Levi explains that he has tried to convey the idea of androgyny in an inoffensive manner by making one of the arms (softly rounded) obviously a woman's and the other (with bulging biceps) a man's.

Properly understood, he says, it is 'an innocent and even pious hieroglyph.' He asserts that the name Baphomet requires to be read backwards, when it resolves itself into the abbreviations, TEM OHP AB standing for *Templi Omnium Hominum Pacis Abbas* (the father of the temple of peace for all men. This seems tortured. Montague Summers favours a derivation from Greek *Baphe* and *Metis*, meaning 'Absorption into Wisdom. Gerald Yorke prefered Persian *bahumet*, 'a calf'.

One evening in 1912 Crowley was visited at his flat in Victoria Street by Theodor Reuss (Merlin) head of a German Order entitled the Ordo

Templi Orientis which, founded in 1902, claimed to continue the original Order of the Knights Templar, re-invigorated by new teaching from the Orient.

Reuss reproached Crowley with having come near to divulging the secret of the Ordo Templi Orientis in one of his books and said that, if he had arrived at it on his own, he had better come in formally so that everything should be in order; he would then receive from it a charter which would make him head of the Order in England. Accordingly, while Crowley was on the continent in 1913, he was initiated into the Ordo Templi Orientis, taking as his name Baphomet. It was agreed that the English Order be called the Mysteria Mystica Maxima. When Orders of this sort bud, the new Order is normally independent. Crowley did not need two Orders so he fused the Mysteria Mystica Maxima with the Argentinum Astrum, while retaining the Golden Dawn ritual and scheme of initiations. It is significant that he gave to the homosexual act the title of Rite XI, eleven being the number to which all the equations add and therefore of the Great Work, to which he now summoned Victor to join him in Paris, where somebody had lent them a flat.

13
The Paris Working

I had brought the story to date when I received from Gerald Yorke *The Paris Working*. I held in my hands at last the record of the strange homosexual procedure undertaken by Vicky and Crowley which was regarded as their magnum opus. It was bound in two fascicules; the first was entitled:

The

Book of the High Magic Art

that was worked by

Frater O S V 6=5

and Frater L T 2=9

The Paris Working

Jan-Feb 1914, EV

This is document C in the account of the progress of

NEMO to TO MEGA THERION

OSV was Crowley; LT (Lampada Tradam) was Vicky. This fascicule contained the record of what they actually did. The other was entitled:

Esoteric Record of the

Workings

of January, 1914, EV

and contained the questions they asked when at the height of ecstasy and the answers they believed they received.

The preamble to the first, dated 4.30 of the afternoon of the last day of the year 1913, explains that a 'casual' act of sex between them 'produced a great marvel', and this, together with the realization that it was close upon the 600th anniversary of the martyrdom of Jacques de Molay, gave them the idea the time was ripe for starting upon the Great Work.

The text bore notes in the hand of Gerald Yorke who assisted me by sending me further notes. I quote one of these as it stands though I think he has made a slight slip:

The Latin hexameters declaimed at the moment of orgasm were taken from a genuine Latin source and were not composed by AC. He was trying to see if they worked. The object of the repetition was that the will or mind of both partners be concentrated on the God at the vital moment. The whole thing was done religiously rather than sexually.

When I say I think Gerald Yorke makes a slip it is because it appears from the text that the hexameters were composed by Walter Duranty, then foreign correspondent for the *New York Times*, who died in 1957. What I think likely is that Crowley and Victor supposed the rituals to have an origin anterior to the Knights Templar; and that, supposing they were performed to verse, Crowley got Duranty, who was apparently a better Latin scholar, to make up something for the purpose. This would fit with what Vicky himself told me, that they made up a ritual along the lines of those they imagined to have been practised in antiquity, and that the chief clues they had came through Roman texts though they believed the traditions they glimpsed through them went back to an antiquity far more remote, and to a culture which seemed to have been more general to the countries round the mediterranean basin.

The record begins with Crowley's reflections at 4.30. I think Victor and he can only have joined forces after Christmas or they would have started at the Winter Solstice instead of the profane New Year. Crowley decided that while the whole Work was for Pan it would avail nothing without Wisdom; Hermes therefore should be first invoked. They must have had an evening meal and then pushed furniture out of the way so as to make a space to be considered the Temple. They laid out incense, fire (I suppose this means a lighted candle), bread, wine, a chain, a scourge, dagger and oil. At 11.30 they started. After Crowley struck two strokes on a bell, Victor danced the Banishing Ritual. They then recited together the portion of The Golden Dawn ritual beginning: 'Hail Asi! Hail, Hoor-Apep!' In more usual spelling, this means: 'Hail, Osiris! Hail, Horus-Apep!' (Apep is the name of the great Snake.)

Next they performed an invocation to Thoth (the Egyptian form of Hermes.) Taking the instruments from the altar Crowley scourged Victor, cut a cross over his heart and bound the chain round his forehead.

Gerald Yorke wrote to me that at this stage of the ceremony clothes, or rather robes, were generally worn, and the scourging would have been done over the fabric, the cutting not so deep as to draw blood. These gestures were performed symbolically to concord with the words:

> *The scourge, the dagger and the chain*
> *Cleanse my body, breast and brain!*

Crowley then anointed the wounds, saying:

> *Let the oil*
> *Balance, assain, assoil.*

After this they uttered together words which will almost be recognised by those belonging to Masonic, Martinist and possibly other Hermetic Orders, words in which the immortal soul confesses its ignorance and its dilemma:

> *I do not know who I am.*
> *I do not know whence I come.*
> *I do not know where I go.*
> *I seek, but what I do not know.(1)*

They had endeavoured to time the ritual so that the preparations should be completed by midnight, and succeeded so well that the last hours of the old year were striking as they uttered the words that were to cóincide with the physical act:

> *Jungitur in vati vates, rex inclyte rhabdou*
> *Hermes tu venias, verba nefanda ferens.(2)*

Victor had to perform the active part. As he was too nervous and excited, it came to nothing. Crowley said he saw thousands of yellow and gold snakes, all writhing in the form of caducei.

There being nothing further they could do they closed the Temple again, with proper ceremony, finishing at 1.40 am. Victor then reverted to his role of scribe and in the dawn wrote up the record, the first of the New Year, 1914.

They made *The Second Working* on the evening of the same day, opening the Temple at 11.20pm, reciting this time three of Crowley's poems, including the invocation of Mercury from the *Rites of Eleusis*. This brought them back by 11.40, to the versicle: Jungitur in vati vates, etc...

This time there was no failure on Victor's part. He was now supposedly possessed by the God and Crowley put questions to him:

The Paris Working

CROWLEY: Are we working right?

VICTOR: No

CROWLEY: What's wrong?

VICTOR: The time and, to a lesser extent, the place.

CROWLEY: What is the right time?

VICTOR: Three hours before dawn.

CROWLEY: Does this apply to Mercury alone, or to all the gods?

VICTOR: To Mercury alone.

CROWLEY: Are we to invoke Mercury again?

VICTOR: Yes.

CROWLEY: Tomorrow?

VICTOR: No.

CROWLEY: When then?

VICTOR: On the day of the full moon.

CROWLEY: What God shall we invoke tomorrow?

VICTOR: Thoth.

CROWLEY: Thoth *is* Mercury.

VICTOR: You will get another aspect.

CROWLEY: Shall we not use the same versicle?

VICTOR: It does not matter.

CROWLEY: Shall I make statues of all the gods?

VICTOR: No.

CROWLEY: Shall I make tablets of all the gods?

VICTOR: Yes.

CROWLEY: What tablets?

VICTOR: Tablets with names only.

CROWLEY: In what order shall we invoke the gods?

VICTOR: The proper order is: Venus, Mercury, Jupiter, Luna, Sol.

CROWLEY: Will he help in geomancy?

VICTOR: Yes

CROWLEY: And also in the conduct of affairs?

VICTOR: In some, not all.

The Magical Dilemma of Victor Neuburg

CROWLEY: In business?

VICTOR: In some business.

CROWLEY: Which ones?

VICTOR: Those in connection with the writing of books, with money and with love.

CROWLEY: How can one invoke Mercury better?

VICTOR: Use a gold pentragram, placing the same in a prominent position; drink yellow wine and eat fish before the ceremony. Let the clock be removed.

CROWLEY: Can you suggest any improvement in the ceremonies, especially that of Jupiter?

VICTOR: Scarlet and silver should be worn, and the crown by OSV, LT is to wear the scarlet robe. Violets are to be strewn and trodden with bare feet.

CROWLEY: Give a distinct proof of your presence appreciable to the intelligence of OSV.

VICTOR: Let the wand, or one, become nine, this is the sign of Priapus but afterwards nothing.

CROWLEY: I understand and agree the proof.

VICTOR: Shall I let him take full possession now?

CROWLEY: Yes.

VICTOR: I am going...Yes. What do you want to know now? There are other things I can tell you, or else ask me questions.

CROWLEY: Tell.

VICTOR: You will receive good news in respect of money on the eleventh of January in the forenoon. Fra LT will be concerned with it; it will be quite unexpected. Money will be given by someone to whom LT introduced OSV. A change in OSV's affairs in February.

CROWLEY: I am going to ask a very important question. Concentrate hard. N.C.G.M.H.D? (this meant when would he become a Magus?)

VICTOR: L.P. L is 50; and P is 6.(3)

CROWLEY: Fifty-six what?

VICTOR: I don't know...Wait...Hours? I am not quite sure, but it is connected with time. The ceremonies should be done every other night.

There follows a long and rather nebulous speech by Crowley. Then the Dialogue resumes. They have changed roles, Victor now questioning.

VICTOR: When will the reconciliation of which I am thinking take place?

CROWLEY: There is no real enmity, it is a mere tiff or misunderstanding.

The Paris Working

VICTOR: When will the pressure of which I am thinking be relieved?

CROWLEY: The answer to both these questions is Death but I don't know in what sense.

VICTOR: Will the most important prediction of December be fulfilled?

CROWLEY: Better than you think.

VICTOR: When?

CROWLEY: It is imminent.

VICTOR: Conventionally?

CROWLEY: Like the sword of Damocles it impends always but may never fall. The answer, however, that I get is five months.

VICTOR: Satisfactory?

CROWLEY: I haven't got that...

There follows another exceedingly long speech by Crowley, mainly concerned with the nature of Mercury; some of it is not without interest, but it could mostly have come out of the books with which they were familiar. He says the association of Mercury and Christ is 'absolutely new' to him, yet I could have given him the source from which I believe he drew unconsciously; *The Secret Doctrine* by H P Blavatsky (vol 5, page 369 in the Adyar Edition.)

They closed the Temple at 2am.

I shall summarize the following workings fairly briefly.

The Third Working, Saturday, January 3.

The Temple was opened at midnight and they finished that part of the ritual consisting of the preliminary recitations by 0.57am. After the act Crowley made a very long speech about semen and Mercury. He said Hermes should be invoked on eight consecutive nights, beginning with a Wednesday. 'He says we should feed in greater abundance. He will protect us.' They should invoke him on the morrow (Sunday) by geomancy, without rite. Beginning on Monday they should invoke Jupiter for four consecutive nights. They would get from Jupiter not so much information as aid. 'It is very important to have banquets...What fools to bother about the room, you don't think I am in the room do you? He wants us to overcome shame generally and says, "There is no shame about me, is there?" He suggests an obvious method which I blush to repeat.' There is an asterisk here, and a note corresponding to it: 'A holy act before the world. (This was done at the house of the lay-sister JC [Jane Cheron]. The Art-Bachelor W D [Walter Duranty] was the victim.)' I ask myself if Victor knew, and if this was a point at which he drew the line.

Finally, 'He again exhibits his contempt for the art of conversation by making a suggestion with which, owing to the lateness of the hour, we comply only in symbolic form.'

It was 2.15 am when they closed the temple.

Later in the morning Crowley woke and, noticing that the previous night's record had not been written up, woke Victor and told him to finish it. This led to 'two fine fights.' Probably Vicky thought Crowley might have let him have his sleep out which is why he showed, as Crowley complains, 'ill temper' throughout the day. Crowley was suffering from a cold. In consequence they did not work, not even the geomancy.

On Monday morning it occurred to Crowley that Hermes's suggestion (evidently that they should make a further sex act) was meant to be obeyed; 'The attempt to replace the real thing by its symbol had led to (a) O S V having a bad cold which confined him to his bed, (b) the continued ill-temper of LT' and other misfortunes.

I draw attention to Crowley's use of the word 'led'. Crowley and Vicky had set out to free men's minds from the superstitions of orthodox religion. The antique Gods have now become as tyrannical as Jehovah! How *could* Crowley imagine Hermes would punish him with a cold in the nose because of failure to perform an act of sex?

The omission was, however, made good at 12.15 mid-day.

The God was questioned in the usual way. Crowley, as the medium, spoke at great length. There occurs this passage: 'Respectability is the greatest of all blinds. The general key in reading ancient documents of a magical nature is to suspect the worst.' (It could certainly be applied to the reading of Crowley's!) He is told that he needs the devotion of four men, all deformed, and finds Victor qualified, having 'spinal curvature, variococele, bent arm.'

Eventually they closed the Temple but sat talking. Victor became entranced and said the Rite was unloosing a huge force. Twenty people working at it would be very dangerous. International complications were to be feared. It was important not to initiate into this any persons under the age of thirty. The dangers of the rite appalled him. 'Those who adopt this Rite will either succeed completely or fail utterly. There is no middle path, for it is impossible to escape the ring of divine Karma created.'

Crowley then became entranced and said their roles should not be interchangeable in any series of rites. He would only assume the active role in the invocation of feminine deities (they never did invoke any). The supreme Rite would consist of the immolation of a willing victim, preferably a girl, whose parts would be offered to the Deities interested.

Coming out of the trance he agreed with Victor that these last recommendations partook of the character of Black Magic and were not to be followed. They thought it significant that they had closed the Temple when this came through, which would explain his having been vulnerable and therefore unprotected. Despite this warning experience Victor now went into a trance. Crowley questioned him about some practical matters.

Hermes returned and kissed Victor on the lips, navel and phallus.

Crowley continued asking questions and Victor prophesied concerning himself. 'LT will be released within two months from everything; he will get into a new stratum of karma. He is going away eastwards. In June he marries but returns to the great work in September.' (Against this Crowley has written at a later date. 'All quite wrong without a single exception. Its conditions are quite altered, LT having acquired a great fortune.') Victor continued: 'Let OSV not allow 493 to enter into Scorpio'.

CROWLEY: What is 493?

VICTOR: Connected with Water and with Cremers. It is she that stirs up strife.

CROWLEY: What is 493?

VICTOR: It is connected with OSV's dealings with Cremers. OSV has told her too much.

CROWLEY: What is 493?

VICTOR: A book of a Mercurial nature stolen by Cremers. Don't let that get into Scorpio. Cremers will either write to LT or communicate indirectly with him. [It is curious to find Victor speaking of Cremers in this strain: later they were friends - but it was just after this they came in contact.]

Hermes gave further instructions. Crowley was always to be the first to skry and Victor should always scribe. Victor should always take the masculine role. (Hermes seems to have forgotten this had been agreed already.) Excepting for the rites of Hermes, Rites were never to be performed on more than six consecutive nights and four was a better number. They should never begin earlier than 9.0, or last more than three and a half hours.

The Fourth Working, Monday, January 5.

They opened the Temple at 9pm, and, contrary to the principle enunciated in the afternoon, Crowley took the active role, exceptionally, probably because Victor was tired after the afternoon's exertions. As they were invoking Jupiter they used for it a different verse:

> Haud secus ac puerum spumanti semine vates
> Lustrat, dum gaudens accipit alter acquas;
> Sparge, precor, servis, hominum rex atque deorum
> Jupiter omnipotens, aurea dona, tuis.(4)

As Crowley was suffering badly from his cold they closed the Temple at 10, though they sat talking until 1.20 when Victor had a vision of Jupiter and of the words: *Via est hodie. Nomina sanctissimorum in felicitate habent viam. Deus dedit signum in via.*

The Fifth Working, Tuesday, January 6.

The temple was opened at 9.30. Victor returning to his usual role the Rite was performed 'ut ordinatur.' The Temple was closed at 10.30.

The Sixth Working, Wednesday, January 7.

The Temple was opened at 9pm. Crowley reproached Victor for not keeping up his strength and taxed him with having 'failed in due banqueting'. The Rite was performed in another manner and the Temple closed at 9.45.

The Seventh Working, Thursday, January 8.

The Temple was opened at 10pm. Crowley was feverish and they closed at 11.20 when Walter Duranty, the lay sister Jane Cheron and somebody called 'Sir Lionel' called. They talked until late.

The Paris Working

The morning's post brought Crowley three Jupitarian things, a letter from his lawyers, a pot of opium, and a set of proofs from his printers.

The Eighth Working, Sunday, January 11.

They invoked Hermes and got 'a good result.'

On Monday Victor was indisposed. Perhaps he had caught Crowley's cold.

On Tuesday afternoon they had to give the Mass of the Phoenix in the house of a friend, PDF.

On Wednesday and Thursday Victor was still indisposed. Crowley realized that further Workings would have to be put off until the next Monday, and took him for a walk in the 'forest'. (Presumably this was one of the several woods in the environs of Paris.) They both felt they benefitted from this day in the open.

The Ninth Working, Monday, January 19.

They opened the Temple at 9.45pm and invoked Jupiter under his Egyptian form as Ammon, with the versicle:
> *Per regni sancti signum da Jupiter Ammon*
> *Da nobis plena munera plena manu.(5)*

During the final recitation Victor, kneeling at the altar, beheld the colossal form of Jupiter, *manibus plenis.* They closed at 12.30 and considered that this, though short was one of the best workings they had made to Jupiter.

The Tenth Working, Tuesday, January 20.

They opened at 11.30 and closed at 12.15, die Mercurii: 'The Ceremony as usual.'

The following day 'the brethren were out of harmony but conquered the feeling of animosity by Will,' and after the banquet repaired to the temple.

The Eleventh Working, Wednesday, January 21.

They opened at 11.00. After the act Victor obtained a message that the Gods wished to regain their dominion upon earth and had chosen Crowley and himself to be fiery arrows shot in the war against the slave-gods. A fourfold sacrifice was demanded 'and that an act of cruelty'. This was apparently executed but its nature is only described by some symbols and Hebrew letters. The Temple was closed at 1.45 and at 1.55 Victor was still lying entranced. By 2.0 he was sufficiently recovered to murmur, 'Telestai' (it is over.) Crowley noted that this was the formula of 7=4.

All the following day, according to Crowley, Victor was 'overshadowed by Jupiter. The world about him appears a vision of the future. His eyes are dilated; he cannot read; his manner is as one stupefied or entranced.'

The Twelfth Working, Thursday, January 22.

They opened at 9.45. - all the invocations from now on are to Jupiter - and closed at 11pm

By Friday morning Crowley was perplexed by the results of these workings. Five people who were to have come to see him in Paris had all failed to do so and both business and private letters remained unanswered. He mentioned this to Victor, who told him that with regard to letters he had had the same experience. The response of Hermes had been direct. They supposed 'that Jupiter being a slow and steady god moves not so easily but with more power.' On Saturday the drought broke and letters and visitors appeared.

The Thirteenth Working, Monday, January 26.

They opened at 11.30. After the act and a recitation from one of Crowley's poems, Crowley 'became inspired in a Terpsichorean manner,' and did the dance of a 'seductive fugitive order'. They closed at 2.0 but sat talking.

Crowley said he had been a priestess(6) in a Greek civilization of Oriental type. Victor tuning in, said this was Crete and he saw a green figure dancing round an altar. The ceremony was one of initiation and it was a temptation dance.

The Paris Working

Crowley said when he had been this girl his name was Aia. The temple had a black marble floor, pillars and mirrors among which she turned. Victor came in. He was a handsome youth with a square golden beard and his name was Mardocles. The candidate had to face an ordeal by temptation; he had either to remain cool and unmoved or else capture and rape her however hard she fought. Failure to do either one or the other was punished by castration and death. Mardocles was unable to remain indifferent but, wrestling with her, was reluctant to be brutal and of his tenderness spared her, so that the penalty was forfeit.

Yet because he was a favourite of the high priest and his father was a very rich corn merchant it was not exacted. He was merely expelled from the temple, Aia with him. He was then about 24 or 25 and resented her because she had ruined his career; yet because he realised he had ruined hers also he was too chivalrous to leave her. They went penniless into the town, and afterwards had further misadventures.

Crowley said to Victor: 'I am always unlucky for you, you know; you always have to sacrifice everything for my love. You don't want to in the least; that is because we both have hold of the wrong end of the stick. If only I could leave you and you could love me. It would be lucky. But that apparently has never happened. Mutual indifference and mutual passion, and so on.'

The Fourteenth Working, Tuesday, January 27.

They opened at Midnight and closed at 1.07. During the day they went to the house of Jane Cheron and smoked the opium she gave them. This rested them but afterwards they felt unwell.

The Fifteenth Working, Wednesday, January 28.

The Temple was opened at 11.15. 'The versicle was prolonged and very quiet, probably owing to the experience of the afternoon.' However, the atmosphere was excellent. They closed at 12.10.

The Sixteenth Working, Thursday, January 29.

They opened the Temple at 10.20 and the effects of the opium persisting the *Haud secus* was as on the previous evening. Afterwards the God demanded blood so Crowley cut the figure 4(7) on Victor's breast, collected the blood and offered it at the altar. Victor then became inspired and 'did a wonderful dance', which Crowley sat down to watch. Becoming entranced, Crowley said that at the four workings next week a sparrow was to be slain each night before the physical act and its blood used to trace the figure 4 on Victor's heart, right breast, left breast and navel, its body being afterwards burnt. From Sunday midnight until Thursday midnight no food was to be taken excepting at the banquets and nothing to be drunk at all 'save only pure water'. The Temple was closed at midnight.

The Seventeenth Working, Monday, February 2.

They opened the Temple at 10.30. Crowley dedicated the first of the sparrows to Jupiter and set it free. Victor then cut the figure 4 on his right breast, shedding his own blood instead of the sparrow's. He was afterwards too exhausted to speak and though they closed the Temple at 12.50 was still in this condition at 1am. Crowley doubted whether they had done well to avoid literal compliance with the command that a sparrow should be sacrificed. Victor must have interceded for the sparrow's lives.

The Eighteenth Working, Tuesday, February 3.

The Temple was opened at 10.30 and the usual act was followed by one performed in another way. The Temple was closed at 1.45.

During the day which followed Crowley had a feverish attack resembling influenza. He obtained more opium from Jane Cheron; it made him feel better though afterwards he thought he had taken too much of it.

The Nineteenth Working, Wednesday, February 4.

The temple was opened at 10pm and closed at 11. Nothing is said about this operation or what happened to the sparrow. I think they must all have been allowed to fly out of the window. Crowley now had fever and bronchitis and retired to his bed for the next four days.

The Twenty-first Working, Monday, February 9.

The Temple was opened 'mentally' at 9.10. What I take this to mean is that Crowley did it from his bed instead of moving around the room to perform the proper gestures. He appears, however, to have got up for the essential act which, in spite of his illness 'went exceedingly well'. They closed at 9.25, and when he took his temperature again he found it had gone down by 0.4 degrees C !!!! (The four exclamation marks are his.)

The Twenty-second Working, Tuesday February 10.

Crowley had recovered, and they opened the Temple at 9.30. The *Haud secus* was 'brilliant and inspired and the result overwhelming - a glow of stupendous success.'

The Twenty-third Working, Wednesday, February 11.

The time of opening and closing the temple is omitted, surely by an oversight. At 3.18am Victor received a message for Crowley that he should go to the house of Hathor for AG (whoever or whatever this is). Victor was more exhausted than on any of the previous occasions.

The Twenty-fourth Working, Thursday, February 12.

The ceremony was very short. They opened the Temple at 6.15 and closed it at 7.0.

One has the impression they were both, by this time, really tired.

The Paris Working was finished.

Victor performed divination by *Thelema*; that is he opened Crowley's book at random and put his finger in it, without looking, and it was seen to be pointing to the line: 'I am thou, and the Pillar is established in the Void.'

So ended what must surely be one of the strangest religious exercises in history.

(1) When I first read this apostrophe it seemed to me like something extracted from *The Book of the Dead*. It is not, however, from *The Papyrus of Ani*. I read through the whole to see whether these lines are in it, and they do not occur. Nevertheless, I would think they are extracted from something authentic.

(2) *Seer is joined with Seer; do thou, Hermes, renowned king of the rod, Come, bearing the word not to be spoken.*

(3) Against this is a note which must have been added by Crowley some years later: 'PS Time from December 3, 1909, to October 12, 1915, is 6 years less 50 days!!!' The former date was that of the act on Dal'leh Addin after which he thought he became a Master of the Temple; the latter is the date on which, while in America, he imagined himself to have become a Magus. I can only say these tremendous pretensions seem to me the proof he was living in a completely delusional world.

(4) *As the seer with seed lustrates him who receives,*
So do thou, I pray thee, king of men and gods,
Almighty Jupiter, shower thine own with gold.
(5) *By the sign of the sacred kingdom, give, Jupiter Ammon,*
Give us full gifts with full hand.

(6) There is nothing peculiar in Crowley's thinking he had had an incarnation as a woman. The doctrine of reincarnation includes the idea of sex change from one incarnation to another; the most usually held belief being that incarnations are taken in sets of seven of one sex and seven of the other, alternately, unless there be some reason to vary the pattern; homosexuality being more likely to take place at the beginning or end of a series than in the middle of one.

(7) 4 is the numerator of Jupiter in the Kabbalistic system.

14
The End of It

The reason I had wanted to see the text of *The Paris Working* was that I hoped to be able to discover from it what Victor and Crowley were trying to do. Assuming that they saw themselves as continuants of the Templars, in what sense did they interpret Templar practice?

I recalled Heim's words, 'They played upon the subtle currents in the spine.' This referred, obviously, to Kundalini; but generally it is the celibate condition which is held to favour the ascension of Kundalini, the reason being that the energy is not drained away. There exists, however, a branch of yoga which permits an embrace without emission because the erotic tension forces the ascension if coupled with aspiration. The partner is always referred to as a woman but I thought Vicky and Crowley might have made a homosexual adaptation of the principle. Inspection of the text made it clear that this was not so.

The questions they put to the supernal beings they invoked were of a triviality which beggars description, and I did not believe in the authenticity of the communications. These came from their own unconscious.

Gerald Yorke came to see me and began a delicate interview by saying, 'These rituals were performed with a serious intent.' I nodded gravely and he continued, 'This was not two homosexuals playing. You must understand what they were trying to do.'

'That's what I am trying to understand,' I said.

'They were using the sex act as a kind of starter to get themselves on to the astral plane,' he said.

'But Victor Neuburg never had any difficulty in getting on to the astral plane,' I said. 'He didn't need anything like this to sent him there.'

'It gave them an initial fillip,' said Yorke. 'It was an experimental attempt to invoke Hermes and Jupiter, using the sex act to inflame the seer.'

I said, 'The only thing that distresses me is that they petitioned tl gods for money.'

He started slightly. 'Surely, only by surfeit! Casually, at the end, use up any surfeit of the power brought down.'

This did not seem quite to meet the case as the petition was built in the Latin. Yorke agreed that the 'communications' were worthles 'But', he said, 'The value of the ritual to the participants should not l judged solely in relation to the communications.' Because it wa dedicated to the gods, he added, it had a purity which could l approached by no earthly experience of sex.

'It's a pre-Christian technique,' he continued. 'Instead of praying t the god you said you were the god. The first step is to imagine tl god. If you have any power of visualization you do see him. The you have to imagine him moving, coming towards you, becomin you, speaking through you. It is the god speaking. The idea is that you do it properly you are really inspired.'

I believed this might have been an Egyptian technique. In *The Book* the Dead*, the deceased is made to say at his post mortem initiation, am Osiris'.

Yorke continued, 'Rosicrucianism was the ancient ritual with sex le out under the Christian influence. Crowley's Argentinum Astrur was Rosicrucianism with sex put back.'

I am not sure that it was only Crowley who put back sex into Rosicru cianism. I have been told of a Frenchman called Sar Peladan wh during the first decade of the century and up to 1914, at least, cor ducted a circle in Paris at which the books of Eliphas Levi wer studied and initiations conferred. My informant was Hayter Prestor who went through the first of these and found he had at one point t lie with a woman. He did not tell me if the group had a name but have been shown recently by Anthony d'Offay two handwritte letters, signed Sar Peladan. There is nothing in them about sex bu they are on notepaper headed *Rosae Crucis Templi Ordo*.

Richard Burton (Terminal Essay to *The Arabian Nights*) writes 'I Rome as in Egypt the temples of Isis were centres of sodomy,' but imagine he had in mind the Egypt which was contemporary with th grandeur of Rome.

Because Yorke spoke almost as Crowley's representative I contende with him. I respected Yorke's loyalty to 'old Crow' as he called him, (The first syllable of Crowley's name is, indeed, pronounced as *crow*, the big black bird; I mention this because I have heard moderns, who had had no contact with the Crowley circle, pronounce it as in *crown*.) Crowley was older when Yorke knew him than when Victor did. Yorke, like Victor before him, had left Crowley, and thought he was a pseudo-Messiah, yet in retrospect he felt an indebtedness to him which he did not wish to repudiate. 'He did me good,' he said, to my surprise. And I recognized the accents of truth when he added, 'I still have an affection for the old sinner. I'm sure Vicky kept that, too.'

He asked me if I would let him see what I wrote about the magic, in case there was anything in Crowley's scripts which I did not understand. Later, I did let him see, and he sent me several sheets of meticulous notes, some of which I have incorporated.

Before he left, that afternoon, he made an endeavour to sum up. 'The object of any ritual of this sort of communion. There are only two basic ways in which you can embody the idea of communion. You can eat something, which is considered as being the God. Or, you can do something sexual. If you aren't going to do either, then you have to think of something else to do. You've got to make a gesture of some sort, which stands for the idea.'

'You can light a candle,' I said.

'It's all a question of the extent to which you can refine your symbolism, without losing the intensity of the experience', he answered thoughtfully.

'Actually, you don't need a gesture, of any sort,' I said.

'Then it wouldn't any longer be ritual magic.' He said he had, in fact, given up ritual magic, and had become a Buddhist. He was merely trying to explain the principle of the magic which Crowley had taught. 'I am not contending that it was a specially good way. But it is a way, which is valid,' he said.

I was impressed by the bearing of Yorke, and also by the readiness with which all the men connected with Crowley and his Argentinum Astrum had made themselves accessible. Everyone had come forward. I had only to let it be known I was interested in the Crowley-Neuburg magic and there was a willingness to help.

Summing up, it would I think be entirely false to consider *The Paris Working* as an operation in Black Magic. It may be questioned whether an act so gross as that of which the Rite consisted can be hallowed completely, but their intention was to hallow it. As a White operation it would be vitiated by the appeal for gold in the invocation of Jupiter; Crowley vitiated it by the materialism of his concerns. But they fenced the Temple with holy symbols in the Banishing Ritual performed at the beginning and were horrified when, at one moment, they thought they were receiving instructions of an evil or Black nature. It was meant to be White; but it was impure.

What I still did not know was what caused the break between them. To *The Paris Working* there is a *post scriptum* by Crowley that Victor 'became Jupiter the bestower, and many unworthy folk became his guests.' In other words, Victor was generous with his money but spent it on other people. This is the last reference to Victor which I find in any of the Crowley papers. Though pages of his autobiography are devoted to his quarrels with people he knew less intimately, Victor disappears from the story without explanation.

Victor must have returned to London without delay. Preston knew he had been to Paris with Crowley but did not feel that he was away long. In May 1914, at Victor's, Preston had a violent row with Crowley. He knew Victor's family were desperate about the association. 'His Uncle Edward became apoplectic if Crowley was mentioned and his mother was in tears.' Perhaps because Preston was the only friend of Victor's they knew who did not belong to Crowley's circle they made him party to their distress. 'They were heavy, overeating, orthodox Jews,' he said. 'How they produced *him* is a biological mystery.'

From Mrs (Joyce) Saunders I learned that Victor had accepted an invitation from her mother, Olivia Haddon, to spend the summer with them at Branscombe, near Seaton, South Devon, where they had taken a row of three cottages. One of the cottages was taken by Cremers. Cremers used to call Crowley 'that impostor' and 'that charlatan'. She and Victor would sit up talking after the rest of them had gone to bed. They were all there when the war broke out on August 4, Cremers's birthday. They were sitting playing cards when somebody came in and told them.

The End of It

Cremers remained at Branscombe for a long time but Victor left about the end of September, giving Joyce as a parting gift a book of selections from Browning inscribed with the date: Seaton, Devon, September 23, 1914. It must have been between this date and October 24 when Crowley left for America, that Victor saw him for the last time. It is my belief that Victor's feeling that he must make the break with Crowley dated from earlier in the year. Victor had rushed back from Paris with almost indecent haste after the conclusion of the Working, apparently shunning Crowley's company in favour of others, which caused Crowley to take the unusual step of coming to Victor's room to look for him. Victor had made himself even more inaccessible by going to Devon. Crowley was probably afraid of Cremers. Victor had got himself a demon protector - perhaps nothing less would have sufficed.

On the positive side Crowley was a man of erudition, and I should feel at fault were I to omit tribute to the depth, in many ways, of his esotericism. I can understand why he held Victor's respect for so long. On the other hand he suffered from megalomania and this pulled all his concepts out of shape. Also, he did physical things, homosexual practices apart, of so revolting an order that I have thought it preferable not to repeat the examples I have been given. And he exploited others upon every plane, material, emotional and psychic. He had a sponge-like activity, unconsciously exercised at the level where it hurt his victims most, though conscious of the financial.

He was not a black Magician, neither was he a charlatan in the vulgar sense; but his personality being so out of hand, he was an impossible teacher.

Victor was brave enough to see him in London, and tell him he could go with him no further, and disavowed the oath he had taken at his reception into the Argentinum Astrum.

Then Crowley ritually cursed him.

15
The Army and After

After Crowley cursed him he had a nervous breakdown. The next two years are a blank, but Cammell has in his possession a drawing of him by Howard Sommerville dated 1915 and inscribed on the back, 'To my sweet Leech, Ernest Thomas Jensen, Esquire, M.D. From his defaulting poet-patient, Victor B.Neuburg, XIII; XII: MCMXVI.'

By the following year he was in the Army. I wrote to the War Office and received a reply saying there was a record in the medal rolls of the British War and Victory Medals of the 1914-18 war of one being awarded to S/355614 Private Victor B Neuburg, R A S C, but that his personal documents were assumed to have been among those destroyed at the records depository at Walworth when it was bombed during World War II.

One of the replies to my appeal in the *Daily Telegraph*, however, was from a Mr H.F.Burgess who had been one of a contingent which sailed from Southampton on September 19, 1917, arriving at Le Havre on the 20th.

We had to march from the boat to the camp and during the march I became conscious of a ludicrous figure not far ahead of me - ludicrous because he was carrying a rifle over his shoulder (as we all were) but in addition he was using a walking stick. I then saw that he limped badly. Before very long, someone in authority noticed this too and found him a place on the baggage wagon.

This, needless to say, was Victor Neuburg. On September 21 they arrived at Rouen where they remained fourteen days after which they were divided up.

I found that Neuburg was in the same contingent as I, destined for Abbeville, where we were posted to the No 9 Detail Issue Store.

They arrived at Abbeville on October 1. By an extraordinary coincidence Hayter Preston had been at Abbeville since the previous year and was Orderly Room Sergeant. A Sergeant Major gave him the nominal roll of a new Detachment of details which had arrived. There were about thirty names on it, and as his eye ran down the list it fell on Neuburg, V.B. The spirit of fantasy seized him, as he told me, and he said to a Corporal standing by, 'Arrest that man! I want him brought to me.'

A few moments later poor Victor was brought in between guards. Seeing Preston, and realizing the joke, his relief was so great he burst into tears.

Preston was able to keep Victor employed on light camp duties. 'He was only kept together by string and sealing wax. He could never shave without cutting himself and so he always looked like Death from a Thousand Cuts. He had no manual dexterity. His movements were not synchronized. His hands and feet worked from two different dynamos. He was the walking mockery of the entire Army system and everything it was meant to be.'

Neuburg was given the job of lighting the Orderly Room fire each morning. He was invariably found before the empty grate reading the newspaper with which he was supposed to be lighting the fire.

It was at Abbeville that Victor translated the 'Chant Royal d'Horace' from the Old French of the sixteenth century while Hayter Preston took it down on the typewriter. In the latter part of October 1917 Preston was posted to Italy and took with him his carbon copy of Victor's 'Chant Royal of Horace'. But before he went he sought repatriation for Victor.

This was evidently achieved. A Mr A.R.Rothwell, replying to my letter in the *Daily Telegraph*, remembers Victor at the Army Convalescent Camp in Neanda, Cornwall. Victor gave him a snapshot of himself taken in the grounds of an army hospital in France and two books in the Mark Rutherford series inscribed: *From this poor Army Service Corps*. Then Victor was moved to a convalescent camp near Eastbourne.

By the autumn of 1919 Victor was out of the Army and living with his Aunt Ti in the village of Steyning, nestling at the foot of Chanctonbury Ring. Vine Cottage, their home, the front of which was covered with a real vine, was, except for an extension, a genuine Tudor house of such charm that a photograph of it adorned carriages of the Southern railway. Preston was now demobbed also, and Victor suggested he should join them. Preston was in at the birth of the Vine Press therefore. It was he who discovered the curious font with the wide W and linked double O which helped to make its productions distinctive; they got it from Millar & Richards, Edinburgh; the other big purchase was a hand-press for Victor to work. The foundation was financed by Aunt Ti.

One day when Victor and Preston were looking at a railway embankment, Victor said, 'Crowley murdered Ione de Forest.'

This came quite out of the blue. Having regard to the suicide notes which she left, accusing Merton (1) I do not think it can be true; but that he said it showed the direction in which his mind had been working. Victor had been completely mystified and could only think that during the week-end while he waited for her in Essex, Crowley had bullied or magicked her to death.(2)

Victor now talked to Preston more than he had done previously. He felt Crowley had ruined his life.

In January 1920, Crowley returned from America. Victor and Preston read it in the paper. 'Victor was terrified of Crowley!' Preston said. 'He was afraid he would come to Steyning to look for him.' Preston kept vigilant watch until they read he had gone to France. Yet Preston recognized the pull which existed between them. 'There was an umbilical cord,' he said. 'Crowley was mother to him. And the cord was made of the Dionysiac poetry they both wrote.'

Preston was there when one day Cremers came to visit Victor. The scene which took place must have been the ante-type of the one I witnessed so many years later. She was apparently very baldly spoken; she referred to exhibitions Crowley had made of himself which are utterly disgusting.

Preston said, 'Victor was very quiet after she left. I had the impression he was distressed that I should have been there and heard it all. He was embarrassed to talk about it.'

What still puzzles me is how Cremers knew so much about Crowley. Though she had glimpsed him in the States in 1901 it seems that she only entered the picture again when she came, as a spectator, to the publicly performed *Rites of Eleusis* in 1910. Obviously, there is something here that I do not know and have not been able to get out of anybody.

Victor was going through an Elizabethan period, even to the dress. He wore leggings with breeches that suggested the sixteenth century, and read sixteenth-century poetry, mainly Donne, Preston recalled.

This was before the general revival of interest in Donne, fostered by Leavis. 'I can't ever remember his quoting Shakespeare!' said Preston. Now it is mentioned, neither can I; Victor's interest lay in lyric poetry not the drama.

Victor took no interest in free verse. They challenged each other to a duel, the weapons to be sonnets, of which each wrote the other a series of six defending the kind of verse which he preferred.

Their poetic meeting ground, however, was in their common admiration for James Thomson, the younger. 'Before his shrine, we were both worshippers,' said Preston. *The City of Dreadful Night* was especially meaningful for Victor, who had had such occasion to feel:
>*That all the oracles are dumb or cheat*
>
> ...
>
>*Because there is no light behind the curtain.*

The first Vine Press book was *Lillygay* in 1920, the Dedication, Prologues, Epilogue, Colophon and certain poems, 'Lillywhite','Rantum-Tantrum' and 'Sick Dick', are by Victor (information from Cammell) though all are printed as if anonymous.

('Sick Dick' later appeared over Victor's signature in an anthology of drinking songs, *The Merry Go Down*, edited by Rab Noolas, otherwise his friend Philip Heseltine, alias Peter Warlock.)

The strangest things in the book are the poems written in Scottish dialect. Vicky told me about these himself. He had not written anything for nearly a decade, he said, and did not think he was ever going to be able for poetry again. 'When it started coming through again, it was in Scottish dialect.' This puzzled him, because he did not know where he could have picked it up. 'I'd only spent a fortnight in Scotland, years before, and that was in the house of a friend and I was indoors all the time.' (It was before I knew the friend was Crowley.) He had hardly had occasion to hear any of the local people talking. Yet the lines kept coming in his head. 'I didn't know whether I was making them up, or remembering them.' When he read the reviews, he gathered that they were well-known Border ballads 'That had been in existence for hundreds of years!' He added, 'Afterwards, I found I could write in English again.'

Swift Wings, a book of his own poems, was published by the Vine Press in 1921. All the subjects have to do with Sussex. In 'William Collins' he describes how he made a reverent pilgrimage to the birth-town of 'the perfect poet of the evening.'

Solid in red brick that breathes the Georges,
Redolent of port and beefsteak orgies,
Is somnolent and Tory Chichester;
For this I love her dullness;

In 'Old Steyne', he compares the leafy, light-filled heart of Brighton through which the trams slide in the dusk, to something created by Keats, Corot, Turner, or 'the feathery pencil of Paul Verlaine.' It is the only trace of the French Symbolist poet which I find in his work. Of a slope of daffodils, he writes in 'Frenchlands':

Here's the worlds' yellow. Here the cosmic yolk
Broke.

Standing between sea and gorse, in 'White Hawk Hill', he feels there were earlier incarnations in which we knew this spot. It seems to him that as far back as he could go, he was always the one who sought the mysteries.

He has been burned, and the element of fire is no more strange to him for it has consumed him; neither is water, in which he has drowned; or earth in which he has often been laid. After this life, too, has given way to a period of oblivion he will come back:

I shall return; the Green Star has me still,
Brain, body, soul and heart. My spirit's will
From tranced sleep of splendour will be drawn
Back to the Green Star of the Golden Dawn;
I shall return; even to White Hawk hill.

16
Marriage

At the end of the year Victor married. It was while visiting his mother in Hove some years previously, that he went into the Post Office and met the girl with contralto voice, prominent teeth and a smile who served behind the counter, Kathleen Rose Goddard. She was born on November 22, 1892, at 77 Lincoln Street, Brighton, and her father described himself on her birth certificate as a waterworks labourer. Her background was staid and narrow; it was also religious in a conventional way. Yet Kathleen must have had a spark of rebellion.

Raymond Casey a retired violinist running a tea-room, in whose home the Steyning Labour Party met, tells me he understood from Kathleen that she had 'taken Vicky away from Crowley'. I do not think Victor's decision to leave Crowley had anything to do with Kathleen, but John Symonds says Crowley spoke of Kathleen as a love of Victor's in pre-war days. He may therefore have known her since 1912, when he spent the latter part of that year with his mother, following the shock of Joan's death. A faded snap in the family album, showing Victor and Kathleen sitting beside each other on a gate, is dated in her hand, 1917. And while he was in the army his mother, who found his writing impossible to read, took his letters to Kathleen to decipher.

Eva Baker, who with her husband, Ivan Baker, took over the tea-rooms when the Caseys gave it up, became a special friend of Kathleen and confirms that she and Victor were having an affair for some years before they married; it was Kathleen's idea they should marry. 'She told him she thought she would like to have a child, and he did not think it right to deny her.'

Prior to the marriage Kathleen had a job as secretary to Margaret Morris, at her school of revived classical Greek dancing in London. Mrs Baker says it was Vicky who got this for her. Kathleen wanted, when presented to his friends as his wife, to be able to say she had previously been somebody's secretary. It would sound a little grander than working in a Post Office.

The Magical Dilemma of Victor Neuburg

I wrote to Margaret Morris. She could not remember how Kathleen had come to her, but she remembered her as a good secretary.

Victor and Kathleen were married at the Registrar's Offices in Hammersmith. The marriage certificate shows their addresses as 5 and 5a Maclise Road, Hammersmith. The date was November 8, 1921. Kathleen was almost twenty-nine and Victor was thirty-eight. Victor and Kathleen made their home at Vine Cottage and Aunt Ti returned to her flat in Victoria Street while Hayter Preston also moved out.

The same year, Victor published *Songs of the Groves*, the book he gave me, which I think contains his best work, an opinion shared by Charles Cammell. Though his name does not appear on the volume, Victor's authorship is attested in the British Museum Catalogue, the volume being indexed under its title. His authorship is also acknowledged in later printed hand-outs, some of which I acquired from d'Offay, and it was acknowledged in the *Sunday Referee*. One of the poems in it, 'Downwood', was also printed under his name in *An Anthology of Modern Verse*, compiled by R.L.Megroz (Pitman 1936).

In the following year, 1922, Victor published *Larkspur*, again anonymously. The Dedication, Prologue, Epilogue, Colophon and the poems signed Christopher Crayne, Paul Pentrath, Harold Stevnes, Lawrence Edwards, Arthur French and Nicholas Pyne are by him (information from Cammell). The lyric 'Trollie Lollie', printed over the last pseudonym, was later set to music by Roger Quilter, Victor's authorship being acknowledged in his proper name in the title sheet of the score. Most of the lyrics in this volume are somewhat light; I prefer one in which he admits his haunting by the old mood, 'Yellow Moon':

Amidst the dark penumberous
Slow green foliage
Vast, vast and slumberous,
She dallies for an age -
Our Moon of Vision Valley
Light of Yellow Blaze,
Sombrely to rally
Men of forgotten days,

He feels the moon's call to those who know her power as she moves over the evening clover. Her ancient worshipper must again be reborn to consciousness of the pain and the ecstasy, but not at this present time; let her not disturb him, nor

*..twang with wanton finger
The old exciting strings.*

..ading these lines, I realized the force of a remark Preston had made
. me,'Victor, at Steyning, was a dead man; he gave up magic and
.ent the whole of the rest of his life feeling he was not doing what he
.as meant to be doing.'

. the same year, Victor published *Songs of a Sussex Tramp* for Rupert
..roft-Cooke; so far as I know it was the first work he did for an
..tsider. Croft-Cooke, then only seventeen, did not know who ran
..e Vine Press but having seen some of its productions submitted the
..oems by post. In the correspondence which ensued, Victor Neuburg
..praised the poems as poetry, passed to considerations of typogra-
..hy and lay-out, and the book went into production without any
..ference having been made as to the manner in which the financial
..sponsibilities, or proceeds if any, were to be shared between author
..nd printer-publisher. After its appearance Croft-Cook was invited
.. spend a week-end at Vine Cottage and found the atmosphere
..nformal and cheerful. Victor quoted from James Thomson and, with
..usto, 'ostrobogulous' passages from Aphra Benn, John Cleland and
..etronius Arbiter. In his book *Glittering Pastures* (Putnam 1963), page
..5, Croft-Cook records Victor as saying while Kathleen poured tea,
..'m just an old queen and make no bones about it.' The phrase is of
..ourse a homosexual cliché but it seemed not quite applicable to Vic-
..or. It was an awkward point to take up by letter with a person I had
..ever seen but I wrote to Croft-Cooke asking him about it. Perhaps
..ny letter puzzled Croft-Cooke for I received a reply from Morocco in
..vhich he said, 'The Vicky bird was not, I think in any way classifiable
..s a homosexual. But there is such a thing as a heterosexual old queen
..nd that is what he probably meant.'

..lso in 1922, Victor produced an 'ostrobogulolus' volume which
..ame to me in d'Offay's collection. Entitled *The Way of A Virgin*, it
..ontains excerpts from Casanova, Boccaccio and the Arabian Nights,
..lus crude folk tales. It was published by *The Brovan Society* (the
..seudonym contains Victor's initials and perhaps those of a collabo-
..ator) but the distinctive typeface of the Vine Press gives it away; also
..t is indirectly 'signed' by a quotation from *Songs of the Groves* which
..mentions the Vine Press. Gorgeously bound, it was obtainable by
.private subscription only, at five guineas.

.Other Vine Press books which came to me from d'Offay include

The Magical Dilemma of Victor Neuburg

Teams of Tomorrow and *Songs of the South* by G D Martineau, cricket correspondent of the *Daily Telegraph*, who wrote to tell me Victor took him up to the roof to look at Chanctonbury Ring, 'from the top of a house which formed a picturesque addition to what might have been acclaimed the loveliest street in England.' Also *Before the Storm* by Princess Ouroussof, and *Night's Triumphs* by Ernest Osgood Hanbury. All these were hand-printed by Victor.

About 2 am, March 8, 1924, a son was born to Victor. While waiting news of the delivery (according to Walter Raeburn), he wrote a visionary poem, 'The Waterbearer'. He was delighted with the 'Infant Brat' which he called 'my first and only edition.' Victor's son was named Victor Edward Neuburg but in the family he was called Toby, as the diminutive, Vicky, was already in use for Victor, the father.

It was from Casey that I first heard of Kathleen's lover. I wrote to this man, Colin Evans, the astrologer, saying I was writing a biography of Victor Neuburg and would be glad of anything he was able to tell me. He rang and said, 'I shall have to think about this. It's awkward, because I knew his wife much better.'

I went to see him. He was a big, burly man with spreading beard and dusty typewriter. On the bookshelf was a framed photograph of Kathleen which he brought over to show me. 'Her only fault, concerning which she was self-conscious, was that her teeth projected.'

'Slightly projecting teeth are not always considered unattractive,' I said, trying to help things along.

'She was a great deal too attractive to me!' he said, and closed his eyes for a moment. 'I was introduced to Mr and Mrs Neuburg at a semi-private dance in Brighton. I thought they were both charming people. I danced with Mrs Neuburg. We became lovers within the week.'

'What date was this?' I asked.

'Toby was about three months old. It was before he could eat food.'

The liaison lasted about ten years. He was not her only lover but the most serious.

'Did Victor know?' I asked.

'I don't know. We never spoke about it. I didn't deceive him. I would call to fetch her perfectly openly. I would say, "I'm taking your wife away for the weekend." He would hand out her case and see us off, smiling. I took it for granted he understood. I thought it was in accordance with his principles.'

'Did Victor have other affairs?' I asked. He did not think so.

He owed a great deal to Victor. 'He had wisdom. And he combined two worlds for me. Before I met him I had lived alternately in a world in which one could only talk bawdiness, and a world in which a bawdy word would have been unthinkable. With Vicky, one could crack a bawdy joke one minute and be discussing a fine point in philosophy the next. That was something I had not met before. It was for me integrating.'

I had not seen Arthur Leslie Morton since the days at Springfield Road so it was really an event when he answered my appeal and climbed my stairs. He was even taller then I remembered him, almost scraping the ceiling with his crest of now grey hair. He had gone to Steyning in 1924 to teach at the Grammar School, his first job after coming down from Cambridge. It was a live-in job and he was not happy in it; he did not get on with the staff or with the locals. 'Vicky saved my life in Steyning!' He spent most of his evenings at Vine Cottage and they talked about Blake.(1)

We talked about the days in which we had both known Vicky, and the Zoists. Morton said, 'It really speaks volumes for Vicky that he was able to dominate that circle of young men - all of them just at an age when young men can be difficult - and in spite of all the rumours, which must sooner or later have reached everybody's ears, I never heard him addressed with anything less than complete politeness. He was *listened* to. With *deference*.'

In 1926 Victor sent some poems to the *Argosy* which were formally accepted by the Editor and then not printed. Mrs Odle, the Editor's widow, told me the Managing Director had told her husband publication was impossible as Neuburg was blacklisted as an associate of Crowley. She wrote to me of Victor:

He understood that his work could never be published in *The Argosy*, but he became a friend of our family. I remember his carefully removing a worm from his path so as not to walk on it. From the top of a bus in the Edgware Road I once watched him walk on the pavement. He picked up a twig of privet and looked for somewhere to place it out of harm's way - and deposited it on the blind of a shop. He had that empathy with all living things that, had he never written a line, would still make him a poet. He was completely vulnerable, unable to perform an unkind action, unarmed.

The Magical Dilemma of Victor Neuburg

Arthur Calder-Marshall, then still at school, spent his holidays in his parents' house near Steyning. He came to know Vicky and wrote to me that he was:

Buddhistically kind to every form of life...liable to remove a cockroach from the passage from the pantry to the yard to prevent its being crushed by Kathleen.

Victor did some reviewing for the *Bookman's Journal*. In March, 1924, he reviewed the Rider edition of Eliphas Levi's *Transcendental Magic*. It was a poem by Victor in the *Bookman's Journal* which caught the eye of Mr C R Cammell, the Scottish poet, critic and student of folk-lore, then living in Geneva:

The Green Ladie:
As I went strolling one morning in May,
I met a young ladie, all green clad and gay.
...
Oh come with me strolling
The white clouds are rolling,
The sky's blue is pale and the chaffinches sing;
The sun is full shining,
It's time for divining
The birth of the year from the heart of the Spring.
....

The ballad delighted Cammell, and he wrote to the Editor asking to be put in touch with Victor Neuburg. Victor then sent Cammell copies of *Lillygay* and *Larkspur* in which he had marked the poems which were by himself, and *Songs of the Groves*. Speaking to me, Cammell described Victor's 'Chant Royal of Horace', which appears in it, as 'the greatest feat of rhyming in the English Language.'

I mentioned the affair of the Border Ballads. Mr Cammell examined a number of published versions which he had in his own collection, and showed me that Victor's Scottish ballads were, in fact, not copied.

'He's composed something of his own in the vernacular. I grew up on the Border, with these sounds in my ears.' It was, he explained to me, a speech different from the Ayrshire of Burns; while that of the Highlands was different again. This was something local to the counties of Berwickshire and Roxburghshire. He would have thought it impossible for anyone who had not been brought up on the Border to command it. He read through Victor's stanzas again, and said, 'There is no flaw in the vernacular which I can detect.'

Cammell corresponded with Victor for some years. Their letters were mostly about poetry but now and then Victor's afforded a biographical glimpse:

April 7th 1926.

My dear poet,

...The struggle of carrying on single handed, save for my wife, who is secretary and treasurer, is slowly slaying the poet! We shall win, though optimism and sheer will; but the process is a devastating one.

Sincerely and fraternally,

Victor B.Neuburg

On July 8 of the same year he wrote, 'Had I known what was due to me in this incarnation, I might have hesitated before taking it on.'

A slight fillip, however, was given to his spirits by the impending General Election. Through the Steyning branch of the Labour Party, of which Vicky had become treasurer, Walter Raeburn, later the well-known QC, then the Labour Candidate for Horsham and Worthing, was put in touch with him. It was arranged that Vine Cottage should become Raeburn's headquarters for a fortnight during the campaign. Commander Eric James King Bull drove Mr and Mrs Walter Raeburn and Mr Harold Payton (later a County Court Judge) down to Vine Cottage. Kathleen was away, but they and Vicky used to have, according to Raeburn, 'glorious late breakfasts,' over which, discussing everything under heaven, they would linger 'until it was time for lunch.' In the afternoons, King Bull would drive them all to to wherever Raeburn was booked to speak, and in the evenings there would be more talk, ranging often over every kind of philosophic question. Raeburn noticed that if Victor's chair was occupied by the cat, he would go out and get another chair rather than disturb it. 'It was his sensitivity.'

Victor kept in with both the Raeburns and the King Bulls for some years. Mr Raeburn placed at my disposal a number of Victor's letters to him, and though most of them refer to the day-to-day activity of the campaign, they are entertaining, and reveal that he could be unexpectedly tough with a Candidate who notified him at the last moment that he would be unable to attend a meeting at which he was booked to speak.

The Raeburns held Victor in regard as a genuine mystic.

(1) A L Morton wrote *The Everlasting Gospel: a study in the sources of William Blake* (Lawrence and Wishart 1958) and a *People's History of England.*

17
The Sanctuary

Victor's place of recreation was the Sanctuary. This owed its existence to Vera Pragnell. Her father, Sir George Pragnell, knighted for his services to commerce, had been in textiles and his death left her with independence at an early age. She was a student at the London School of Economics when, fired by the teachings of Dr W.E.Orchard, she decided that 'man's first necessities are faith in God and access to the land.' At the end of 1923, she bought at the foot of the South Downs near Storrington 'a beautiful tract of about nineteen acres of common, eight acres of arable land, a lovely heather-covered, sentinel-like hill and two semi-detached derelict cottages.' She gave free use of this to any who wished to plant vegetables or build themselves houses. She had always thought that the poor were humiliated by having to prove they were 'deserving.' No questions were asked therefore of intending settlers. Neither were there any rules.

Such an Arcadian Anarchy, presided over by a young and beautiful woman, could not fail to attract attention from the Press and Miss Pragnell found herself on the one hand described as a 'lady Bountiful', and on the other hand taxed with everything from 'encouraging tramps' to 'encouraging free love'. Indeed, when Hayter Preston came down from London to see Victor and made his own way into the Sanctuary, the first thing that crossed his line of vision was 'a pair of white buttocks disappearing into the bracken. I wondered if I had entered a nudist colony!'

When I went down I was met by Vera Dennis Earle, as she had become. She was a warm personality, reassuringly realistic. She drove me through Storrington and we soon reached a house which nestled at the side of the wood. I was ushered into a spacious, beautiful room where I met Dennis. He seated me by a roaring fire and offered a choice of red wines while Vera brought down from the shelf *The Story of the Sanctuary*, published by the Vine Press. It was when she had wanted some leaflets done, that she had in the first place written to inquire whether they did outside work, and so she came to know Vicky, who later produced her book. On the fly-leaf was written *Leonora Pragnell*; Vera explained this had been her mother's copy. The book was dedicated in print to Edward Carpenter. Victor was the author of the verse:

To the Master
Fitly and truly be this book to you
Given;....

...

All that we prize as true
Was held by you of old!

...

Be sounded through the world: This man was true.

...

O my brave Hellene

...

...our youth's doyen, Edward Carpenter.

Edward Carpenter had visited the Sanctuary. He was then over eighty and for some time before he came he had been sending along his fans, 'mainly puzzled young men whom he felt I could help by giving them a break, living toughly among all sorts in the open air.'

She had been surprised by the emotion Vicky showed on first meeting Carpenter. He told Carpenter that as a young man he had been helped by reading his books, and said, 'It's a privilege to be able to shake you by the hand and say Thank You!'

It was in the wake of Edward Carpenter that Dennis Earle came down. He had been Carpenter's devoted secretary, a young man of twenty-eight or thirty. Vera married him.

Vera said, 'I always associated the Sanctuary, so far as Vicky was concerned, with a kind of release after the Steyning menage.'

At Vine Cottage he was oppressed by Kathleen's dominant practicality and complete lack of poetry. She damped his inspiration. But when he escaped he recovered his spontaneity and sense of fun. We talked about Kathleen's infidelity. Dennis thought it possible Vicky knew but that it belonged to an order of things which had no reality for him. Looking at me, he said, 'Vicky was the most truly sexless human being I have ever met. He was absolutely innocent.' We had been speaking, before this, of his relations with Crowley, so this was a penetrating remark.

Dennis asked, 'He was a spirit riding on a cloud. He wasn't human.

The Magical Dilemma of Victor Neuburg

He was a pixie.'

He had used almost the same words as Ethel Archer. Cammell had expressed to me his theory that Victor was a being belonging to the kingdom of faery which had, by mistake, taken human birth.

Vera Dennis Earle gave me among other souvenirs the programme of a pantomime, *Babes in the Wood*, written by Victor and produced by Dennis on December 31, 1927. Morton was present. So was Toby, who had to be carried out, crying. Vera told me they had folk dancing, in which Vicky took part, while Hugh de Selincourt stood gravely watching. It was at the Sanctuary that Victor met C.W.Owen, the Anarchist, who spent his last days at Vine Cottage and when he died left Victor his bitch, Nell. Attached by accident to a letter from Owen to Emma Goldman, Vera found a page from her old diary:

June 16th: Oddly momentous one. Vicky Bird came out to me in the Cottage Garden and we conversed on this and that while I leant on my hoe and fiddled with the fork. In the course of conversation we got on to the likeness of various of our friends to animals - usually animals they possessed till, sort of, the animals possessed *them*. DJF, for instance, is like her pampered pekinese, whereas Fred, who spends more time in the stables than with his wife, is exactly like a horse. Edward Carpenter says Dennis is like a camel; and I was round and cuddly, said Vicky, like a bear crossed with a dove.

'And you - you are awfully goat-like,' I began, when I noticed he stiffened and under his sallowness he seemed to go deathly white.

'Darling Vicky,' I said, throwing my arms around him. 'I love goats, don't you?.'

'No - no, not really.'

'But why are you so upset?'

He sat down and buried his face in his hands. After ages he muttered, 'I was one. A goat was my curse.'

Within minutes he was fooling again. 'Forget it.' But it was weird; one just couldn't forget.

As I read this I felt the cold creep of goose-flesh, for I realized that here was the clue to the curse Crowley had pronounced on him. I had never taken seriously the legend that Crowley turned him into a camel. The idea of magicians being able to turn people into animals, literally, is of course absurd. Nevertheless, a goat is the lower or averse side of Pan. From the loins down Pan is a goat.

When entering the Argentinum Astrum the candidate was warned that if he left he would evoke the Avenging Current. This was not a malediction pronounced on him by another person but the kick-back of any power he had brought into operation but failed to bring to a proper conclusion and would be appropriate to the nature of the enterprise undertaken and abandoned. Crowley had taken it upon himself to interpret this and declared that Victor would become possessed by the lower side of the Deity they had invoked in their sex magics in Paris and on Dal'leh Addin.(1)

His real innocence protected him, but the fear would only have left him slowly.

(1) Crowley might have done well to reflect upon the dictum of Eliphas Levi, that curses expend themselves upon him who pronounces them, unless he is without malice.

18
Crowley again:
Arcanum Arcanorum

Vera Dennis Earle drove into Steyning one day, and saw Kathleen coming out of Vine Cottage, her face livid beneath her make-up. 'It's happened!' Kathleen gasped. 'After all these years! Crowley came!'

He had come to the door, banging his stick on the ground and said, 'I want Victor'. Victor was not at home and she had said so; after insisting for some time Crowley seemed to realize that Victor was not in the house. He left, but Kathleen was afraid he was still in the vicinity and would try to intercept Victor as he returned. Vicky had taken the dog up on the hill and Kathleen managed to intercept him before he returned to the cottage. Victor went to an address unknown to Crowley and he remained there until Crowley seemed to have left Steyning.

This was about 1927. In the years which had elapsed since Victor terminated the relationship, Crowley's notoriety had been built up by the press until from being a private person whose strangeness was known to few, he had become inflated to the status of a public bogey. *John Bull* in the Spring and Summer of 1923 ran a series of articles about him under the lurid titles, 'The King of Depravity', The Wickedest man in the world,' 'A man we'd like to hang', and 'A human beast'. 1920-3 was the period during which Crowley presided over the grandiloquently called Abbey of Thelema (1) at Cefalù in Sicily.

The *Sunday Express* ran a series of articles titled: 'Young Wife's story of Crowley's Abbey', 'A Young English Bride Reveals' and, finally, 'Angel Child Who Saw Hell and Came Back'.

'The facts', said the *Sunday Express*, 'are too utterly filthy to be detailed in a newspaper, for they had to do with sexual orgies that touch the lowest depths of depravity.' Crowley's defenders have made much of the fact that the 'girl-wife' who testified concerning these 'unspeakable orgies' was misleadingly described; she was Betty May.

228

Crowley Again: *Arcanum Arcanorum*

Her name was suppressed in the newspaper but in her autobiography, *Tiger Woman*, which was later published by Duckworth she makes no mystery of herself. She was born in Limehouse where her father kept a cheap brothel near the docks. He kept her out of contact with this by arranging with some people who kept a barge on the Thames to keep her there. A man took her to France and she was 'adopted' by a gang of Apaches operating in Montmartre; her role was to lure rich-looking men into places where they might be robbed. It was her prowess in fighting with rivals of her own sex which earned her the soubriquet, *La Femme Tigre*, but it was because she lost confidence in the ability of her *confrères* to protect her against the vengeance of one of the men she had decoyed that she returned to London. In the Café Royal she met Jacob Epstein and became his model. Raoul Loveday, the young Oxford graduate who met Crowley and became his acolyte almost as soon as he had married her, and who died of typhoid at Cefalù was her third husband. Perhaps this is not what most readers of a Sunday newspaper would understand from the phrases, 'angel child,' girl-wife' or even 'young English bride.'

I met Betty May in 1941, after Vicky's death. I had been to see Runia and walked with her from Boundary Road to the bus stop on the Edgware Road. In Springfield Road I think, as we passed in front of the garden of one of the houses, a woman looked over the top of the privet hedge she was clipping and said to Runia: 'How are the cabbages?' Runia looked uncomprehending and the woman said: 'Your sons! I call them cabbages because they were fed on cabbages. They used to sit in front of big plates of salad. You gave them raw cabbage!'

She had henna'd hair and liberal lashings of eye-black but she was not young, and her face was at once pasty and wasted. Her manner was bluff but might have hidden a heart; I formed the impression she was lonely, glad of the few moments' conversation and anxious to prolong it.

When at length we moved off, Runia said, 'That was Betty May! The most notorious of all the women associated with Crowley. She was called The Tiger Woman! Did you notice the piece of fur?'

I was surprised and thought that as a tiger she was not comparable to Cremers. The bit of worn fur on the old black coat had suggested nothing feline to my mind. 'Did Vicky know her?' I asked.

'Only when we both came here.' Runia explained that Betty May had not met Crowley until years after Victor had separated from him. 'But when we found we were such near neighbours it seemed unkind not to ask her in for a cup of coffee'. She thought Vicky had been reluctant to make the acquaintance, though 'of course they compared notes on AC; they were both victims.' Vicky had taken a philosophical view and said the important thing was not to let experience sour one but to learn comprehension and compassion from it, and that one should regard it all as contributing to the education of the soul on its long journey. She thought the conversation had done some good for Betty May though it upset Vicky. 'She wouldn't be able to tell you anything about Vicky!' she said suddenly, as though she read my mind.

That Betty May should have been willing, nearly twenty years after her horrible experience with Crowley in Sicily, to talk about it with Vicky, who would instantly have detected the slightest false note is, to my mind, proof of her sincerity. She might have been moved by rage or the payment to supply the material for the articles in the *Sunday Express* and *John Bull*. It may have been her letter to the British Consul in Palermo when Loveday died - she had accompanied him to Crowley's place in Sicily only in the pathetic hope of preserving some minimal shreds of relationship - which caused the Italian authorities to expel Crowley from Italian soil; but there could have been no motive of vengeance or advantage in speaking to Vicky about it.

In reading her published accounts one must remember that she shields Loveday's reputation with gallantry. The reader is never in possession of the distressing details found in the red notebook discovered by John Symonds amongst Crowley's papers.

Hayter Preston spoke with Betty May after her return from Cefalù, he spoke with Mary Butts also, who returned from Cefalù before Betty May went. Of the perversions that Mary Butts witnessed in Cefalù, one can only say that they are not printable. But accounts of these, too, which formerly rested upon her verbal statement to shocked listeners, have been found by John Symonds in the record kept in Crowley's hand in the red notebook.

Symonds suggested to me that Crowley's behaviour resulted from his masochism; he pointed out that the connecting thread running through the diversity of his perversions was the idea of submitting himself to some kind of vileness or humiliation. This could be true.

Crowley Again: *Arcanum Arcanorum*

There is an insistence on passive experience, and even some of the exhibitionism could be classed under this heading; to make humiliation complete there had to be beholders. In the most ordinary sense there is no doubt that Crowley loved to suffer. I was very conscious of this in his manuscripts. He loves to be 'exhausted', whether by playing billiards, walking in the desert, or sex. His motto in The Golden Dawn, which long puzzled me, become clear: *Perdurabo* means *I shall endure.*

Gerald Yorke said to me in all earnestness, 'Crowley didn't enjoy his perversions! He performed them to overcome his horror of them!'

This of course, is what Crowley said. It seems to me fatuous, because if one is to start doing things in order to overcome one's horror of them there is no end - which is exactly what Crowley found.

What is more interesting is the philosophic validation he gave himself; this is what I tried to discover and I think I have done so. It lies in the = sign, The Golden Dawn system of equations. The clue is given in several places, even in his published writings where he says that every movement in one direction must be balanced by an equal movement in the opposite one. Thus, for him, every movement upwards had to be balanced by an equal movement downward. He thought it was because he had been born with the Sun in the sign of the Balance, Libra, that he was specially fitted for the perception of this mystery.

As I perceived that the equals sign lay at the root of his problem, I suddenly saw in my mind's eye an = in white light. It formed the two transverse ridges across the root of the nose of an ape with red and blue cheeks. I wondered what species of ape it was; the word mandrill occurred to me. I looked this up in a dictionary of zoology and discovered that the technical name for the animal was *Cynocephalus Maimon*, and that it as described as 'offensively libidinous.' This seemed to me appropriate as Crowley was not only 'offensively libidinous' but the Cynocephalus is the Ape of Thoth, the averse side of the god of Knowledge. Though I had often come upon the term in occult literature - Crowley himself uses it to signify knowledge foolishly used - I had not previously considered it in relation to the live, zoological animal. Of course such a vision is not a portrait of the total man, for it ignores the higher qualities which were not entirely absent; but it is a picture of that aspect of him I was trying to understand.

The Magical Dilemma of Victor Neuburg

Having come so far in my appreciation of the trap into which he had fallen, something else occurred to me. I re-opened, at the last chapter, Eliphas Levi's last book, *Key to the Mysteries*. On the final pages are three almost full-plate diagrams; the first shows the black pentagram, with the apex downward, in the middle of which is written Satan Est La Haine; the second is the pentagram of White occultism, with the apex upwards in which is written, Dieu Est. The third consists of the white pentagram with the other behind it, yet drawn in white, with the spokes pointing inwards instead of outward; the words in the middle of this are L'Esprit Saint Est. It the brief accompanying legend, on page 204, Levi says:

Good personified is God. Evil personified is the Devil. To know the secret or formula of God is to be God. To know the secret or formula of the Devil is to be the Devil. To wish to be at the same time God and the Devil is to absorb in one's self the most absolute antimony, the two most strained contrary forces; it is to shut in one's self an infinite antagonism. It is to drink a poison which would extinguish the suns and consume the worlds.

Below this is a footnote of Crowley's:

'An allusion to Shiva, who drank the poison generated by the churning of the milk Ocean (see *Bhavagata Purana Skandha VIII*, Chaps 5-12), Levi therefore means in this passage the exact contrary of what he pretends to mean. Otherwise this 'be good and you will be happy ' chapter would scarcely deserve the title 'Arcanum Arcanorum' - AC'

Now, the whole issue lies in this. I doubt whether Levi alluded deliberately to the Hindu scriptures for in his previous book he disparaged them. Yet it does seem to me that he is trying to say something very daring, something which he feels to be unsayable in plain words. What Crowley has said to himself at this moment is obvious: he has said that he must postulate, and live the postulate that he was 1=10 and 10=1, the light and the darkness, the alpha and the omega, evolution and involution, the heights and the depths, good and evil, the Devil and God. If ever a man went off his head through the occult sciences it was Crowley.

(1) A box-like dump of a villa so I was told by the late Elizabeth Nicholas, then the Travel Correspondent of the *Sunday Times*.

19
Steyning - The Latter Days of the Marriage

Meanwhile, unaware how strange was his background, Victor's young son was growing to the age of fragmentary memories. A blue teddy-bear. Two eggs for his tea. They were in Shoreham where his father had taken him for the afternoon. They went into a tea-room and he had an egg for his tea, and when he had finished it he said, 'Can I have another egg?' his father said, 'Yes'. He could never remember his father refusing him anything or telling him not to do anything.

Uncle Ben came to see them; his mother told him it was important to be nice to him but all he could remember of this august being was a tummy, with a gold watch and chain. And a walking stick with a knob. Aunt Hannah came 'with toys and delicious fish.'

Each year at Christmas time they gave a party to which poor children from the surrounding villages were invited. His father used to dress up as Father Christmas.

In the *Freethinker* there is a picture entitled *Moses frightened of a snake*. Toby liked the snake. (When after his father's death Runia gave Toby some of his books, he found a slip inserted opposite this picture, on which his father had written: 'For Toby'.) I was able to tell him that in a ps to a letter to Cammell dated 26.7.27, Victor had written 'I love Toby'.

Gertrude Stein and Philip Heseltine came to see Vicky: Lord Alfred Douglas called but Kathleen shut the door in his face. One day when Toby was in his bath his father brought in a huge man to whom he announced, 'This is my son!' It was Paul Robeson. Tallulah Bankhead was another exotic visitor to Vine Cottage.

The Vicar once called on Vicky. He was not expected, but returning from the Sunday morning service saw the door open and, after knocking, stepped into the hall. Vicky came out of the bathroom with nothing on but a towel wrapped round him. 'I don't believe in the Lord Jesus Christ,' he said, 'But you're very welcome, sir!' Kathleen made him stay for lunch.

In Steyning Vicky was regarded as a mild eccentric. Eric Richmond, a retired variety artist who lived opposite Vine Cottage, recalled a peculiarity of his gait. 'He walked the way a bird walks, the legs rather wide apart and thrusting out straight in front as he made little runs.'

Some of the snaps in the family album show Kathleen standing jauntily with one foot upon the seat of a chair, evidently a favourite pose of hers, the better to show off different suits of pretty, flowered pyjamas, a cigarette in hand or mouth. When in these gay moods she must have been an entertaining companion and one can understand why Vicky, in the days before the relationship went sour, found her society relaxing. But now the smiles were less often for him.

The albums also reveal sun-bathing as one of the occupations of Vine Cottage. There are photographs of Kathleen's favourite young men, in the near nude, or fake nude, partially screened with innocent art by tubs or bushes to give the illusion, perhaps of Adam in the Garden of Eden, or a wild man in the woods. Captions are in Kathleen's hand.

Calder-Marshall wrote to me:

You can take it as definite that Vicky would have no intellectual or moral objection to Kathleen's infidelity. He might have objected to deception. He belonged to an inverted Puritan generation that did not regard reticence about such things as a form of good manners. She was in no sense an artist or an intellectual. She would, I felt, have been happier with almost any man who could provide her with bed, board, lodgings, babies and a balance in the bank. An utter bourgeoise.

On the question of Kathleen's infidelity, I asked Arthur Leslie Morton when he came, whether he thought Vicky really accepted it with indifference. Morton said he might have wanted to make it clear that he did not regard a married woman as her husband's property - as Shelley did not - and therefore might have told her she was 'free'. But perhaps rather hoping she would not use her freedom. 'Between one's theory and one's feelings there can be a gap. Could one say, there are occasions when a woman is wiser if she does not take a man at his word, and this was one of them?'

Calder-Marshall said Kathleen had no sympathy with Victor's producing his own books, as the sales were insufficient, and so he had by this time given up his treasured hand-press. He still produced, for outside people, who paid, books under the imprimateur of the Vine Press, but the type was now machine-set, at West's. Now, Kathleen was irked by seeing him physically idle.

I see Victor at Steyning as a spiritually tall man amongst pigmies; but that was not how he was seen by people there. They saw a sad little man with a dominant wife, who was unfaithful and did not care for him sufficiently even to mind his clothes; a man who was largely dependent on his aunt. This was the weakness of his position. Devoted to the highest art and principles, he scorned to do anything merely for the purpose of making money; at the same time he bestowed it in loans that were virtually gifts. In short, he had the aristocratic attitude but without the means except at the expense of his family.

Though he tried to make the Vine Press books pay their way he looked to any possible proceeds to supply altruistic causes. At the beginning of 1928 he accepted editorship of the local Labour paper, the *Dawn*, which was losing money; in a hopeful letter about this to Walter Raeburn, on March 20, he wrote, 'Soon I'll be able to defray the loss myself.'

Kathleen, installed at Vine Cottage, became a tyrant. She ran everything. He let her, because practical things were without significance for him.

His humiliation was complete with the letting of Vine Cottage to paying guests. The money made was Kathleen's money, more than he made with his press; as values of the mind had no reality for Kathleen, this situation caused her to treat him as an appendage of complete uselessness. He let himself be driven, more and more, to the Sanctuary, which had become a sanctuary in more than name. He was less alone when he could escape up on the Downs by himself. There in the dusk, his imagination could shape other times, other faces. There, as he wrote, in his poem, 'Downwood'(1):

> I stand
> On the old hill,
> Chill,
> In a forgotten land
> With an unknown name.

(1) Chanctonbury Ring

235

20
The Institute for the Study and Treatment of Delinquency

Meanwhile, a revolution had been taking place in Victor's life. cannot establish the date of that summer afternoon on which he an his cousin, Stanley Davis, emerging from the tall bracken at th Sanctuary, set eyes for the first time upon Runia, seated on the ve randa of one of the chalets beside the woman friend who had brough her down; nor of the subsequent period when Victor went to sta with Stanley at the latter's house in Uckfield where Runia came t visit them.

Runia at the time of her meeting with Vicky was still in her earl fifties, the mother of two sons and a daughter and still living with he husband. Julian Tharpe was a society portrait painter and they live in Primrose Hill. Vicky met Tharpe, Runia met Kathleen, and ther was a transitional period during which relations were at least superfi cially friendly.

Writing to Walter Raeburn on 14.4.31, Victor gave a Primrose Hil number and Runia's address though he put it as though he wer staying there temporarily, and said, 'I am now a filmist.' In fact, one o Runia's sons was making films, and Victor had been invited to com in with him in some capacity; I imagine it was mainly the ideas which he contributed.

Victor's letters to Cammell show 17.4.31 as the day appointed fo their meeting, which took place in a pub of Whitehall, Cammel having just arrived in England from Geneva.

After he returned to Vine Cottage, Victor began to suffer acute pai because of a hernia. An operation was considered to be necessary and Kathleen and Colin Evans brought him up to an hospital i

The Institute for the Study and Treatment of Delinquency

London. They were still with Victor when Runia arrived. Subsequently Cammell, accompanied by another poet, came to visit Victor in hospital; he recalls that it was in mid-winter. While they were there Runia arrived and Victor introduced them. After a little Runia said, 'Victor is tired. It's time for you to be going.' She herself did not appear to be preparing to go and Cammell did not see why he should be pushed out, so he said, 'Victor himself will tell me when he is tired. I shall go when Victor tells me. Or when the nurse tells us.' So he stayed, until presently the nurse said it was time for them all to go.

Later, Cammell was invited to lunch with Runia and her husband at Primrose Hill; Victor was there and so were Kathleen and Toby. When Cammell said, 'I must be going,' Kathleen rose and said she must be going too. She and Toby left with him and travelled on a bus to Highgate, Victor having remained behind. This was Cammell's first intimation there was something wrong.(1) Kathleen had gone to dine and eventually to live with Colin Evans, taking Toby with her.

In the first letter I received from Walter Raeburn, he wrote, 'I do not know if you realise it was he (Victor), who was one of the originators of the idea which finally took shape as the Institute for the Study and Treatment of Delinquency (ISTD). The first meeting was at our home.' I had not known. Mr Raeburn explained that in 1931 Victor came to see him, bringing Runia and Dr Grace Pailthorpe. Victor said, 'We want to start a Society for the Prevention of Cruelty to Criminals'.

King Bull tells me he is sure Victor's concern with this went back to the affair of a little printer whom he and Kathleen had befriended over one Christmas at Steyning, and who was later charged with fraud. Victor enlisted both Raeburn and King Bull in the endeavour to help him, but he was sentenced, and it turned out that he had eight previous convictions. He was of the type that would today be classed as a psychopath delinquent, and Victor felt that there should be curative rather than punitive treatment.

I wrote to the ISTD to ask whether they had any records showing Victor Neuburg's association with its early days, and received this reply:

Dear Miss Fuller,

Thank you for your letter of 10th March enquiring about the connection of the late Mr V. B. Neuburg with the ISTD.

The Magical Dilemma of Victor Neuburg

I have had a very brief look at the first Minute Book of the Institute - which started life as the Association for the Scientific Treatment of Criminals (ASTC) - and it appears that he was present at the very first meeting, held on the 22nd July, 1931. He then appeared as one of the original members of the Executive Committee and as Honorary Secretary at the beginning of 1933.

If you would like to come along to the Institute yourself to look through the Minute Book you will be very welcome to do so.

Yours sincerely

Eve Saville

General Secretary

Arriving at the Institute, I was welcomed by Miss Saville and conducted into the E.T.Jensen Memorial Library.

Miss Saville gave me the Minute Book and left me to peruse it at my leisure. I saw that the original officers had been: Ernest T.Jensen(2), Chairman; Victor B.Neuburg and Runia, Secretaries; and Dr Grace Pailthorpe. The first meeting recorded in Runia's hand, was at Primrose Hill; thereafter, with one exception, meetings were held at 56 Grosvenor Street. Dr Pailthorpe may have been Runia's friend, but it was certainly Victor who brought in Jensen, and Walter Raeburn and, through Raeburn, Harold Paton, as legal advisers. Victor also brought in Lady Pragnell (Vera Dennis Earle's mother) who was invited to be a Vice-president.

Victor attended almost all the meetings (I remembered that Raeburn had told me that it was about the end of November 1931 that, calling at Primrose Hill, he found Runia's husband distressed because Runia had that afternoon left him with Victor.) The last meeting at which Victor was present was on July 27, 1932, when the title of the Institute was changed to that it bears today. The reason for his disappearance is not given, but it was suggested by Dr Edward Glover that he was one of several who withdrew when, for a time, the preoccupations of the Institute became so narrowly medical that there was not much for other people to do.

I looked through a report for the year 1934 and saw that a list of thirty-nine Vice-presidents which the Institute had by then acquired included the names of Professor Sigmund Freud, Professor C G Jung, Professor Adler, Dr Havelock Ellis, Lord Dawson of Penn, Lord Horder, Lord Allen of Hurtwood, Mr H G Wells, the Very Rev Dr Herz, and His Grace the Archbishop of York. I thought: 'It's the mad ones who start things; the respectable who follow up and confer

The Institute for the Study and Treatment of Delinquency

respectability.'

(1) As this is Cammell's last appearance in the story, I should say that some time later, though not until 1936, Cammell met and became friends with Aleister Crowley. When Victor knew that Cammell was in contact with Crowley he became reluctant to meet Cammell. So the contact ceased. It was Cammell, himself, who told me this.

(2) Formerly of Crowley's circle.

21
The *Sunday Referee* and the Discovery of Dylan Thomas

Hayter Preston had become Literary Editor of the *Sunday Referee*. In early 1933 Calder-Marshall, just down from Oxford, called to see him at the office. Preston asked him about Victor; as the Calder-Marshall family had left Steyning the news was not up to date, but he told Preston that Victor had been looking poorly and miserable when last he saw him.

Preston was distressed to hear this and felt he should have kept in closer touch. He wrote to Victor and received an invitation to tea with him at an address in London: Adelaide Road. When he arrived Victor introduced him to Runia. She remained present all the time. Preston said to me, 'I saw in her something of Aunt Hannah!' There was no sign of Kathleen and when he saw Victor privately he asked what had happened. Victor said simply, 'We parted.'

Preston arranged an interview between Victor and Mark Goulden, the Editor of the *Sunday Referee*; and Goulden decided to allocate a column in the paper for a poetry feature to be conducted by Victor. No national newspaper had ever published such a feature, but for that matter no national newspaper had ever introduced a weekly supplement devoted to literature, art, music, etc, such as Goulden did in the *Sunday Referee*. The idea behind the poetry column (to be known as *Poet's Corner*) was to encourage new talent and entries were invited for a weekly prize competition, the pick of the contributions to be published in the paper together with comments on them by Victor.

His fee for the work was two pounds a week - the standard wage in those days, of a typist.

The *Poet's Corner* appeared for the first time on April 9, 1933, and was an instant success. Victor favoured no school; reading a poem, he heeded only an inner frisson which caused him to say, 'This is poetry.' He had this when he read a poem called 'Chelsea Reach', about gulls and barges. The signature was Pamela Hansford Johnson, a name then unknown. He printed it on April 23 as a weekly prize winner.

Encouraged, and indeed emboldened by the spate of excellent verse that flowed into the office Victor conceived the idea of a more important prize to be awarded every six months. The recipient would have his collected work published in book form. For the first winner - provided he could get the scheme through - Victor clearly had in mind the unknown Miss Hansford Johnson whose lyric gift had so impressed him. He put the proposal to the Editor, Mr Goulden, who accepted it without hesitation.

On May 31 Pamela Hansford Johnson met Victor for the first time at a house in Carlton Hill, where he had rooms. The second time she saw him was on July 31, in Steyning. Runia was acting as hostess at Vine Cottage(1), and talked about herbs and nature cures and put plates of jam in the garden for the wasps! Present also were David Gascoyne, who was also a contributor to the *Poet's Corner*, and the composer Dr Daniel Jones, not to be confused with my friend Professor Daniel Jones, the phonetician. The volume of entries, most of them handwritten was all the time increasing. The chores of the job became considerable, and Arthur Leslie Morton, who was in London, used to come in one evening a week to help Victor at Fellows Road where he now was. Victor was reading his eyes out, when he came to a handwritten poem beginning, 'That sanity be kept...' It came from South Wales and the signature beneath it was a new one, Dylan Thomas. He printed it on September 3, as weekly prize winner and describe it as 'the best modernist poem that I have as yet received.'

It was the second poem he received from Dylan Thomas beginning, 'The force that through the green fuse drives the flower', which made the bigger impact on him. 'Mr Thomas's 'Poem' is cosmic in outlook...a large poem, greatly expressed,' he wrote in the *Sunday Referee* on October 29. He had already designated Pamela Hansford Johnson as the first of the *Sunday Referee* poets whose work was to receive the distinction of publication in book form. She, reading the poems by Dylan Thomas as they appeared, felt that they belonged to a different order from her own, and asked Vicky for the poet's address so that she might write to him and tell him how much she admired them.

On January 7, 1934, Victor published 'Song' by Dylan beginning, 'Love me not as the dreaming nurses', and on February 11 published Dylan's poem beginning 'A process in the weather of the heart'. Of this, Victor wrote that it was 'admittedly difficult,' but would 'repay careful scrutiny by any poetry lover. It is a microscope poem, that is each phase may be separately and closely studied and yield a separate beauty facet.'

Pamela Hansford Johnson had been corresponding with Dylan and on February 24, he came to London as the guest of Pamela and her mother at their home in Clapham. He was younger than Pamela yet she felt as though he were older because of his 'literary sophistication,' as she put it to me. On the second day of his visit, Sunday, February 25, 1934, at her home Victor and Dylan met for the first time. Meanwhile the Editor of the paper, having read Victor's glowing praise for the work of the unknown Welsh poet, asked to see more of the author's poems.

Mr Goulden, later head of the publishing house of W.H.Allen and Company, told me that when he read these further poems he could not believe they were written by a boy of eighteen. 'They were extremely complex, abstruse compositions', said Goulden, 'and I thought we were being hoaxed. Maybe it was a rather brilliant eclectic effort by some highbrow prankster who had cleverly plagiarized the work of those contemporary poets - especially the Americans - who were writing abstract verse of this kind.' Neuburg insisted that the poems were genuine. Finally, Goulden said, 'There is only one way to settle this argument. We will send for the author and all take a look at him.' He then gave instructions to his secretary (Miss Gwen Thomas) to invite Dylan to come from Swansea for an interview at the *Sunday Referee* office. The paper would pay his fare and expenses and put him up at the Strand Palace Hotel, which was not far from the Fleet Street premises of the paper. The poet accepted and duly presented himself escorted by Neuburg, Runia and Hayter Preston.

'He looked a little slim, pale boy,' said Preston, 'with a head two sizes too large for his neck. He had the cockiness of a sparrow but this was merely a cover for his nervousness. Victor was pulsating like an electric wire.' It was an unnerving situation for an unknown young author. He was facing literally, his judges. 'We grilled him about his work,' said Goulden. 'I remember asking him point blank how he came to write involved, intricate verse like this. How did he make a start on a new poem and how did he sustain the mood?' 'And how well I remember the unforgettable reply,' adds Goulden. 'This young man, who looked more like a farm hand than a poet, was obviously perplexed. He ran his fingers through his bush mop and with a kind of embarrassed boyish grin he suddenly exclaimed, "Oh, you know, it just seems to flow." It was perhaps a trite remark but it was spoken with that resonant Welsh lilt which gives music to simple words. The voice was the most remarkable quality of this otherwise unremarkable and gauche young man.'

At the end of the inquisition the Editor's doubts about the authenticity of the poems submitted by Thomas were completely allayed, Victor's choice of him as the prize winner was ratified.

On Sunday, June 17, there was a party for Dylan at Vicky's.

It was decided that Dylan's book, to be entitled *18 Poems*, would be produced at the Parton Press under the aegis of the *Sunday Referee*. The cost of production was £50, and of this the *Sunday Referee* paid £30 and the Parton press £20. A royalty was payable to Dylan.

In the middle of the summer Pamela's book, *Symphony for Full Orchestra*, appeared, with a Foreword by Vicky. To launch it, he gave a party for her, in his Aunt Ti's flat in Victoria Street. *The Argosy*, which had black-listed Victor, now started a competition on lines imitating those of the *Poet's Corner*. It was not destined to discover names of such lustre. Victor was now printing in the *Sunday Referee*, Dylan Thomas, Pamela Hansford Johnson, Ewart Milne, Francis Berry, Herbert Corby, Idris Davies, Ruthven Todd, Margaret Stanley Wrench, Eileen Brennan, Hugo Manning, Leslie Daiken, A L Basham, Ken Etheridge, Julian Symons, David Gascoyne and Laurie Lee. Gradually, they found their way to where Vicky lived. Morton, Dylan and Pamela formed the original nucleus to which others added themselves.

Margaret Stanley Wrench (Newdigate Prize Winner of 1937) remembered:

A large head and a mane of hair, a room full of assorted people and untidiness, the debris of living, scattered books, papers, table tops stained with the marks from wet glasses, ash scattered, letters scattered.

The Magical Dilemma of Victor Neuburg

Francis Berry, who today has a considerable reputation, wrote to me:'

The claim made that 'Francis Berry , whom the old *Poet's Corner* had, with Professor Wilson Knight, the honour of discovering'...is, if you read Victor Neuburg for *Poets' Corner* (ie of the *Sunday Referee*) exactly true- granting that it was an honour? Knight first discovered...but then Neuburg gave what Knight could not give, publication and the encouragement of his praise set out in print. He gave one one of those enormous leaps and bounds of joy which one needs at that age, and I have an image of him - which I summon or which comes unannounced - an image of a frail yet strong bird yet man.

Berry's visit to Victor must have been just before his move to Springfield Road. I had brought Victor's story to the point at which I entered it.

On March 10, 1935, there was a feature article in the *Sunday Referee* which surprised me very much: 'My Search for the Absolute' by Aleister Crowley. I asked Hayter Preston about this and he told me its appearance had nothing to do with Victor. He himself was responsible. He had received a telegram from Crowley asking him to go down and see him at the Old Ship in Brighton. He was surprised and puzzled because their contact had terminated in the violent row in May 1914, but he went nevertheless.

It turned out to be a stunt in the sense that Crowley was only trying to sell him an article. In a moment of softness Preston bought the article and, by drastic editing, made it publishable. But it did not meet with the approval of the Editor.

Mr Goulden recalls: 'I considered the article altogether too abstruse - with its overtones of ontology and epistemology - for the readers of a Sunday newspaper. It seemed to me that this was material which Crowley (whose work as a poet I knew and admired) had dredged up from some of his old manuscripts and was now trying to foist off on his friend Preston. I agreed, however, to let it go - after considerable revision by Preston - and I actually chose the heading for it - a title about as meaningless and metastic as the text itself. I told Preston we didn't need any more of this stuff but on the Tuesday after publication (Sunday newspaper staffs do not come in on Mondays), Aleister Crowley, a sinister figure wearing an overlarge black Homburg (like spies in pre-war fiction affected) presented himself at the office and dumped a sheaf of typescript on my desk. These, he said, were the 'future instalments'.

'When I told him I didn't intend to publish any more articles from him he became furious. He said Preston had given him a contract for a series of articles but Preston (whom I thought was slightly afraid of Crowley) stoutly denied this. Crowley became abusive and I ordered him out of the office. 'I'll sue you,' he shrieked and indeed he did start proceedings for breach of contract. Preston urged me not to defend the action because he believed that Crowley could put "a curse on us", but I was not intimidated either by Crowley's threats or by his alleged magical powers of evil.'

'Crowley in the witness-box put up a very poor showing. But during his evidence he appeared to be making what Preston claimed were "mystical signs"' to the judge with his hands. His Lordship, however, was obviously impervious to this esoteric radiation. "I prefer Mr Goulden's version of this affair to that of the plaintiff" he announced at the end of the case and looking directly at Crowley standing in the well of the court, the judge added "You have no justification in law or morality".

'"You'll regret this," Crowley snarled as we passed him on the way out of court.

'Preston seemed to take this imprecation very much to heart and it is my belief that our victory over Crowley distressed Preston for a very long time afterwards. When the *Sunday Referee* eventually ceased publication Crowley sent me a postcard with the words, "So you didn't win after all." Apparently he wasn't aware that I had left the paper two years previously.'

'In the years that followed, Preston continued to be associated with me in my various journalistic and literary enterprises and I never lost the feeling that the court episode with Crowley had cast a sort of shadow on Preston.'

'Then, one day, he came to tell me Crowley was dead. I saw at once that a burden had been lifted from Preston's shoulders. A spell had been broken.'

There comes back to my mind something Runia told me when I saw her in 1941. She was with Vicky in the Atlantis Bookshop in Museum Street when he was rummaging through old books. Suddenly he drew closer beside her, so as to be able to speak in a voice that would not be heard by others, and said, 'Let us leave'.

As they emerged into the sunlight, she saw that he had turned deathly white. He said, 'AC came in. He was standing looking at books. Almost next to us. I don't think he saw me.' (2)

(1) I enquired of the local authorities as to the ownership of Vine Cottage and how long it remained in the family, and had a reply from the Rating Officer of the Chanctonbury Urban District Council, 'until the end of 1933 Mr V.B.Neuburg was the rated occupier and Mrs Theresa Royce the owner.'

(2) This is Crowley's last appearance in Victor's story; he died in a Hastings boarding house on December 1, 1947. His estate, as I discovered at Somerset House, was valued at death at eighteen shillings and sixpence.

22
Remeeting with Pamela Hansford Johnson

I had not seen Pamela for years but when she opened the door to me she looked exactly as she did at Vicky's. I had written to her - she was now Lady Snow - telling her I was writing his biography and she replied saying she would love (she underlined it) to talk with me about Vicky. As she brought me in, helped me off with my coat and poured me a gin, she seemed just the same. 'I was very fond of him,' was almost the first thing she said,'I never saw the slightest impropriety in his house.'

'There wasn't any,' I said, surprised she should think it necessary to assure me.

She insisted, 'I do want to say that in the whole of the time during which I was a frequent visitor I never saw anything in the slightest degree indecent, or indecorous, or unseemly, or in any way capable of shocking a young girl.'

'But I know there wasn't!' I protested, touched by her loyalty. 'I was there every Saturday for a year! And the Sundays and Fridays! I know what it was like!'

'I do want to say that any young girl was safe with him,' she said, speaking with great earnestness.

Her defence of Vicky endeared her to me.

'And not only safe,' she added. 'Protected. Any young girl would, in his house, have been protected. If one had been getting into any kind of trouble, he would have seen it and intervened and protected one.'

Assured at last of my friendship for Vicky she said, 'I've got out my diaries for you.' On the table was a pile of small pocket-diaries, and I saw how much preparation she had made for our meeting when, by means of slips of paper already inserted in places to be found again, she was able immediately to read out the entries for the significant dates, beginning with her first meetings with Vicky and with Dylan, which I have used in a previous chapter. We talked about Dylan.

She told me of a ghastly occasion when she and Dylan and Geoffrey Lloyd brought in some beer, and Runia, when she and Vicky came in later had been terribly angry about it. 'She spoke to me on the telephone next day, Sunday, and accused me of giving the place over to orgies and bear-gardens!'

Reading aloud from her diary, Pamela said, 'I cannot believe it was that bad, even with Dylan present!'

It was only when she copied out the extracts from her diaries and gave them to me that, seeing the date of this was Saturday June 29, 1935, I realised that this was the occasion on which I had been present.

After this Pamela had stayed away for some time. When the change of policy and editorship on the *Sunday Referee* caused Vicky to lose his column, Runia telephoned her and asked her to organize and lead a procession down Fleet Street with a banner demanding the reinstatement of the *Poets' Corner*. Pamela would have done anything she thought could help Vicky, but she did not believe this was his own idea and did not feel she could do it.(1)

Pamela said that on one occasion when Runia went out to the shop round the corner to buy pasties for their supper, Vicky said, 'She looks after me very well. Perhaps too well.' And he told Pamela a story. He had needed to buy some shoes. Runia accompanied him to the shop and did all the talking. He tried the shoes on and the assistant turned to Runia and said 'Do you think they hurt him, Madam?'

Pamela explained why she had been at such pains to assure me of the propriety of everything she had ever seen at Vicky's. An obscure climate of scandal attached to his name and it had troubled her. 'A barrister, having heard that I went to Vicky's, warned my mother that Victor Neuburg was a man of bad reputation!' she said. 'My mother, being a wise woman and generally trusting what I told her - she also trusted her intuition, having met Victor herself - did not attempt to withdraw me from Victor's circle.'

Pamela had been very much concerned. Sitting forward in her chair, absolutely vibrant, she said, 'I can't tell you the amount of perturbation it caused me! I spent years of my life trying to find out what Vicky had done!'

Not liking to ask anybody she had simply lived, as she explained, with her ears skinned in the hope of picking up some clue.

I hesitated for a moment, wondering what her reaction to the truth would be; and as she saw me hesitate she asked, in tones absolutely ringing with impatience, 'Have you discovered? What did Vicky do wrong? Or that people thought he shouldn't have?'

I told her in one sentence. 'He had homosexual relations with Aleister Crowley.'

She hadn't thought of that. 'Then my mother need not have worried for me!' Once, when Runia had gone out to buy pasties - all her real conversations with Vicky seemed to have been when Runia had gone out to buy pasties - Vicky had read her some of Crowley's poetry and asked her opinion. 'He said that he had known him.' When Runia came back, she asked them what they had been talking about. Pamela said, 'Aleister Crowley.' Runia said, 'That name is never to be spoken in this house.'

Perhaps that should have given her the clue! It hadn't because, as Pamela explained, she had always thought of Vicky as essentially masculine.

At this moment Sir Charles Snow(2) came in and Pamela brought him up to date with the story. After this the conversation broadened out, and Sir Charles asked me about Vicky's days in Cambridge.

We remained in contact. At my request Pamela sent me the photographs of herself and Dylan Thomas taken during the time they belonged to Vicky's circle (see plates). I asked her if she would like to write me something about Vicky which I could quote. In reply, she sent me this:

VICTOR NEUBURG: 1934

He was uncommonly like a bird: small, bony, with a fine large beak and hair curling high and loose like a bird's crest from his high forehead. His eyes were cobalt blue and very clear, a young man's eyes, startlingly young in his middle-aged face. He wore a sloppy black jacket not infrequently marked with egg (alpaca, I think it was) and poet's tie, which would be a Ted's today.

Whether I should have expected anything arcane in his history if I had not been warned of it, I don't know, but I don't think I should. My immediate impression, which

The Magical Dilemma of Victor Neuburg

I have never had reason to change, was that he was infinitely kind: that he was a good man. I was young enough and shy enough to be frightened by freakishness of manner, and his was often freakish; but the freakish-ness was of a kind to charm the young and make them feel admitted into the secret of it. It delighted them and liberated them. He could be, and often was, remarkably silly; but when anyone went to him with a personal problem he could be as worldly-wise as Kipling's 'Prooshian Bates,' always ready to point to 'a safe way round, out or under.'

His conversation with the young, or with anyone else, was cleanly; he used no bad language, substituting oaths he had invented for himself; and if he was sometimes given to airy blasphemies, they made no more impact than if he had been deriding Father Christmas.

In his light tenor voice he spoke the most beautiful pedantic English: I used to wish that I, too, dared to say, 'ac-TOR', 'composi-TOR':, etc, as he did.

When he was on the subject of magic, I felt he was suffering from a deeply divided nature. At times he no longer believed a word of it; if it was 'all rot' to me, it seemed, for the moment, 'all rot' to him. Yet the terrors of the past still held him, like a nightmare which persists when the curtains are drawn, the sun is streaming in, and breakfast is on the table.

He must, I think, have developed in a very few years this profound latent cynicism: and latent it must have been, during the Crowley days. Did he really think the Master's poetry was any good? When he read Crowley's awful verses to me, it was with his tongue in his cheek. And yet - and yet - (you could feel him thinking all the time) could he, even now, revenge himself upon a defaulting worshipper?

Pamela Hansford Johnson

Some time later the Snows came to spend an evening with me. Inevitably, Pamela and I talked about Vicky. Sir Charles made himself at home and found something to look at (he liked my paintings, which was flattering.)

I asked Pamela if she thought it was the rumours surrounding Vicky's past which had been responsible for Dylan's falling away from the circle.

'No,' she said. There were several things. The Name Zoists. 'He thought it sounded *zooey*.' (I remembered with dismay the unfortunate cognates I had given him!) And Runia. He didn't get on with her. 'If it had been just Vicky, by himself, he would probably have stuck, to the end.'

Still puzzled by the magic side, Pamela said, 'I'm a Christian. I can get on quite well with people who say they don't see any reason to believe in all that. Much better than with people who believe in magic signs!' On this front, there had been a wall between herself and Vicky.

Although Pamela's period at Vicky's overlapped with mine in the main it belonged to the two preceding years and she talked to me of this earlier period, when there were fewer people and, as the hour grew later, every conversation between Dylan and herself ended in politics. Vicky thought this extraordinary. 'It worried him,' Pamela said. 'He thought it unnatural for young people to be so very much concerned with politics. He used to say, "But you reduce everything to politics!"

'And that was back in the days when it was only Dylan and me. Dylan was Left, but with his middle-class background he couldn't go very far to the Left. Later, there was a really determined Marxist element.'

She herself went less often to Vicky's after she married because her first husband, Neil Stewart, was not in sympathy with the ambience and was rude to Runia about 'yogis and bogeys'.

The Marxists were impatient with what they considered the 'silly side' of Vicky. For some time they thought they could take him along with them. He had moved some way towards the Left and they thought they could use him. But when he said he was not a Communist, he meant it. 'He began to feel the Communists were trying to take over control,' Pamela said.

He dug his toes in. He would not allow *Comment* to become a Communist organ. When the Communists realized that, they withdrew their support and the whole thing collapsed.

Morton must be exempted, however, from this analysis of the behaviour of the Communist element as a group. His friendship with Vicky, going back to the Steyning days, was a personal one. He always respected the fact that Vicky was not a Communist, and had too much regard for him to wish to use him against his wishes. He was, in fact, one of the truest of all Vicky's friends.

---

(1) I learned later from Hugo Manning that he collected signatures to a petition in this sense. Hayter Preston told me that, before things had reached this pass, Runia endeavoured to interest the Labour peer, Lord Hurtwood (formerly Clifford Allen) in putting some money into the *Sunday Referee*, which would avoid the need to change its policy. She, Vicky, Hurtwood and Preston had tea at the Reform Club to discuss this but nothing came of it.

(2) Later Lord Snow.

23
After I Knew Him

Holding Pamela's tribute to Victor, I wondered if I could place others beside it. Dylan was dead, but I still had his letter containing words which might have been Victor's epitaph. And in the British Museum, in the Dylan Thomas Memorial Number of *Adam International Review*, I found in the editorial column this:

'Vicky encouraged me as no one else has done,' Dylan Thomas declared on hearing of Neuburg's death in June, 1940. 'He possessed many kinds of genius, and not the least was his genius for drawing to himself, by his wisdom, graveness, great humour and innocence, a feeling of trust and love, that won't ever be forgotten.'

A touching detail for future biographers is the following inscription in the first copy of *18 Poems*:

'From Dylan to Victor, with the utmost thanks!'

Geoffrey Pollett was dead. Geoffrey Lloyd had been killed in the Spanish Civil War. Idris Davies had sent me, when my own first book was published, one of his, *Tonypandy*, probably because it contained a reminiscence of Vicky in the poem beginning:

> I used to go to St John's Wood
> On Saturday evenings in summer
> To look on London behind the dusty garden trees
> And argue pleasantly...

But I had heard nothing since. Faber, who published all his books, had produced his *Collected Poems*. I wrote to them. They told me he was dead.

Death seemed to have taken a heavy toll. But from Siam I received a green air-letter. It was from Herbert Corby. He had seen my letter in the *Daily Telegraph*, and wrote:

I remember him [Vicky] as sympathetic and encouraging with a catholic taste and a belief in all of us; and some of his geese really were very lovely swans indeed: Dylan Thomas and Pamela Hansford Johnson.

By now Corby had four volumes of poems published. Leslie Daiken

After I Knew Him

telephoned to speak of 'dear Vicky, who helped us all so much.' Daiken had been Features Editor at Reuters, had numerous publications to his name and was now connected with television. He came to tea, and astonished and touched me by telling me he had cut out from *Comment*, and preserved for all these years, my story, 'Many are Called'. 'You came from the well-dressed world, and put all us Bohemians to shame!' he said. He had kept in touch with Dylan to the end, and Caitlin had spent some time at his home during one of her pregnancies. He said, 'What made Vicky remarkable was that, whoever he was talking to, he could be instantly on the beam.'

I said, 'He was more than a Poetry Editor. He was a spiritual teacher.'

Daiken said, 'I'm glad you said that. He was a sage. If this had been an Oriental country he would have been regarded as a Holy Man, and we should have been considered his pupils.'

'Did Vicky cough?'

I asked suddenly, for my inability to remember this worried me, in view of the cause of death given on the certificate.

'Oh, he did cough,' said Daiken. 'He hadn't got a chronic cough, but he coughed when there was fog. He would muffle up even to go down to the *Sunday Referee*. He recalled Vicky's saying he only smoked Woodbines, because they were little and he wasn't supposed to smoke at all: 'They're coffin nails for me. I've got a bad lung. We don't talk about it.'

I asked him if he would like to write something about Vicky, and he sent me this:

V.B.N.

V.B.N. was the leavening of my drifting, bohemian, anarcho-politico-mish-mash of a literary lifeline in London. True, after the footstools and draught-excluders of Rathgar, where we all sat with bated breath under the beard of A.E. and the brow of W.B. bohemian London, with its pubs and its 'political poets' was something very special...and I owe something to Mike Sayers for letting me touch the T.S.Eliot hems. But one missed the rooting, the direction, the sense of vocation that V.B.N infused into one. He had that fantastic catholicity, that generosity of heart, that 'in my father's house-are-many-mansions' approach to younger writers which made our motley crowd all tick as though their special thing mattered. Room for the free verse people, for the sonneteers, the sprung-rhythmers; the bolshies, the anti-politicals, the Irish, the Scots and the Welsh (cohorts of them) all of whom had chips and manias amid the myriad manifestos. Agreed, I had got a big kick when Orage's paper printed a story...but that was nothing beside the sense of reaching an audience I got when Vicky Neuburg published 'St Patrick's Day' in his little magazine *Comment*, on March 21st,

The Magical Dilemma of Victor Neuburg

1936.

What of the V.B.N. circle of poets? As variegated as a race-meeting ground on Easter Monday, we all met in the Swiss Cottage sitting-cum-reading room that Jean Fuller no doubt has described vividly in other pages of this study. From all points of the compass, each his/her own navigator. Many of us had been companions-in-print in Victor's *Sunday Referee* corner, but here we could meet in the flesh, and laugh and listen, and brood and argue, that essential pollination process to which all socially-minded poets are addicted. And, whatever our respective clarion-calls, we were nothing if not socially conscious. I listened to Geoffrey Pollett arguing the toss with Geoffrey Lloyd on Marxist ethics; Dylan Thomas fighting (against no odds) for regionalism in poetry; Jean Fuller, blonde and svelte and willowy as a shy nordic myth-maiden, smiling when we all congratulated her on the first story she had printed, 'Many are Called'; diagnostic, she would be a dab at narrative prose; Ruthven Todd and Idris Davies exchanging passionate ideas about poetry. There was glamorous Pamela Hansford Johnson deep in conversation with, say, Walter Ford, while when it came to the wrongs of Caitlin ni Houlihan, my newly found compatriot, the poet Ewart Milne just back from serving before the mast, gave heroic support. Talk, talk and more talk - but after the heady hangovers of Irish Hooley, a more constructive tensile-strength to it all; we were learning our trade; we were all in a sense novices at the Neuburg Temple, thrusting, testing, working our passage along the via dolorosa which is Poesy's path. We took. We probably influenced each other's work and helped each other more than we shall ever know. And thanks to V.B.N.

'Thanks to V.B.N.' should be, perhaps a sub-title to any memoir that anybody in that group concocts today. Looking back from my present-day work for a then unimaginable medium called television, after 25 years of writing, writing, writing, earning my living with words, words, words, I suppose I can say that after the encouragement I received from Sean O'Casey, my greatest debt is to V.B.N.

Presiding there, over us all, a sort of A.E. without the Irish mystic's self-dramatized hooha, he helped, guided, amused, encouraged, like a father-figure who was to most of us, I think, a brother figure! 'That's good stuff, let's have 600 words for *Comment* - there's a C.H.O.G.' His private joke words have always stayed with me as vividly as his nervous fingers holding his cheap cigarettes ('have a gasper, do! Go on, have one. I only smoke coffin-nails. Try one!') which he interminably offered to us all, the poor sharing out to the poor. Absurd words, which in themselves, and his pilpulistic talent for religious purism, became a ritualistic charade. 'Are you a FROG?' While I mutely searched for a reply, he chortled, 'A friend of God!' His irreverence had a touch of the prophet dissenter. And so it was in an amalgam of roles as high priest of poetry, and a catalyst to our often mutually cancellative chemical personalities, editor-in-chief and pantomimic extraordinary, his 'At Homes' were vibrant. But overriding them all was his role of patron. He was patron to all us apprentices, sweetly and with a sixth sense of compassionate apprehension, showing us just how each and every talent we writers should develop.

V.B.Neuburg, had he devoted less energy and time to teaching other poets their trade, might have produced a vaster corpus of original writing. But what could the latter, however brilliant, embody beside the tributes of mature men and women who have grown into better people because of their mentor and friend.

Leslie Daiken. (1)

I have quoted this long passage because, while I have described the evenings at Vicky's myself in the earlier part of this book, it pleases me that the reader should not be left solely with my description.

I wrote to Daiken's compatriot, Ewart Milne, who had ten books of poetry to his name. He replied from Ireland, explaining how he had come to see Victor:

I think that was in the late summer of '36. We sat in the back garden, and Victor talked and I listened. But though he talked, he also observed. I took to him, with his great ugly beautiful head, and his small body, and his great soul - and his appalling use of syntax, and his obsession with punctuation - immediately. I didn't think he was a great poetry editor; he loved the esoteric and magic too much for my liking; and yet I found myself loving him. He really cared nothing whatever for conventions of any kind, and I could appreciate that. And he had a completely tolerant mind, wide, catholic, receptive. Moreover, though in his editing days on the *Referee* he often encouraged many he did not think would go far, yet he knew the poets, the real poets. He was completely trustworthy there. I remember his speaking to me of Dylan Thomas, of Pamela Hansford Johnson, of Herbert Corby, of Francis Berry and A.L.Morton before I met any of them, and before any of them were at all well known.

If you will, try to picture him with his great head of a real gnome, sitting up in bed in a filthy dressing-gown in a room full of books, with Runia occasionally looking in and myself on the end of the bed, gingerly listening, and suddenly Vicky stopping, looking at me and saying , shaking the great mop of his hair, "You'll get through, you'll win out, but I won't." I said, "How do you know, Victor?"' But he only repeated that he knew. That was one of the last times, if not the last time, that I saw him.

I knew, because Runia had told me, that he was quite seriously ill, and yet I felt death was really very far from Victor Neuburg; his interest, his zest for life, was huge...I just think that if anyone did get through it was Victor Neuburg. Without his help and encouragement, and above all his acceptance of the poet, I really don't know where I would be today. If I was to be dedicated, if I did not care what I had to do for the sake of the poetry I could write, Vicky showed me that he at any rate understood - so what could I do but be grateful for what I imbibed from him, the steeling of all belief that it was worthwhile.

Maurice Sarver, who used to be Manager of the Unicorn Press, wrote:

I still think that had Victor lived he would have created a great revival in the quality of English poetry, by his encouragement and teaching of the ardent poet.

At first, I suppose, Victor was only in bed at times. There was the move from Springfield Road to Boundary Road. Oswell Blakeston, answering my letter in the *Telegraph*, wrote:

Before the war I lived in Boundary Road and I called on Victor Neuburg to see if I could get his signature to a pacifist manifesto denouncing Power Politics. He was very kind to me, and he asked me about my life. I tried to tell him some of the problems of existing on a shoe string. I remember he said, "It must be very hard for you, being so undefended."' He pointed to the shelves of his magnificent library. "'I have my armour against the future. All these books."He gave me an invitation to come back and borrow books whenever I felt inclined. Strangely enough, I cannot remember whether he signed the manifesto.

But before long, it seems, Victor was in bed most of the time. Hugo Manning telephoned me; he remembered me almost by definition as 'the girl who stood up to the Only British Nazi!' I asked him to tea, and he came, bearing as a gift his latest volume of verse, *The Secret Sea*. 'What did Vicky die of?' he asked me. 'Was it a cancer?' He was not the first person to have asked me that. I told him what was on the Death Certificate.

Manning saw Vicky for the last time just before leaving for South America. Distressed at finding him bedridden, he asked him what he was suffering from. 'In my youth I was too great a sensualist,' Victor replied.

'I think he must have imagined it.' Manning said. 'He said he had "worn himself out". But he did not look like a great sensualist. The white of his eyes were clear, and his gaze was pure and steady.'

Manning found it impossible to believe him dead. 'All that understanding, that great intellect and sensitivity, all that he was, can't have ceased to be. In some state, he must still be.'

'What I felt about him,' said Manning, 'was his humbleness. He served life instead of, like most people, trying to make it serve him.'

In the library of the British Museum with, I know not what idle curiosity, I looked up *Comment* in the Catalogue. I saw that it had continued until January 30, 1937. Even after so many years, it caused acute pain to discover it had gone on for thirty issues after I had thought it had stopped.

Why had I not received them? I was fully paid up. Returning home, I looked at the last issue I had received through the post. The date was June 13, 1936. It contained an acknowledgement for a small contribution I had made towards a fund. I wrote to Corby and asked him if he could cast his mind back to the last evening at Vicky's, when Runia had told us it would not be necessary for us to come any more on Fridays to do the wrappers. He replied saying he believed Runia thought we had become too much part of the establishment and decided to make our presence unnecessary.

I went back to the British Museum and got out the *Comment* file to see what I had missed. I wanted particularly to see how his semi-fictional autobiography had progressed, and I read that Frankie, a visionary child, had experienced his first revelation when at the age of six he had been invited to a house where, on one of the walls, was a reproduction of Botticelli's 'Primavera'. As his eyes met it, his whole consciousness seemed to be gathered into them, and he almost came out of himself towards the picture. Now at last I was able to identify the figure in that early poem of Victor's, 'A Nocturne', the figure of his true love. 'Tiny rosebuds girt thy green mantle, and thy yellow hair...' I opened *Il Sogno Nostalgico* da Sandro Botticelli at the reproduction of 'La Primavera'. I think, actually, it is carnations or pinks that are embroidered on the mantle of the figure scattering the flowers, which had become in his memory of that first vision rosebuds. A whole world seemed to be unlocking itself, and it was connected with the Grey Friend who met him beside the wood, before he was born.

As Frankie grew, the clarity of his vision diminished. He went to school and learned to play boys' games, and by twelve years old he was living in the tangible world as though it were the real. Yet something in him rebelled against the prison; he was reluctant to eat, and his mother took him to the doctor. In the waiting-room he was left alone, and it was here that his second revelation came to him. On the table there were some magazines; he opened one of them and for the second time in his life found himself looking at a reproduction of the 'Primavera'. The effect on him, 'was very much what the first vision of Laura "in her light green dress" must have been to Petrarch. "Spring, spring, in how many lands have I known you?" - the dawn-rose flushed Frankie's cheeks...Frankie's eyes brimmed with hot, radiant tears; in the absolute, the abandonment of happiness he rose and went to the window.'

He had recognized 'the Green Lady whom he had known, and whom to know was the only life that mattered.'

There is little more to say. Among the books I acquired from Anthony d'Offay was one entitled *The Popular Faith Unveiled*, (1884).

The fly - leaf was inscribed:

Victor B Neuburg ˙/.

London NW8 ˙/.

summer solstice, 1939 ˙/.

Many of the margins bore his comments, and at the foot of a chapter relating stories in the Gospels to the sun's course through the Zodiac, he had written:

The practice of this allegory, on the principle that man is a microcosm to the universal macrocosm, is the basis of mysticism, occultism and masonry, a blend of both. The esoteric apprehension of the exoteric rubbish of 'popular' religions was, and is, called 'initiation' or the going into things.

'/.

Vera Wainwright saw him in an upstairs room at Boundary Road and he gave her an introduction to Austin Spare, who was going to do illustrations for a fresh volume of his poems. 'He was in bed, being nursed by a devoted Lady, and could only speak. When I left, I knew I should not see him again.'

Arthur Leslie Morton saw him for the last time in the late summer of early autumn of 1939. It must have been about the time the war started, though he cannot remember their speaking of it. Vicky appeared very weak although his personality was unchanged.

His mother died, at Boundary Road, on 24th November, 1939.

Probably the last person from outside to see him was H.Cutner from the *Freethinker*, in 1940 when he took the photograph of him in bed, his head propped against the pillow. A beard had grown on his face because he could not shave.

On May 30, 1940 he passed from the body in which those who loved him had known him in this life.

For me, he lit a flame which can never be put out. I felt in him, in a way which holds the imagination for ever, the heroic spirit. His story is still the most awful that I know.

In the association of Victor with Crowley, a personality of exceedingly fine grain was overlaid by one exceedingly coarse. A genuine mystic bluffed and exploited by an inflated pseudo-Messiah. For Victor the association was a disaster; it wrecked whatever career he might have had; it ruined his health and nervous system; and, in the conventional sense, it destroyed his reputation. Victor never recanted; but he did have a feeling that a deep profanation of the mysteries had taken place, and it worried him that he could never put his finger on the point at which things had taken a wrong turning. I think that things had gone wrong with Crowley before he met him, and that the elements which later made his personality so monstrous were there from the beginning only Victor did not at the beginning perceive them.

Yet the whole experience had left him a being whose comprehension seemed infinite.

He was a well from which one could draw to the extent of one's capacity. He received all who came to him, and gave each one back his own image, brightened. If that is not true magic, I do not know what is.

There is a Persian saying that the Master carpet-maker does not undo the pupil's mistakes, but weaves them into the pattern. So the pattern becomes richer. The purity in Victor's gaze meant more to me because I knew through what frightful darkness he had carried the lamp. But that I knew what it had cost him, it could not have meant so much to me that he could still say without regret, 'We went to sea in a sieve.'

(1) Leslie Daiken died in 1965.

Postscript to chapter 23: The Party

On 10 May, 1965, I gave an eve of publication party for the memory of Vicky. Timothy d'Arch Smith came early and helped my mother with the preparations. The next to arrive were the Snows. I said to Charles, 'It's gallant of you to have come!' He said, 'Pamela would never have forgiven me if I hadn't!' Dame Irene Ward came, from the Commons, and then Vicky's son and his wife Ann and their daughter, Caroline, Arthur Leslie and Vivien Morton, Walter and Dora Raeburn, Eric Richmond, Frederick Carlton Smith, Charles and Iona Cammell, Herbert and Margaret Corby, Margaret Stanley Wrench, Mark Goulden, Father Brocard Sewell, Frances Horowitz, Alan Brownjohn, Howard Sergeant, Ronald Davison (the President of the Astrological Lodge), Tamara Bourkoun, Gerald Yorke, Eric and Chloe King-Bull, Anthony d'Offay and Shirley Toulson.

I proposed a toast 'To Vicky' and Pamela proposed the reply. I read them the whole of 'Druids' (which I would on the morrow read before television cameras, standing amongst the trees on Chanctonbury Ring).

General J.F.C. and Sonia Fuller accepted but were held up. Some time afterwards he died; then I received a letter from a firm of lawyers. They told me she had just died, and there had devolved upon them, as their solicitors, the duty of settling up the estate, and they could find no Will. They had, however found his address-book, might they hope that in me they had found his next of kin? I was sorry to have to disabuse them.

Bibliography
Works of Victor Benjamin Neuburg

A: Unpublished
The Magical Record of Omnia Vincam (1909)
Lent me by General J F C Fuller; now in the Humanities Research Centre, University of Texas, Austin, Texas
The New Diana (1912)
70 numbered stanzas with preliminary verses and Epilogue
Babes in the Wood: A Pantomime (1927). Programme only given me by Vera Dennis Earle. Text probably not preserved

B: Books of Poetry
The Green Garland (Probsthain, 1908)
The Triumph of Pan (Equinox, 1908) 181 pp
Lillygay: An Anthology of Anonymous Poems (Vine Press, 1920) 78 p. Certain parts
Swift Wings: Songs in Sussex (Vine Press, 1921), 59 pp
Songs of the Groves: Records of the Ancient World (Vine Press, 1922) 139pp
Larkspur: A Lyric Garland (Vine Press, 1922), 101 pp
Parts only

C: Anthologies Carrying His Poems
Cambridge Lyric Poets, 1900-13, ed A Tillyard (Heffer, 1913)
Another Book of Sussex Verse, ed C F Cook (Cambridge, 1928)
A Treasury of Modern Poetry, ed R L Megroz (Putnam, 1936)
Merry Go Down, ed Rab Noolas, [pseud. P Heseltine] (Mandrake, 1929)
The First Comment Treasury, (ed) pseud. Benjie (*Comment,* 1936)

D: Introductions, etc.
Biographical Introduction to *Footsteps of the Past,* J M Wheeler (Pioneer, 1931)
Foreword to *Symphony for Full Orchestra,* Pamela Hansford Johnson (*Sunday Referee,* 1934)

Bibliography

Note to *18 Poems*, Dylan Thomas (Sunday Referee and Parton Press, 1934)
'To Introduce', *First Comment Treasury* (*Comment*, 1937)

E: Journals, Poems, Translations and Articles Carried In
The Freethinker
The Agnostic Journal
The Theosophical Review
The Equinox
The New Age
Freedom (for which, for a while, he wrote the Leaders)
The Bookman's Journal
Oxford Outlook
The Sunday Referee
Comment (including his semi-autobiographical serial 'The Perfect Stranger')

F: Books carrying references to Victor B Neuburg
Archer, Ethel, *The Hieroglyph*, semi-fiction (Denis Archer, 1932)
Calder-Marshall, Arthur, *The Magic of My Youth* (Hart-Davis, 1951)
Cammell, C.R, *Aleister Crowley* (Richards, 1951)
Croft-Cooke, Rupert, *Glittering Pastures* (Putnam, 1965)
Crowley, Aleister, *The Confessions: An Autohagiography*, (eds) John Symonds and Kenneth Grant (Routledge, 1979)
Crowley, Aleister, *The Paris Working* (unpublished MS). Lent me by Gerald Yorke; now in the Warburg Institute, London
Crowley, Aleister, Miscellaneous unpublished mss lent me by Gerald Yorke, now in the Warburg Institute London)
Hamnett, Nina, *Laughing Torso* (Constable, 1931)
Stephensen, P.R, *The Legend of Aleister Crowley* (Mandrake, 1930)
Symonds, John, *The Great Beast* (Rider, 1951)
Symonds, John, *The Magic of Aleister Crowley* (Muller, 1958)
Valiente, Doreen, *Where Witchcraft Lives* (Aquarian Press, 1962)

H: The Golden Dawn, Rosicrucianism, Kabbalah, etc
Ambelain, Robert, *Le Martinisme, La Franc-Maçonnerie Occulte et Mystique* (Niclaus, Paris, 1946)
Crowley, Aleister, *Magick in Theory and Practice*, (ed) John Symonds

and Kenneth Grant (Routledge, 1973)

Crowley, Aleister, 'The Vision and the Voice', in *The Equinox*, I,v (March 1911) 21-176

d'Arch Smith, Timothy, *The Books of the Beast* (Crucible, 1987)

Farr, Florence, *Egyptian Magic*, Introd. Timothy d'Arch Smith (Aquarian Press, 1982)

Fortune, Dion (pseud Violet Firth), *The Mystical Qabalah* (Williams & Norgate, 1941)

Fuller, J F C, *The Star in the West* (Walter Scott, 1907)

Gilbert, Robert, *The Golden Dawn and the Esoteric Section* (Theosophical History Centre, 1987)

Howe, Ellic, *The Magicians of the Golden Dawn* (Routledge, 1972)

Howe, Ellic (ed), *The Alchemists of the Golden Dawn: The Letters of the Rev W.A.Ayton to F.C.Gardner and Others 1886-1905* (Aquarian Press, 1985)

Levi, Eliphas, *Transcendental Magic*, trans A E Waite (Rider 1896 ed. 1962)

Regardie, Israel, *The Golden Dawn: An Account of the Teachings, Rites and Ceremonies of the Order of the Golden Dawn* (Aries: Chicago 1937-1940), Four Volumes

Mathers, S.S.L.Macgregor, *The Kabbalah Unveiled* (Routledge, 1957, 9th Impression)

Waite, Arthur Edward, *The Real History of the Rosicrucians* (Redway, 1887)

Wittermans, Fr, *A New and Authentic History of the Rosicrucians* (Rider, 1938)

The Equinox, 10 volumes, 1909-1913

I: Egyptian and Hermetic Background

The Book of the Dead, Facsimile of the Papyrus of Ani in the British Museum, printed by Order of the Trustees (1894)

The Papyrus of Ani, a reproduction in facsimile, edited with Hieroglyphic Transcript, translation and Introduction by Sir E.A.Wallis Budge (Medici, New York, G.P.Putnam's London, 1913). Original in the British Museum

Budge, E.A.Wallis, *A Hieroglyphic Vocabulary to the Theban Recension of the Book of the Dead* (Kegan Paul, Trench, Trubner, 1911)

Gardiner, Alan H, *Egyptian Grammar: Being an Introduction to the Study of Hieroglyphics* (Oxford, Clarendon, 1927)

Mead, G.R.S. *Thrice Greatest Hermes: Studies in Hellenistic Theosophy*

Bibliography

and Gnosis, being a Translation of the Extant Sermons and fragments of the Trismegistic Literature, with Prolegomena, Commentaries and Notes (Watkins, 1949), Three volumes

J: Plato
The Works of Plato, translatedwith analyses and introduction by B Jowett (New York, undated)

K: Templars and Assassins
L'Affaire des Templiers, Le Dossier de, (ed) and trans Georges Lizerand (Paris, 1964)

Burman, Edward, *The Assassins, Holy Killers of Islam* (Crucible, 1987)

Bouthoul, B. *Le Grand Maître des Assassins* (Collin, Paris 1936)

Loiseleur, *La Doctrine Secrète des Templiers* (Paris, 1872)

Wood, O.C. *History of the Assassins*, trans from Hammer-Purgstall's *Die Geschichte des Assassinen*, 1818

L: Miscellaneous
Alpers, Anthony, *Katherine Mansfield: A Biography* (Cape 1953)

Archer, Ethel, *Phantasy* (Vine Press, 1930)

Carpenter, Edward, *The Intermediate Sex* (Allen & Unwin, 1908)

Collins, Mabel, *The Blossom and the Fruit* (Author, 1888)

Historical Register of the University of Cambridge to the year 1910 (CUP, 1917)

Hoskins, C.A.(ed), *The Letters of John Middleton Murry to Katherine Mansfield* (Constable 1983)

Maud, Ralph, *Entrances to Dylan Thomas's Poetry* (Pittsburg UP 1963)

May, Betty, *Tiger Woman* (Duckworth 1929).

Tomalin Claire, *Katherine Mansfield: A Secret Life* (Viking 1987)

Thomson Jr, James, *The City of Dreadful Night* (Dobell)

Tarn, Shirley, *Seven Years* (Hermes, Vine Press and Dobell, 1928)

White, Rold, (pseud Harold Dinely Jennings White), *Day of Life* (Vine Press, 1928)

White, Rold, (pseud Harold Dinely Jennings White) *Twain One* (Vine Press, 1930)

Yeats, W.B. 'The Trembling of the Veil', in *Autobiographies* (Macmillan, 1926)

Index

Index

Index

Index

Index

Index

Index

Other *Mandrake* Titles:

Mike Magee's *Tantrik Astrology*,
ISBN 1 869928 06 7, 128pp, £4.95/$9.99
The first volume of Mandrake's Modern Studies in Tantra Series.
A manual of sidereal astrology and more besides

Katon Shual's *Sexual Magick*, 2nd Edition,
ISBN 1 869928 07 5, 128pp, £4.95/$9.99
Not just another 'blue' grimoire, but a survey of magical sexuality.

Snoo Wilson's *More Light*, 1st Edition,
ISBN 1 869928 08 3, 88pp, £4.95/$9.99
A play about the heretic Giordano Bruno as performed at the Bush
theatre, London. The parts of Shakespeare, Elizabeth I and the
heavenly bartender played by women.

Amookos's *Tantra Magick*,
ISBN 1 869928 10 5, 128pp, £6.99/$13.99
The secrets of one of one of the few real tantra groups published for the
first time.

Forthcoming:

Jean Overton Fuller's *Sickert & The Ripper Crimes*

Timothy D'Arch-Smith's *Books of the Beast* (revised edition)

Nadia Choucha's *Surrealism & The Occult*

For full details on these and many other titles
published and distributed by *Mandrake*,
write to PO Box 250, Oxford, OX1 1AP